Analysis of
Delinquency and Aggression

Analysis of Delinquency and Aggression

EDITED BY

EMILIO RIBES-INESTA
National Autonomous University of Mexico

ALBERT BANDURA
Stanford University

 LAWRENCE ERLBAUM ASSOCIATES, PUBLISHERS

1976   Hillsdale, New Jersey

DISTRIBUTED BY THE HALSTED PRESS DIVISION OF

JOHN WILEY & SONS

New York   Toronto   London   Sydney

Lawrence Erlbaum Associates, Inc., Publishers
62 Maria Drive
Hillsdale, New Jersey 07642

Distributed solely by Halsted Press Division
John Wiley & Sons, Inc., New York

Library of Congress Cataloging in Publication Data

Main entry under title:

Analysis of delinquency and aggression.

  Includes bibliographical references and index.
  1. Child psychiatry. 2. Aggressiveness (Psychology).
3. Juvenile delinquency.
I. Ribes-Inesta, Emilio. II. Bandura, Albert, 1925–
RJ499.A536   618.9′28′9   75-40104
ISBN 0-470-15227-3

Printed in the United States of America

Contents

Preface

This volume contains the papers presented at the Third Symposium on Behavior Modification held in January 1973, under the sponsorship of the Department of Experimental Psychology and Methodology of the National Autonomus University of Mexico. The symposium was organized around two central themes: first, the experimental analysis of aggression; second, the application of learning principles to the prevention and modification of delinquency.

The topics for this symposium were selected to show how the problems of aggression which have been interpreted in diverse ways, can be analyzed under controlled laboratory conditions. In addition, the chapters explain how behavior modification techniques, derived from this knowledge, can be used for preventive purposes. Because of the social nature of aggression and delinquency, behavior change techniques are principally aimed at modifying environmental influences. These contributions illustrate how behavioral scientists can contribute to the understanding and amelioration of conditions that give rise to violence.

In the introductory chapter of this volume, Emilio Ribes outlines some methodological and sociological criteria on the problem of aggression. The introduction is followed by a chapter by J. D. Keehn, in which he discusses problems raised by the experimental research on aggression in animals in laboratory settings. Robert Schwitzgebel reviews the technology for measuring and modifying transgressive behavior. The chapters by Benjamin Dominguez *et al.* and Irwin Sarason describe the use of corrective techniques for delinquents in institutional environments. The rest of the contributions, by John Burchard *et al.*, John Reid and Gerald Patterson; Harold Cohen; and Elery Phillips *et al.*, concentrate on preventive measures applied to the social environment of delinquents. Finally, the chapter by Albert Bandura advances a social learning theory designed to encompass diverse forms of aggression, individual and collective, personal and institutionally sanctioned.

We wish to express our gratitude to all the contributors, University officials, professors, students, and others, who so generously helped in the organization of the Third Symposium on Behavior Modification and in the preparation of this volume.

EMILIO RIBES-INESTA
ALBERT BANDURA

Analysis of
Delinquency and Aggression

1
Some Social Considerations on Aggression

Emilio Ribes-Inesta

National Autonomous University of Mexico

In the last decade, there has been increasing interest in violence as a social phenomenon, motivated in some extent by the profound changes taking place in very different types of societies. This interest in violence has not only stimulated experimental studies on aggression but has also propagated a great many different hypotheses and theories about it. Some of these theories have analyzed and explained individual and social aggression within the framework of internal biological processes in the organism (Lorenz, 1966; Tinbergen, 1973).

Explanations of aggression, derived from ethological analyses of these phenomena, have been used to postulate, on most occassions, the inevitability of aggression and violence in living organisms, but especially in vertebrates and man. Even though the ethologists' interpretation of aggression is based on valuable empirical observations, the interpretation itself contains a questionable rationale that leads to dangerous conclusions.

It should be pointed out that criticisms of the ethological position on aggression as an instinct, drive, or internal urgency do not reflect on the animal observations on which this position is supposedly based. On the contrary, the greater evidence for the opposite view comes from the experimental analysis of animal behavior. The ethological interpretation unnecessarily omits the decisive influence of environmental factors in relation to behavior. It is impossible to draw ultimate conclusions about the prevention of aggression and other behaviors without taking into account the decisive role of environmental events.

It is not necessary to go into detail about the ideological and social implications that an ethological conception of aggression has. It is a "scientific" justification of the inevitability of war and violence in human relations and of every sociological position or ethics based on the same propositions.

The generalized observation on which ethologists base their postulated impossibility of eliminating aggression in living organisms rests on the recognition that

1

the ecological environment, through a multiplicity of variables, requires of aggressive behavior as a continuous adaptive mechanism, not only for natural selection but also for its preservation. This ecological mechanism is translated not only to the direct relationships between environment and the organism's behavior but also to internal patterns of stimuli and responses that, in several ways, are incorporated into the hereditary endowment of the species (Lorenz, 1965).

Even though the validity of current ethological assertions, as restricted to conditions in which underlying observations support them, cannot be denied, it is seriously objectionable to logically extend them to human behavior.

The fundamental problems are undoubtedly the remarkable emphasis on the action of ecological variables in the control of inter- and intraspecific aggresion and the assumed phylogenic influence of species endowment. It is a basic proposition that most of inter- and intraspecific aggression is innate in the individual and that environment plays only a *releasing* role. This has led Tinbergen (1973) to say, for example, that

> I do not hesitate to give as my personal opinion that Lorenz's book *On Aggression*, in spite of its assertiveness, in spite of factual mistakes, and in spite of the many possibilities of misunderstanding that are due to the lack of a common language among students of behavior—that this work must be taken more seriously as a positive contribution to our problem than many critics have done. Lorenz is, in my opinion, right in claiming that elimination, through education, of the internal urge to fight will turn out to be very difficult, if not impossible [pp. 466–467].

As a logical corollary of a schematic evolutionistic position, it is concluded that aggression is unavoidable, on the basis of observations about the dominant effects exerted by the ecological environment for thousands of years on vertebrates and, particularly, on man. It is erroneus, however, to consider man and the rest of the vertebrates as phylogenically identical from a functional viewpoint, for although man is the culmination of this phylum, there exists a large discontinuity between him and his other evolutionary companions.

Man, as a living organism, is under the same natural laws as the other members of the zoological kingdom; nevertheless, he is unique, because of his particular development and evolution, in being able to transform nature in an active and thoughtful way. Even though the ecological environment has been a determinant in the "creation" of what we know today as the human species, therefore, it is also undeniable that man has been a large-scale transformer of this ecology. As a consequence, many of the great problems faced by industrial society in our times are products of this conscious alteration of the environment.

In reference to this it is very relevant to quote Engels (1961), who discusses the role of labor in the transformation of the ape in man. He says that

> ... the animal *uses* external nature and introduces changes just through his presence, while man, through his changes, makes it to serve his purposes, *domaining* it. This is the essential and supreme difference between man and the rest of the animals, difference produced by labor [p. 151].

Therefore, the ethological position is not sound in considering aggression as unavoidable, because it is through the scientific knowledge of ecological and environmental determinants of aggression that the necessary and sufficient means contributing to the construction of a social system, or a human ecological environment, in which the emergence of aggression is prevented, will be obtained (Skinner, 1971).

In order to consider the social nature of aggression in man and the appropiate controls for eliminating it, I shall briefly review the more relevant findings in the experimental analysis of aggression.

LABORATORY FINDINGS ON AGGRESSION

A great number of investigations have been carried out in order to isolate the major determinants of aggressive behavior. These studies have encompassed a large variety of species and behaviors. I shall review the experimental data in order to put into context some of the aggression phenomena that humans display in society.

The first quantitative and systematic laboratory studies were those carried out by Ulrich and Azrin (1962) on the effects of aversive stimulation on aggressive behavior. Since then, the range of variables has increased, including many experimental operations other than electric shock. I shall examine the literature in terms of the conditioning procedures employed and taking into account the various observed effects under particular parametric conditions.

Many of the aggressive behavior elements that may be conceived of in terms of respondent control correspond to a certain extent to the phenomena described by Lorenz (1966) and that Skinner (1969), very adequately, has called "phylogenic aggression" in order to distinguish it from the directly environmentally shaped ontogenic aggression.

It may be said that there is a respondent control relationship when the antecedent stimulus controls a high-probability occurrence of prespecified response, without previous training or exposure to such a stimulus. It may be assumed that behaviors under respondent control are outstanding examples of the initial phylogenic repertoire of an individual organism before the modulation and shaping of future or "learned" behavior development by the environment. Among the variables experimentally identified as relevant in the production of respondent aggression, the following are the most important. First, the administration of electric shock elicits unconditioned aggression to other species, to the same species, or to inanimate objects (Ulrich & Azrin, 1962; Azrin, Hutchinson, & Hake, 1967; Azrin, Hutchinson, & Sallery, 1964). The same effects may be obtained using intense air blasts (Azrin, Hake, & Hutchinson, 1965) or discontinuing reinforcement [extinction] (Azrin, Hutchinson, & Hake, 1966).

There are some reports on respondent conditioning of aggression in which previously neutral stimuli have acquired the functional capacity of eliciting such a behavior (Ulrich, Hutchinson, & Azrin, 1965; Creer, Hitzing & Schaeffer, 1966; Vernon & Ulrich, 1966). Individuals of the same species, as well as tones of different frequencies and intensities, may become conditioned stimuli for adopting fighting postures.

The most interesting experimental data, however, come from operant conditioning procedures. Reynolds, Catania, and Skinner (1963) have shown the possibility of food reinforcing and discriminatively controlling aggressive behavior in pigeons. Similar effects have been obtained by Ulrich, Johnston, Richardson, and Wolff (1963) with tame rats (Sprague-Dawley variety), using water as the reinforcer. The employment of intracranial reinforcement (Stachnik, Ulrich, & Mabry, 1966) has shown that these effects are reproducible with a wide variety of reinforcers and that aggression may be directed to very different species (rats, cats, monkeys, etc.).

Azrin, Hutchinson, and McLaughlin (1965) have found that opportunity for aggression can be used as an operant reinforcer during aversive situations. The use of electric shock as a consequence for aggressive behavior has shown the feasibility of punishing and suppressing this behavior, even when the effects depend on the intensity of shock and on a sufficient number of sessions to overcome the initial eliciting effects of the stimulus. The use of electric shock as a negative reinforcer seems to produce, as expected, an increment in aggressive behavior (Azrin *et al.*, 1967). Hutchinson, Azrin, and Hunt (1968) have found that aggression can also be produced as a side effect of ratio schedules of reinforcement. Ulrich and Favell (1970) have replicated part of the previously mentioned findings using human subjects in a laboratory-type situation.

These experimental data are relevant in showing the plasticity of aggressive behavior, its multiple causation, and the definite influence exerted by rather arbitrary consequences, from a phylogenic viewpoint. Emphasis on environmental factors, and the possiblity of controlling through them the occurrence or elimination of aggressive behavior, leads to conclusions oppossite to those of ethologists'.

Skinner (1969) says that

> . . . the environmental solution becomes more plausible the more we know about the contingencies. Phylogenic aggression may be minimized by minimizing eliciting and releasing stimuli. Behavior acquired because of an inherited tendency to be reinforced by damage to other can be minimized by breaking up the contingencies—by creating a world in which very little behavior causes the kind of damage which are reinforcing. . . . In short, we can solve the problem of aggression by building a world in which damage to others has no survival value and, for that or other reasons, never functions as a reinforcer. It will necessarily be a world in which non-aggressive behaviors are abundantly reinforced on effective schedules in other ways [p. 216].

When behavioral principles identified in the laboratory are extended to social environments and to human social behavior, it is necessary to consider some basic aspects in interpreting individual or collective aggression.

SOME SOCIAL CONSIDERATIONS

Human society, excepting primitive communism, has been historically divided into classes and, of course, our present society is not an exception (Engels, 1955). Skinner (1953) has analyzed how social institutions, as agencies representing dominant social classes, play the role of behavior control systems, through regulation of biological and social satisfactors (positive reinforcers) and the administration of aversive stimuli to reduce the likelihood of various behaviors that threaten social structure and organization.

A wide variety of social phenomena that have been approached as individual or small group problems are actually consequences of the particular functioning of the social structure as a whole. Delinquency is perhaps the most illustrative phenomenon. There are behavioral analyses (Burgess & Ackers, 1966; Ribes, 1972) of how delinquent behavior is socially determined and emerges as a consequence of concentrating social satisfactors in a limited nucleus of society and of repressive use of aversive behavioral controls to "eliminate" the problem. From these examples and many others, discussed by Bandura in another chapter of this volume, it is safe to conclude that sources that produce, feed, and maintain "antisocial" and aggressive behaviors are intrinsic to a society divided into classes. Violence in the human being is not an individual but a social phenomenon. As such, violence emerges from the system and not from the individual. Individual and small group aggression cannot be analyzed isolated from the social system context, which actually generates violence as a defining property of its structure.

Even when the problem of aggression is analyzed as a macrobehavioral phenomenon, as in hostility in international relations or in wars (Andreski, 1964), simplistic and deforming explanations that ignore the relevant determinants should be avoided as appealing to aggressive drives or similar biological "causes." In these cases, as in those related to relatively closed systems, the basic determinants are the same: appropiation of satisfactors by a reduced number of people and the use of aversive control in order to maintain this system of appropiation and distribution of reinforcers. Some thinkers have clearly asserted (Lenin, 1960) that war is nothing else than the extension of politics, stressing the social nature of violence in man.

If the Skinner box is considered as a perfectly defined model of a closed economic system and extend what has been learned of aggression in this experimentally contrived situation to society, some measures to eliminate aggression and most forms of violent social behaviors in man become clearly definable.

The basic operations needed to produce aggression are three: (a) extinction or decreases in reinforcement density, (b) presentation of aversive stimuli, and (c) positive reinforcement for aggressive behavior toward another organism or an object. Social changes should be directed, according to our knowledge, to: (a) equally distributing social wealth, (b) eliminating social aversive controls and, (c) eliminating conditions that legitimatize violence and aggression as means of appropiation of socially produced wealth.

To eliminate aggression as a human phenomenon it is necessary to change and transform the social system, currently based on a class-division structure generative of violence. Without this change in the complex social contingency systems that define and rule the wealth production and appropiation social relationships, it is impossible to raise the potential existence of a world without aggression and violence.

Behavioral scientists, knowing the determinants of aggression by means of their experimental analyses, have the moral obligation of extending this knowledge to all the members of society. Their increased awareness of the roots of aggression will channel their efforts to changing and transforming the social system. The construction of a new world, without class divisions, in which relations among men will be ruled just by positive reinforcers (Marx & Engels, 1955; Skinner, 1956, 1961) is a future possibility if conditions are met. Paradoxically, the solutions suggested by behavioral science to the problem of human aggression are within the competence not of science itself but of responsible political activity.

REFERENCES

Andreski, S. Origins of War. In J. Carthy & F. Ebling (Eds.), *The natural history of aggression*. London: Academic Press, 1964.

Azrin, N. H., Hutchinson, R. R., & Sallery, R. D. Pain-aggression toward inanimate objects. *Journal of the Experimental Analysis of Behavior,* 1964, 7, 223–228.

Azrin, N. H., Hutchinson, R. R., & McLaughlin, R. The opportunity for aggression as an operant reinforcer during aversive stimulation. *Journal of the Experimental Analysis of Behavior*, 1965, 8, 171–180.

Azrin, N. H., Hutchinson, R. R., & Hake, D. F. Pain-induced fighting in the squirrel monkey. *Journal of the Experimental Analysis of Behavior*, 1966, 9, 191–204.

Azrin, N. H., Hutchinson, R. R., & Hake, D. F. Attack, avoidance and escape reactions to aversive schock. *Journal of the Experimental Analysis of Behavior*, 1967, 10, 131–148.

Azrin, N. H., Hutchinson, R. R., & Sallery, R. D. Pain-aggression toward inanimate objects. *Journal of the Experimental Analysis of Behavior*, 1964, 7, 223–228.

Burgess, R. L., & Ackers, R. L. A differential association-reinforcement theory of criminal behavior. *Social Problems*, 1966, 14, 128–147.

Creer, T. L., Hitzing, E. W., & Schaeffer, R. W. Classical conditioning of reflexive fighting. *Psychonomic Science*, 1966, 4, 89–90.

Engels, F. El Origen de la Familia, la propiedad privada y el Estado. In K. Marx & F. Engels, *Obras escogida*. Vol. 2. Moscow: Ediciones en Lenguas Extranjeras, 1955.

Engels, F. *Dialéctica de la Naturaleza*. México: Grijalbo, 1961.

Hutchinson, R. R., Azrin, N. H., & Hunt, G. M. Attack produced by intermittent reinforcement of a concurrent operant response. *Journal of the Experimental Analysis of Behavior*, 1968, 11, 489–495.

Lenin, V. I. *Obras escogidas*. Moscow: Ediciones en Lenguas Extranjeras, 1960.

Lorenz, K. *Evolution and modification of behavior*. London: Methuen, 1965.

Lorenz, K. *On aggression*. London: Methuen, 1966.

Marx, K., & Engels, F. Manifiesto del Partido Comunista. In K. Marx & F. Engels, *Obras escogidas*. Vol. 2. Moscow: Ediciones en Lenguas Extranjeras, 1955.

Reynolds, G. S., Catania, A. C., & Skinner, B. F. Conditioned and unconditioned aggression in pigeons. *Journal of the Experimental Analysis of Behavior*, 1963, 1, 73–74.

Ribes, E. Methodological Remarks on a delinquency prevention and rehabilitation Program. In S. W. Bijou & E. Ribes (Eds.), *Behavior modification: Issues and extensions*. New York: Academic Press, 1972.

Skinner, B. F. *Science and human behavior*. New York: Macmillan, 1953.

Skinner, B. F. Some issues concerning the control of human behavior. *Science*, 1956, 124, 1056–1066.

Skinner, B. F. The design of cultures. *Daedalus,* 1961, 534–546.

Skinner, B. F. *Contingencies of reinforcement*. New York: Appleton-Century-Crofts, 1969.

Skinner, B. F. *Beyond freedom and dignity*. New York: Alfred Knopf, 1971.

Stachnik, T. J., Ulrich, R., & Mabry, J. H. Reinforcement of intra- and inter-species aggression with intracranial stimulation. *American Zoology*, 1966, 6, 663–668.

Tinbergen, N. On War and Peace in Animals and Man. In T. McGill (Ed.), *Readings in animal behavior*. New York: Holt, Rinehart & Winston, 1973.

Ulrich, R., & Azrin, N. H. Reflexive Fighting in Response to aversive stimulation. *Journal of the Experimental Analysis of Behavior*, 1962, 5, 511–520.

Ulrich, R., Johnston, M., Richardson, J., & Wolff, P. C. The operant conditioning of fighting in rats. *Psychological Record*, 1963, 13, 465–470.

Ulrich, R., Hutchinson, R. R., & Azrin, N. H. Pain-elicited aggression. *Psychological Record*, 1965, 15, 111–126.

Ulrich, R., & Favell, J. E. Human Aggression. In C. Neuringer & J. Michael (Eds.), *Behavior modification in clinical psychology*. New York: Appleton-Century-Crofts, 1970.

Vernon, W., & Ulrich, R. Classical conditioning of pain-elicited aggression. *Science*, 1966, 152, 668–669.

2

Schedule-Dependent Aggression

J. D. Keehn

Atkinson College, York University, Toronto

THE ORGANISM AND THE ENVIRONMENT

One of the first things that students of experimental psychology are taught is that introspection and subjectivity are bad and that objectivity in data collection and interpretation is good. When they pass examinations to show that this is understood they are given a rat to train in a typical Skinner box. Within minutes they complain that the animal is more interested in scratching than in securing food, is stupid, or is angry, for he is biting the lever or the bars of the floor.

The students are gently chastised about this and reminded of their excellent examination results. The reminder they do not need but the chastisement they receive with astonished disbelief. A week later they may again complain that the animal will not work, but now a curious thing appears. The complaint is to the effect the animal has been overfed or that some part of the apparatus is at fault. What has happened, often without their awareness, is that the students have changed from observing a rat that is in a box to observing an environment that dictates the behavior of an organism. When the organism is human this is an extraordinarily difficult change to make, as the student shows in complaining of the stupidity of the instructor in overfeeding the rat. Faced with this accusation the instructor is likely to be as subjective as his pupil, and this brings up the question of psychic-dependent and schedule-dependent aggression.

PSYCHIC DEPENDENCE AND SCHEDULE DEPENDENCE

Criminals and Crime

Burt (1938) began his book on juvenile delinquency with the description of a criminal:

> One sultry August afternoon, in a small and stuffy basement kitchen, not far from King's Cross Station, I was introduced to a sobbing little urchin with the quaint illiterative (fictitious) name of Jeremiah Jones. Jerry was a thief, a truant, and a murderer. When first I saw him, he was just seven and a half years old, a scared and tattered bundle of grubbiness and grief, with his name still on the role of a school for infants. Yet, at this tender age, besides a long list of lesser faults, he had already taken another boy's life [p. 1].

The significance of this case is the typing of Jerry—a thief, a truant, and a murderer—and the salience of the major crime. Murder is a salient crime on any occasion but its drama is heightened in the present instance through the youthfulness of the victim and the perpetrator. The matter is given its full pathos in the words of a judge in a more recent case that involves a girl called Mary Bell.

> "Members of the Jury," Mr. Justice Cusack began his summing up. . . ."
>
> It is an unpleasant thing for any Court to have to try a case in which it is alleged that two little boys, one aged three, the other aged four, lost their lives by Murder. It is even more unpleasant and distasteful when it is alleged that the persons responsible are two girls respectively aged eleven and thirteen . . ." [Sereny, 1972, p. 15].

Instances of child murder by children are not rare, and child battering by adults is an even more common event (Bakan, 1971). The following are more or less random selections from the daily press:

> A 2-year-old baby was slapped on the face, seized from his mother's arms and thrown on to the pavement at the Hospital for Sick Children Saturday after an argument over a taxi fare . . . Police said last night that a man and his wife had taken their son to the hospital with diarrhea. An agrument developed over who would pay the taxi driver.

> A 21-day-old girl was in critical condition in the Hospital for Sick Children last night three days after she was badly beaten. The child suffered a fractured skull as well as extensive injuries to her head, back and buttocks early Friday afternoon.

> A 19-year-old father was sentenced yesterday to five years in penitentiary after pleading guilty to a charge of manslaughter in the death of his 14-month-old son.

As Johnson (1972) says,

> Each year about 700 children kill someone, with about one-third of the victims being other family members. Much more frequent than intra-familial murder is child abuse and neglect (the battered child syndrome) [p. 130].

The quotation emphasises the frequency as much as the salience of the crime, and it is frequency, perhaps, more than salience that causes society concern over crime.

Legal and penal systems are devices that society uses to arrange contingencies on crime. They define criminal behaviors, classify them, and specify consequences of apprehension. The law is concerned with the nature of the crime. It may specify "an eye for an eye and a tooth for a tooth" or even more than this, as in penalties of death for minor thefts and rape. As recently as 1938, Burt, the prime mover of the Child Guidance movement in Britain, was required to argue for a different point of view, one which represented the psychologist's rather than the policeman's stance:

It is not on the investigation of the offence but on the investigation of the offender that (the psychologist's) efforts are primarily focussed [Burt, 1938, p. 51].

From this standpoint Burt classifies a number of crimes according to motivational, emotional, or instinctive characteristics of the criminal, an abbreviation of which is shown in Table 1. Psychological investigations, according to Burt, concern themselves with strengths of emotions or instincts, such as hunger and sex, or with such pathological states as psychopathy or sadism, not the apprehension of offenders. The change of emphasis from law enforcement to psychological analysis is from organism *response* (the crime) to *organism* (the criminal) response. This emphasis may be described as the analysis of *psychic dependence* as it is characteristics of the psyche that are thought to determine the occurrence of behavior, including crimes.

Salience, Frequency, and Contingency

One unfortunate aspect that this viewpoint perpetuates is the disregarding of behavior before an offence is committed. Children, or adults, are labeled habit-

TABLE 1

Classified List of Juvenile Offences[a]

1. Sex
2. Anger
   a. Bodily violence to persons
     (i) Murder
     (ii) Wounding
     (iii) Violence without weapons
     (iv) Cruel injury to children or animals
   b. Angry reactions without violence
     (i) Bad temper
     (ii) Incorrigibility
     (iii) False accusations
     (iv) Insults
     (v) Cruelty
   c. Violence to property
     (i) Malicious damage
     (ii) Mischievous damage
     (iii) Arson
3. Acquisitiveness
4. Wandering
5. Grief
6. Secretiveness

[a]Abbreviated from Burt (1938, pp. 15–16).

ual offenders according to the frequency of their apprehension but not necessarily according to the frequency of particular behaviors emitted. A good example of the value of close attention to frequencies of behavior is the case of one of the girls that Mr. Cusack alluded to above. Mary Bell was accused of two child murders, one certainly and the other probably by strangulation. Sereny's (1972) account of the life of Mary Bell reveals a number of strangling incidents in which Mary was involved. These incidents are summarized in Table 2, which

TABLE 2

Strangling Incicents (or Allegations) Concerning Mary Bell[a]

1. May 11, 1968	John G., 3 years old, injured—"bleeding from his head" [p. 20].
2. May 12, 1968	Cindy Hepple: She put her hands around my neck and squeezed hard . . . The girl took her hands off my neck and she did the same to Susan [p. 21].
3. May 25, 1968	Martin Brown, 4 years 2 months, found dead in derelict house. Date 7/68. Mary said (to friends) "Norma [Bell] put her hands on a boy's throat. It was Martin Brown; she pressed and he just dropped" [p. 34].
4. May 26, 1968	"When Susan's parents heard her scream they dashed out, they say, and saw Mary and Susan standing near the front door of the house, Mary with both hands around Susan's neck [p. 31]."
5. July 31, 1968	Brian Howe, 3 years 4 months, found dead with "pressure marks and scratches on both sides of his neck" [p. 37].
6. Aug. 15, 1968	At remand home in Croydon. Mary could not sleep and was crying. She said she felt she was being strangled [p. 60].
7. Dec. 7, 1968	Policewoman Jean Q., in Detention Center. "I looked up and I saw first that she was holding the cat by the skin at the back of the neck . . . then I realized that she was holding the cat so tight it could not breathe and its tongue was rolling . . . . I said, "you mustn't do that; you'll hurt her." She answered, "Oh, she doesn't feel that, and anyway, I like hurting little things that can't fight back" [p. 82].
8. Mid-1969	"Early in her detention, on at least two occasions, she was involved in the more or less mysterios demise of some hamsters which died of neck injuries" [p. 222].

[a]Constructed from Sereny (1972).

probably contains only a small proportion of actual incidents because it is based on accounts recalled at long intervals after the events.

Psychological analysis in the psychic-dependence paradigm does not operate in isolation from environmental events. Naturally attention is given to heredity, but historical and contemporary situational factors also enter the account. More or less detailed accounts of the social backgrounds, historical situational events, are given by Sereny (1972) for Mary Bell and by Burt (1938) for Jeremiah Jones. These accounts are of immense importance as sources of hypotheses concerning criminality and social delinquency but their value as bases for the scientific analysis of behavior is limited if they describe structural situations rather than specific dynamic contingency events. The manner of dress of a young delinquent shown in the frontispiece of Burt's book says much about the living circumstances of the boy depicted if one is acquainted with life among the London poor (e.g., Quennell, no date), but it is a different kind of information that the following comments convey about Mary Bell (Sereny, 1972):

> *Kindergarten, 1961* (age 5): The teacher told of an occasion when Mary had put her hands around a smaller child's neck and pressed. "Don't do that, you mustn't do that," she had said to Mary. "That's naughty." "Why?" Mary asked, "Can it kill him?" [p. 191].

> *November 15, 1967*: Mary wrote in school Newsbook, "On Saturday I was coming from the park with susan and the (sic) was loads of police cars. I went over. There had been a baby found dead in a polthene (sic) bag" [p. 199].

> *The Trial, December 13, 1968*: ..."Do you know what the Bible is?" "Yes, sir." The general public did not know, but the Court and several members of the press were aware that the Bible had a very special meaning in Mary's life .... Billy Bell was to say later, "She had five of them, she was always reading the Bible." But he did not know that what apparently mesmerized Mary in one of the Bibles was a list of names, dates and addresses that had been glued in—the list of relatives who had died [p. 96].

As Sereny sums it up,

> Mary had always been conspicuous: she had for years hit, kicked, scratched and "nipped" other children, done everything to attract her teacher's attention .... *Few paid attention to her.* On the contrary, most were resolved to ignore her. So she went further. She killed pigeons by throttling them, *"You stop that, Mary Bell,"* they said. She put her hands around the throat of a newborn baby lying in his pram, *"Mary—leave him be,"* somebody shouted ..." [p. 200, italics added].

Mary had indeed "always been conspicuous" and a psychic-dependent disorder naturally comes to mind. However, there is another aspect of Mary's circumstances that the quotations bring to light—the attention she demanded and the throttling that could not be ignored. Contingencies, or reinforcement schedules for throttling, were at work in Mary's life.

On the basis of these it may not be Mary as a person that a psychological analyses needs to describe but the dynamic interpersonal environment in which Mary happened to live.

Structural and Dynamic Environments

The environment of an organism may be described structurally or dynamically in terms of its effects on behavior. Structural descriptions are common, but dynamic descriptions are necessary for completeness in accounting for behavior. Lecture halls are often unexciting sorts of places but at the very least they encourage the roving eye—which is behavior. Looking from one place to another is a dynamic event in which an environmental change accompanies the behavior. The behavior is not impervious to the change.

Experimental spaces are usually topographically barren, more or less, but exhibit such dramatic dynamic properties as delivery of food or electric shock contingent on temporal or behavioral events. "Schedule dependence" refers to the behavioral effects of specific changes in the environment. The term derives from schedules of reinforcement (Ferster & Skinner, 1957), which are rules about contingencies between specified responses and environmental changes. It is the concept of reinforcement schedule that dictates the choice of "schedule dependence" to describe a dynamic environment that contains an organism (in contrast to the conventional organism that is in an environment) as a focus for the study of behavior. However, schedule dependence is not restricted to the contingencies between specified responses and reinforcers. Reinforcement schedules have effects beyond their direct control over schedule-specified responses; these effects are included in the concept of schedule dependence.

I shall illustrate aspects of schedule dependence in the case of aggression with some data on three kinds of schedule effects: direct schedule effects, where biting is a specified behavior; schedule-induced biting; and schedule-dependent effects, where fighting and biting depend on schedules that specify or have specified other behavior.

SCHEDULE DEPENDENCE AND AGGRESSION

Schedule-Specified Biting

Two early experiments, by Reynolds, Catania, and Skinner (1963) with pigeons and by Ulrich, Johnston, Richardson, and Wolff (1963) with rats, investigated the operant conditioning of fighting. In the case of the pigeons, hungry birds were paired and each was trained to peck its partner for grain reinforcement in the presence of a particular colored light—blue or green. With the rats, one in a pair was satiated, whereas the other was water deprived and reinforced with water for making aggressive responses. In both experiments more fighting than was necessary occurred and seemed to consist of two types of behavior: operant fighting that did not exhibit the full characteristics of an "instinctive pattern" and "released unconditioned fighting" (Reynolds *et al.*, 1963). These two types of behavior resemble the nonviolent murders attributed to such child murderers as Jeremiah Jones and Mary Bell, and the violent batterings through which some parents, probably unintentionally, kill their children.

My own studies of schedule-specified aggression have focused on biting by rats. There are two problems involved with using unrestrained animals in pairs: the problem of subjectivity in counting responses and the problem of the elicitation of responses by counterattack. These problems have been resolved by using restrained target animals (Azrin, Hutchinson, & Hake, 1966), stuffed models (Flory, 1969a) and inanimate objects suitable for receiving and recording bites (Azrin, Hutchinson, & McLaughlin, 1965; Azrin, Rubin, & Hutchinson, 1968). In the present studies a bar has been fixed in place of a normal lever in a Lehigh-Valley experimental chamber so that bar bites but not bar presses operate electronic scheduling and recording equipment. The rats are normally maintained at 80% body weight and reinforcements (45 mg Noyes pellets) are scheduled on various fixed- and variable-interval schedules during daily sessions that are usually 100 min long.

Figures 1 and 2 show typical cumulative biting records of two subjects under fixed-interval reinforcement schedules of 15 sec, 1, 2, 3, 4, and 5 min. These records exhibit the typical scalloping patterns characteristic of cumulative records of bar pressing and key pecking under the same reinforcement schedules. They also show numerous aberrations and "breakthroughs" that are also not uncommon in key-pecking records (Ferster and Skinner, 1957). Interpretation of "breakthroughs", or "takeoffs" (Ulrich, Dulaney, Kucera, & Colasacco, 1972) is not clear, for they may represent weak inhibitory control of operant bites by stimuli associated with the beginning of intervals or they may be examples of aggressive bites that are reinforcing in their own right. Azrin *et al.* (1965) have shown that biting is reinforcing in the sense that monkeys will pull a chain if it releases a tennis ball that they may bite.

That the bites recorded in Figures 1 and 2 may be of more than one kind is suggested by work on autoshaping in pigeons (Brown and Jenkins, 1968). Work by Schwartz and Williams (1972) indicates that not all key pecks in experiments of this kind need be under a single source of control, i.e., in the same functional or topographical category. They have shown that under a negative automaintenance condition, in which key pecks postpone the deliveries of grain, pecks are of shorter durations than under conditions in which pecks have no effect on the grain delivery schedule.

It is possible that short-duration pecks are aggressive in kind (Schwartz and Williams call them direct effects of food presentation as against contingent effects of food presentation), a possibility supported by the emotional wing-flapping and neck-stretching behaviors emitted by pigeons during autoshaping training sessions. If this is true then cumulative records of pigeons' key pecks may commonly confound operant pecks and aggression pecks. The rats' biting records shown in Figures 1 and 2 may be similarly confounded. Other evidence on

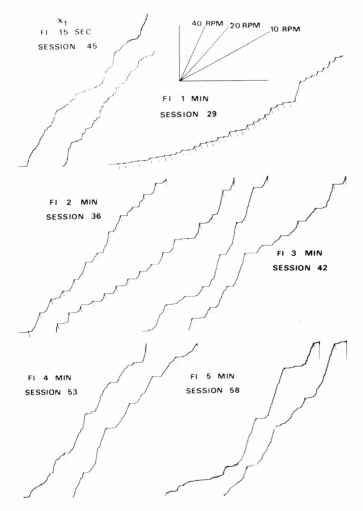

FIG. 1   Sample cumulative records of bar biting by a single rat reinforced with food pellets for bar biting on fixed-interval (FI) schedules as marked. Pellet deliveries are indicated by hatchmarks on the records.

this matter is presented below in the case of response bursts under Sidman (1953) avoidance schedules.

Deprivation and Schedule-Specified Biting

Another way of assessing the self-reinforcing aspect of biting is by control of food deprivation. A response that has no intrinsic reinforcing properties, as is assumed in the case of lever pressing and key pecking, will vary in rate according to amount of weight loss. If biting is supported by factors that are independent of its food-securing function then it may remain at high rate even though weight loss is reduced. In fact, biting for food decreases in rate as body weight increases from 80 to 95% when rats are reinforced for several sessions on a variable-interval 1-min schedule. Session by session data for two rats are shown in Figure 3.

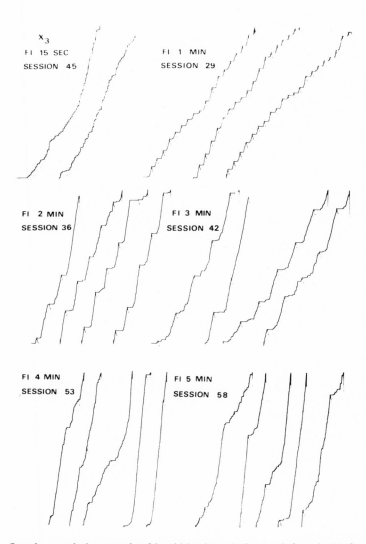

FIG. 2 Sample cumulative records of bar biting by a single rat reinforced with food pellets for bar biting on fixed-interval (FI) schedules as marked. Pellet deliveries are indicated by hatch marks on the records.

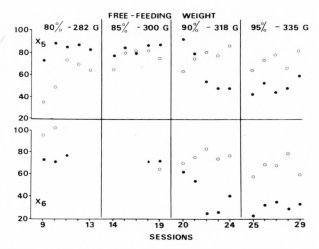

FIG. 3 Bar bites per minute (solid circles) of two rats at the indicated percents of free-feeding weights with biting reinforced by pellets on a variable-interval 1-min schedule. Open circles show licks per pellet in individual sessions in which 100 pellets were normally secured.

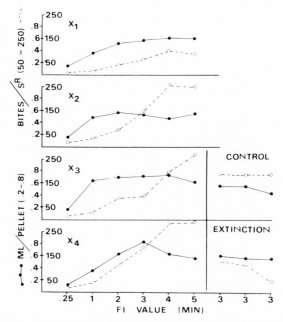

FIG. 4 Mean bites per pellet (open circles) at indicated fixed-interval reinforcement schedules up to 5 min under normal conditions and under "extinction" conditions (X4) when pellets were delivered independently of biting at 3-min fixed intervals. All values are averages of five sessions. Filled circles are average schedule-induced water intakes.

Extinction of Schedule-Specified Biting

"Extinction" is a confusing term that has been used indiscriminately to describe a process and a product. In the case of positive reinforcement it has typically referred to the process of withholding reinforcement, with a typical decline in response emission. In the case of negative reinforcement extinction usually specifies removal of the motivating stimulus, e.g., electric shock, which may not reduce responding for a considerable time (Sidman, 1955). Alternative extinction procedures are the differential reinforcement of other behavior (DRO) with positive reinforcers and rendering the response ineffectual in the negative case.

Figure 4 shows the effect of making bar biting unnecessary for the production of food. The animal (X4) that has received pellets freely shows a decline in bar biting over the 15 sessions depicted in the figure, whereas the control subject, which has still been required to bite for food, maintains its biting rate over the same period. When the conventional extinction procedure of not reinforcing bar biting is used biting quickly extinguishes, as Figure 5 depicts in the case of animal X2. For the first 25 min of the 90-min session shown in the figure pellets are scheduled for bar biting at 1-min. fixed intervals.

Schedule-Induced Biting

Extinction-Induced Aggression with Positive Reinforcement

Schedule-induced aggression was reported by Azrin *et al.* (1966) using pigeons as subjects in an experimental chamber that contained a target bird as well as the usual manipulanda and feeding mechanism. In two experiments, with one bird in a pair restrained and the other free, no reinforcements were presented to either bird. Then, for several sessions the free bird was trained with a multiple schedule of reinforcement in which extinction periods and reinforcement periods, either

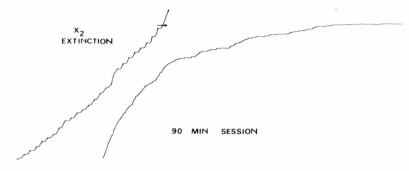

FIG. 5 Typical cumulative record of bar biting. Bites were reinforced at fixed intervals of 1 min up to the arrow and unreinforced thereafter.

response dependent or response independent, alternated. With several pairs of birds the multiple schedule induced fighting that had not occurred when no food was available, and the fighting mostly happened when the extinction periods were in effect. Similar findings were reported with monkeys (Hutchinson, Azrin, & Hunt, 1968) and with rats (Thompson & Bloom, 1966).

Explicit extinction periods are not necessary for the production of schedule-induced aggression, nor need reinforcement depend on a specified response. Flory (1969a) has used an experimental arrangement similar to that of Azrin *et al*. (1966) except that the target is a taxidermically prepared model arranged so that a microswitch closes whenever the model's head is attacked with a force of 35 gm or more. The subjects are two pigeons that are presented food for 4 sec every 15, 30, 60, 120, 240, 480, or 960 sec, with the proviso that food presentations cannot occur within 15 sec of an attack to prevent superstitious conditioning (Skinner, 1948).

Frequencies of attack according to interfeeding times were maximum at 120 sec for one bird and 60 sec for the other. These attacks, Flory reports, mostly occur just after food presentations, or at the beginning of interfeeding intervals. Flory's findings on aggressive pecking by pigeons closely parallel those of schedule-induced drinking by rats (Falk, 1961, 1972), where there is also a bitonic relation between schedule-induced drinking and interpellet interval. This finding has been reported many times (Falk, 1966; Flory, 1971; Hawkins, Schrot, Githens, & Everett, 1972).

Keehn and Colotla (1971) distinguished two kinds of licking that may relate to the aforementioned distinction, made by Schwartz and Williams (1972), between direct food-controlled and contingency food-controlled key pecks by pigeons. With respect to drinking, postpellet drinking is a direct effect of food (actually unavailability of food) and interpellet drinking, which occurs toward the end of interpellet intervals, is contingency controlled (Segal, 1969).

In the experiments on schedule-specified biting described above, schedule-induced postpellet biting does not occur, as the scalloped cumulative records in Figures 1 and 2 indicate. However, opportunities for schedule-induced drinking exist if water bottles are available. Typical postpellet drinking is found, as Figure 6 shows, except that postpellet drinking does not give way to interpellet drinking at long interpellet intervals, and drinking is not bitonically related to interpellet interval.

Doubtless, complex relationships between topographical and dynamic properties of the environment determine how schedule-induced drinking, biting, and other behaviors occur, but phylogenetic factors are important too. In studying postreinforcement pauses in fixed-ratio reinforcement schedules with Maudsley-reactive (MR) and Maudsley-nonreactive (MNR) rats (Broadhurst, 1960; Jay, 1963), Keehn (1963) noticed that the MNR animals almost always drink between reinforcements, whereas the MR subjects more typically bite the bar. This observation has been checked in an experiment in which three animals of

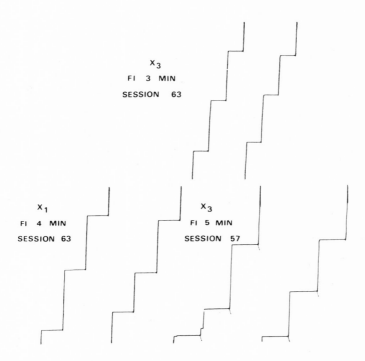

FIG. 6 Cumulative records of schedule-induced drinking by two hungry rats reinforced at fixed intervals of 3, 4, and 5 min for bar biting. Cumulative biting records of these animals are shown in Figs. 1 and 2; fluid intake and response rate data are shown in Fig. 4.

each strain were reinforced for bar pressing on a fixed-interval 1-min schedule in Lehigh-Valley rat chambers equipped with water bottles and bite bars. Figures 7 and 8 show how members of the two strains drink: the MNRs (R4, R5, R6) regularly in interreinforcement intervals, the MR's (R1, R2, R3) erratically and to a much lower level. Figure 9 provides comparison data on a daily basis of the total licks of individuals of the two strains. It shows clearly that the difference in drinking between the strains can develop quickly and that there are no overlaps in intakes after the first few days.

The daily biting records (Figure 10) are not so regular. All animals exhibit biting that rises to a maximum and then declines, except in the case of the MR subject R2. In a study of lever biting during Sidman avoidance conditioning, Pear, Moody, and Persinger (1972) have also noticed that bar biting rises to a maximum and then declines. The erratic nature of schedule-induced biting within a session by individual animals is illustrated by Figures 11 and 12. In contrast to biting, schedule-induced drinking is regular and predictable (Keehn & Colotla, 1970).

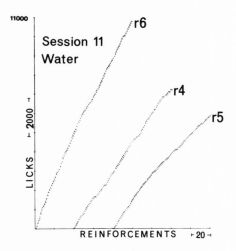

FIG. 7 Constructed cumulative records of schedule-induced licks at a water bottle by three rats of the MNR strain. Primary data were computer printouts of total licks at the times of reinforcement, which are indicated by blips on the record.

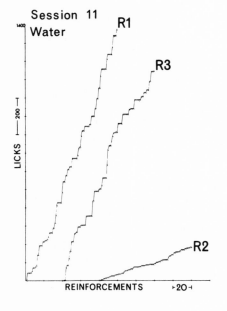

FIG. 8 Constructed cumulative records of schedule-induced licks at a water bottle by three rats of the MR strain. Primary data were computer printouts of total licks at the times of reinforcement, which are indicated by blips on the record. Note that the ordinate scale is one-tenth that of Fig. 7 and that the MR animals did not drink regularly after reinforcements.

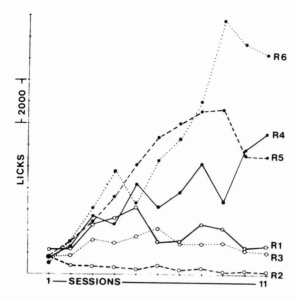

FIG. 9 Total schedule-induced licks per 100-min sessions of three MR (R1, R2, R3) and three MNR (R4, R5, R6) rats reinforced at fixed intervals of 1 min with food for bar pressing.

FIG. 10 Total schedule-induced bar bites corresponding to licks shown in Fig. 9.

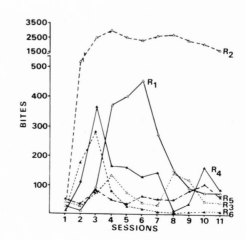

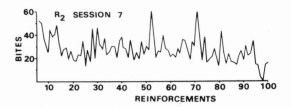

FIG. 11 Total bites following successive reinforcements of MR subject R2 in a typical 100-min session. See Fig. 8 for corresponding licking, plotted cumulatively, by this animal.

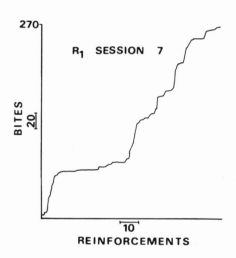

FIG. 12 Constructed cumulative record of bar biting by the MR subject R1. See Fig. 8 for a corresponding record of schedule-induced licking by this animal.

Pain-Elicited Aggression with Electric Shock

Much more regular biting behavior is induced by periodic electric shocks than is induced by periodic feeding, although animals are usually held in a more constrained position when shock is studied. A restraining tube for a rat given tail shock is described by Azrin *et al.* (1968). These workers have used a wooden target, a rubber target and a bite bar. Their general procedure is to give tail shocks every 10 sec over the middle 20 min of 60-min sessions. They have obtained shock-induced biting with all targets. The rubber target, they report, is inferior to the wooden target in eliciting biting but is superior to the metal bite bar on which the rats average only four bites a minute. It is possible that the erratic biting induced with positive reinforcement is a function of the target used rather than the type of reinforcement, for biting rubber may furnish a more favorable feedback for further biting than does biting a metal bar.

The use of a rubber hose as a stimulus for pain-induced biting was initiated by Hutchinson, Azrin, and Hake (1966). In work with squirrel monkeys, biting on the hose manipulandum has been shown to vary lawfully with tail-shock voltage (Hutchinson, Azrin, & Renfrew, 1968) and with shock–shock interval. The regularity of pain-elicited biting as voltage is changed is also reported by Hutchinson and Emley (1972). With continued exposure to recurrent shocks, however, a new pattern of behavior emerges, in which biting continues through the shock–shock interval, and resembles the pattern of behavior maintained by fixed-interval schedules of positive reinforcement. Hutchinson and Emley (1972) also report classical conditioned biting elicited by a flashing light, but other attempts to classically condition fighting in rats have been less successful (Creer, Hitzing, & Schaeffer, 1966; Vernon & Ulrich, 1966). The difference may be a function of species (monkeys vs. rats), response specification (bite hose vs. a live target), or conditioned stimulus (light vs. tone).

Pre- and postshock responding need not both occur on the same manipulandum. Hutchinson and Emley (1972) report the accidental discovery that if a lever is available some monkeys press it during shock–shock intervals. In these cases lever presses (which are nonfunctional) show scalloped cumulative response curves accelerating up to shock, whereas hose bites show typical postshock bursts. Confirmatory data have been reported by Hake and Campbell (1972), who have first conditioned press responses with a fixed-interval (FI) schedule of negative reinforcement (shock termination on FI schedule) and then have added a bite hose as a second manipulandum. As have Hutchinson and Emley (1972), they have found an increasing rate of manual responding until just before shock, when a conditioned suppression occurs, and a brief burst of postshock biting. This behavior bears some resemblance to the maintance of behavior by response-produced shocks, as Hutchinson and McKearney have argued (McKearney, 1972).

A final example of shock-induced biting was the burst of responses that occurred after shocks during Sidman avoidance training (Sidman, 1958). Pear *et al.* (1972) designed a bite bar to see whether these bursts were bar bites rather than bar presses. They did demonstrate that both kinds of responses occurred, confirming an earlier report by Boren (1961) that post-shock response bursts on Sidman avoidance schedules belonged in a different class from those responses that occurred later in response–shock intervals. Boren (1961) separated the two response classes by bar location, Pear *et al.* (1972) by response topography.

Schedule Effects on Aggression

Schedules of reinforcement maintain behavior and the behavior so maintained may be more or less impervious to extraneous effects. It is well known, for example, that behavior maintained by ratio schedules of reinforcement is often hard to disrupt (Sidman, 1960) and that some drugs have different effects on behavior according to the reinforcement schedule in effect (Dews, 1956; Mc-Kearney, 1972). Two broad classes of effects are conceivable with respect to schedule interactions with aggression: historical effects, in which the effects of prior experience on performance under a standard ongoing schedule are compared, and contemporary effects, where comparison is made of the effects of a standard procedure, e.g., punishment, when different contemporary maintaining schedules prevail. I shall give illustrations of the former and of an intermediary case, in which continuous and intermittent punishment of aggression are compared.

Escape and Avoidance Histories

The induction of fighting by painful stimuli may have an advantageous effect if the stimulus elicits fighting against an aggressor responsible for the pain. In other circumstances reflexive fighting may have a detrimental result. Ulrich (1967) has trained rats individually to press a bar to terminate painful electric shock and has then tested them in pairs in which either rat may stop the shock. This results not in improved but in deteriorated performance, because instead of terminating the shock when it appears the animals fight before one of them presses the bar. A similar result has been obtained by Logan (1972) with a signalled avoidance procedure. Logan reports that avoidance wheel-turning performance deteriorates because "a large dominant male rat may hold a small submissive male by the head and prevent him from getting to the wheel. . . . And then, when the submissive rat finally turns the shock off, the dominant rat frequently aggresses him again." (Logan, 1972, p. 1059). A feature of Logan's informally reported finding is that aggression occurred at shock offset, a characteristic not noticeable when fighting occurs in response to *brief* periodic shocks.

The effect of prior histories of avoidable and unavoidable shock on shock-induced fighting by pairs of rats was studied by Powell, Francis, Francis, and Schneiderman (1972). Their experiment was conducted in two stages. Two sets of four white rats were used. In Stage 1, all animals in a set of four were exposed at 2.5 mA shocks of 0.5-sec duration at 2-sec intervals (S—S interval) unless one of the subjects, an isolated "avoid" subject, pressed a bar. In this case shock was postponed for 20 sec for all members of the group. The three other subjects, an isolate and a pair, had no control over the shock. In Stage 2 of the experiment the subjects were tested in various pair combinations, with results that differed according to the animals' roles in Stage 1. Most fighting on the occasions of shocks occurred between the originally paired rats that had histories of fighting in Stage 1, particularly when dominant and nondominant fighters (one from each set of four) were paired in Stage 2. The avoiders, who could continue to avoid, fought only slightly less. Least fighting of all was exhibited by pairings of nondominant, no-response, and avoid subjects. The experiment showed that shock-induced aggression was a modifiable phenomenon according to pre-experimental histories prior to a standard test.

Aggression-Contingent Punishment

Can pain-elicited fighting be controlled by consequent aversive events? The answer appears to be negative insofar as punishment can be expected to elicit further aggression, and insofar as animals that once avoided shock fight when they fail to avoid even though this leads to further shocks. Nevertheless results of the paired avoiders reported by Powell *et al.* (1972) show that fighting may decrease with training; and Myer and Baenninger (1966) have shown that attacking of mice by rats is suppressed by response-contingent shock.

Suppression of shock-induced hose biting by squirrel monkeys was achieved by Ulrich and his co-workers (Ulrich *et al.*, 1972) with response-contingent shock to the tail, but sometimes facilitation of biting occurred. Facilitation appeared when punishment of biting was intermittent and when two bite hoses, one on which biting was punished and one on which it was not, were used. In this case elevated rates of biting occurred on the unpunished hose when biting on the other bar was punished.

Aggression induced by positive reinforcement schedules is amenable to punishment by the withholding of reinforcement (time out) as well as by administration of painful shock. Using the standard experimental arrangement of Hutchinson *et al.* (1966), Flory (1972) has reinforced two food-deprived monkeys with food pellets on fixed-ratio schedules of 50 or 20 responses per pellet, schedules on which stable attack behavior occurs. Following this, the food-producing lever is withdrawn for 10 sec. If the gum-rubber bite tube is attacked in this period the time-out interval is increased until 10 sec pass without attack, at which time the food lever is reintroduced.

Under this time-out condition, one monkey bit less and the other bit more than in the baseline condition. At longer time-out durations, however, 30 sec in one case and 60 sec in the other, attack frequencies were reduced for both animals. As Flory (1972) noted, the time-out contingency was actually a differential reinforcement for other behavior (DRO) than attacking the rubber tube. This aggression-controlling procedure was used by Reynolds *et al.* (1963), who stopped pigeons from fighting by reinforcing them for going to opposite corners of a box. Powell *et al.* (1972) in the experiment described above, also provided evidence suggesting that aggression was reduced through the acquisition of incompatible behavior.

Time-out procedures have been used in practical settings to reduce aggressive behavior in children (Bostow & Bailey, 1969; Corte, Wolf, & Locke, 1971). Comparison of the effects of time out on aggressive behavior induced by various positive schedules of reinforcement has not been systematically studied yet. However, as fixed-interval (Cherek & Heistad, 1971), differential reinforcement of high-rate (Knutson & Kleinknecht, 1970), fixed-time (Flory, 1969a), and multiple (Hutchinson *et al.*, 1966, 1968; Flory, 1969b) as well as fixed-ratio schedules of reinforcement all induce aggressive behavior, the possibilities of direct studies of the effects of a standard procedure (time out) on aggressive behavior maintained by different schedules of reinforcement are clear.

The value of attending to the dynamic properties of the environment and not just to the psychic qualities of the organism has now been abundantly demonstrated in the study of aggression. Understanding of environments that enhance and suppress biting attack is increasing, as is understanding of the differences between schedule-specified and schedule-induced aggressive behaviors. What now needs concentrated investigation are the interactions between maintaining and suppressing schedules of environmental events, as bases on which to build technologies for the control and modification of destructive and aggressive behaviors of both types.

MODIFICATION OF AGGRESSION

Aggression as Reinforcing

Participation

To emphasize the environment in the control of behavior is not to entirely exclude consideration of the organism. After all, it is an organism that is behaving and some forms of behavior may be functionally self-reinforcing. The data presented above on the schedule-specified bar biting of rats shows little evidence of the behavior "taking off" from contingent-food control, but as Reynolds *et al.* (1963) have observed, and as I have tried to demonstrate with other examples, contingency-controlled fighting may differ from elicited unconditioned fighting.

Azrin *et al.* (1965) have shown that the opportunity to bite in the presence of pain-eliciting shock reinforces an arbitrary chain-pulling response, and examples of human behavior that give the impression of pleasurable fighting are common in sport and play. Violence conducted in the name of authority appears in many works of art, and other examples from all parts of the world appear in television and newspaper pictures from day to day. These typically exhibit the exaggerated forcefulness and frequency characteristic of all schedule-induced behaviors (Falk, 1972).

Observation

With humans, direct participation in violence may be less reinforcing than observation of violence or its effects. Boxing as a popular sport, and bear baiting, cock fighting and public executions have not lacked for audiences in their time.

Modern films of violence draw audiences in enormous numbers, as have the spectacles of gladiatorial slaughter promoted in ancient Roman times.

Observation of human violence is one step removed from actual participation, but participation in violence in modern times is itself often removed from the execution of violent acts or the witnessing of their effects. The stirring wartime speeches by Winston Churchill were more to fortify the British people in their determination to continue a long and apparently unrewarding war than to excite them into actual physical attack. Shakespeare's words for Henry V (Act 3, Sc. 1) on the field of Agincourt were written for quite another effect:

> In peace there's nothing so becomes a man
> As modest stillness and humility:
> But when the blast of war blows in our ears,
> Then imitate the action of the tiger;
> Stiffen the sinews, summon up the blood. . . .
> Then lend the eye a terrible aspect. . . .
> Now set the teeth and stretch the nostril wide,
> Hold hard the breath and bend up every spirit
> To his full height. On, on, you noblest English . . . .
> (W. Shakespeare, Henry V, Act III, Scene 1: Clark & Wright, No Date, p. 424)

In both cases, Shakespeare's poetry and Churchill's prose, the words retain their reinforcing effects far beyond the limits of their original intentions. Apart from the poetry, two things are significant in Henry's speech. The first is that it cannot have been necessary in the case of men already belligerent and committed to warlike acts; the second is that it specifies behavioral techniques for inducing belligerence—techniques that anticipate the James–Lange theory of emotion and the imitation theory of aggression.

Modeling and Avoidance of Aggression

The two major classes of theories of aggression, reactive and spontaneous (Eibl-Eibesfeldt, 1970), both have evidence to support them and both are incomplete, for aggression as schedule specified and aggression as schedule induced are under different sources of contol. Neither theory, however, needs to focus attention on intrapsychic qualities as determinants of fighting, for fighting and other aggressive behaviors are always under environmental control. The problem in the control of aggression is whether it is better to arrange environmental contingencies so that aggressive responses never occur, or to arrange for countercontrol measures to suppress aggressive behavior when it appears. It is impossible to answer this question fully now but it is possible to assert that aggression is a controllable phenomenon. Only its complete reliance on environmental circumstances must be understood, and from the evidence reviewed above it seems that environments that support behavior incompatible with aggression are the most hopeful circumstances for bringing aggression under control.

A question to resolve in the case of human aggression is the extent to which the reinforcement of the observation of aggression serves to strengthen behavior other than the participation in aggression or serves to provide models for the shaping of aggressive behavior itself. There is much evidence to suggest the latter (Bandura & Walters, 1963) but the possibility remains that the modeling behavior, like response-specified biting in rats, monkeys, and pigeons, is something less than the phylogenetically determined instinctive behaviors observed in predation and territorial defence.

CONCLUSIONS

Let me conclude with a remark made by Miron (1966) concerning the punitive control of aggression:

> One morning, I attempted to terminate some aggressive behavior by one of the patients; I used the squirt bottle, and the response was so immediate and reinforcing to my own behavior that I found myself watching her very closely, squirt bottle in hand; observers commented that I appeared almost to be "stalking" the patient, anticipating the opportunity to use the squirt bottle. I must admit that I was surprised at the sudden feeling of mild disappointment when her forbidden behavior was not forthcoming [p. 9].

This can be recognized as an example of operant schedule-specified aggression—the squirting, stalking, and feeling behaviors are all under response-contingent control. These behaviors clearly differ from the temper responses to "frustration" with which we are equally familiar. The experimental analysis of aggression has begun to isolate the environmental conditions responsible for the establishment and maintenance of both schedule-specified and schedule-induced aggression and may eventually serve to help bring these behaviors under benevolent social control.

REFERENCES

Azrin, N. H., Hutchinson, R. R., & Hake, D. F. Extinction-induced aggression. *Journal of the Experimental Analysis of Behavior*, 1966, 9, 191–204.

Azrin, N. H., Hutchinson, R. R., & McLaughlin, R. The opportunity for aggression as an operant reinforcer during aversive stimulation. *Journal of the Experimental Analysis of Behavior*, 965, 8, 171–180.

Azrin, N. H., Rubin, H. B., & Hutchinson, R. R. Biting attack by rats in response to aversive shock. *Journal of the Experimental Analysis of Behavior*, 1968, 11, 633–639.

Bakan, D. *Slaughter of the Innocents*. Toronto: CBC Learning Systems, 1971.

Bandura, A., & Walters, R. *Social learning and personality development*. New York: Holt, Rinehart & Winston, 1963.

Boren, J. J. Isolation of post-shock responding in a free operant avoidance procedure. *Psychological Reports*, 1961, 9, 265–266.

Bostow, D. E., & Bailey, J. B. Modification of severe disruptive and aggressive behavior using brief time-out and reinforcement procedures. *Journal of Applied Behavior Analysis*, 1969, 2, 31–37.

Broadhurst, P. L. Experiments in psychogenetics: Applications of biometrical genetics to the inheritance of behavior. In H. J. Eysenck (Ed.), *Experiments in personality*, Vol. 1. *Psychogenetics and psychopharmacology*. London: Routledge & Kegan Paul, 1960.

Brown, P. L., & Jenkins, H. M. Auto-shaping of the pigeon's key-peck. *Journal of the Experimental Analysis of Behavior*, 1968, 11, 1–8.

Burt, C. *The young delinquent*. (4th ed.). London: University of London Press, 1938.

Cherek, D. R., & Heistad, G. T. Fixed-interval-induced aggression. *Psychonomic Science*, 1971, 25, 7–8.

Clark, W. G., & Wright, W. Aldis (Eds.), *The complete works of William Shakespeare*. Garden City, N.Y.: Nelson Doubleday, no date.

Colotla, V. A., Keehn, J. D., & Gardner, L. L. Control of schedule-induced drinking by interpellet intervals. *Psychonomic Science*, 1970, 21, 137–139.

Corte, H., Wolf, M. M., & Locke, B. J. A comparison of procedures for eliminating self-injurious behavior of retarded adolescents. *Journal of Applied Behavior Analysis*, 1971, 4, 201–213.

Creer, T. L., Hitzing, E. W., & Schaeffer, R. Classical conditioning of reflexive fighting. *Psychonomic Science*, 1966, 4, 89–90.

Dews, P. B. Modification by drugs of performance on simple schedules of positive reinforcement. *Annals of the New York Academy of Sciences*, 1956, 65, 268–281.

Eibl-Eibesfeldt, I. *Ethology: the biology of behavior* (E. Klinghammer, transl.). New York: Holt, Rinehart & Winston, 1970.

Falk, J. L. Production of polydipsia in normal rats by an intermittent food schedule. *Science*, 1961, 133, 195–196.

Falk, J. L. Schedule-induced polydipsia as a function of fixed-interval length. *Journal of the Experimental Analysis of Behavior*, 1966, 9, 37–39.

Falk, J. L. The nature and determinants of adjunctive behavior. In R. M. Gilbert & J. D. Keehn (Eds.), *Schedule effects: drugs, drinking and aggression*. Toronto: University of Toronto Press, 1972.

Ferster, C. B., & Skinner, B. F. *Schedules of reinforcement*, New York: Appleton-Century-Crofts, 1957.

Flory, R. K. Attack behavior as a function of minimum inter-food interval. *Journal of the Experimental Analysis of Behavior*, 1969, 12, 825–828.   (a)

Flory, R. K. Attack behavior in a multiple fixed-ratio schedule of reinforcement. *Psychonomic Science*, 1969, 16, 156–157.   (b)

Flory, R. K. The control of schedule-induced polydipsia: frequency and magnitude of reinforcement. *Learning & Motivation*, 1971, 2, 215–227.

Flory, R. K. Punishment of fixed-ratio schedule-induced aggression in monkeys. Paper presented at the 18th Annual Meeting of the Southeast Psychological Association, Atlanta, Georgia, 1972.

Hake, D. F., & Campbell, R. L. Characteristics and response-displacement effects of shock-generated responding during negative reinforcement procedures: pre-shock responding and post-shock aggressive responding. *Journal of the Experimental Analysis of Behavior*, 1972, 17, 303–323.

Hawkins, T. D., Schrot, J. F., Githens, S. H., & Everett, P. B. Schedule-induced polydipsia:

an analysis of water and alcohol ingestion. In R. M. Gilbert & J. D. Keehn (Eds.), *Schedule effects: drugs, drinking and aggression*. Toronto: University of Toronto Press, 1972.

Hutchinson, R. R., Azrin, N. H. & Hake, D. F. An automatic method for the study of aggression in squirrel monkeys. *Journal of the Experimental Analysis of Behavior*, 1966, **9**, 233–237.

Hutchinson, R. R., Azrin, N. H., & Hunt, G. M. Attack produced by intermittent reinforcement of a concurrent operant response. *Journal of the Experimental Analyses of Behavior*, 1968, **11**, 485–495.

Hutchinson, R. R., Azrin, N. H., & Renfrew, J. W. Effects of Shock intensity and duration on the frequency of biting attack by squirrel monkeys. *Journal of the Experimental Analysis of Behavior*, 1968, **11**, 83–88.

Hutchinson, R. R., & Emley, G. S. Schedule-independent factors contributing to schedule-induced phenomena. In R. M. Gilbert & J. D. Keehn (Eds.), *Schedule effects: drugs, drinking and aggression*, Toronto: University of Toronto Press, 1972.

Innis, N. K., & Keehn, J. D. Comment. In R. M. Gilbert & J. D. Keehn (Eds.), *Schedule effects: drugs, drinking and aggression*. Toronto: University of Toronto Press, 1972.

Jay, G. E. Genetic strains and stocks. In W. J. Burdette (Ed.), *Methodology in mammalian genetics*. San Francisco: Holden-Day, 1963.

Johnson, R. N. *Aggression in man and animals*. Philadelphia: Saunders, 1972.

Keehn, J. D. A reversal effect with pauses on mixed schedules of reinforcement. *Nature*, 1963, **200**, 1124–1125.

Keehn, J. D. Review of F. R. Brush (Ed.) *Aversive conditioning and learning. Behavior Therapy*, 1972, **3**, 374–377.

Keehn, J. D., & Colotla, V. A. Predictability of schedule-induced drink durations. *Psychonomic Science*, 1970, **18**, 297–298.

Keehn, J. D., & Colotla, V. A. Schedule-induced drinking as a function of interpellet interval. *Psychonomic Science*, 1971, **23**, 69–71.

Knutson, J. F., & Kleinknecht, R. A. Attack during differential reinforcement of a low rate of responding. *Psychonomic Science*, 1970, **19**, 289–290.

Logan, F. A. Experimental psychology of animal learning and now. *American Psychologist*, 1972, **27**, 1055–1062.

McKearney, J. W. Schedule dependent effects: effects of drugs, and maintenance of responding with response-produced electric shocks. In R. M. Gilbert & J. D. Keehn (Eds.), *Schedule effects: drugs, drinking and aggression*. Toronto: University of Toronto Press, 1972.

Miron, N. Behavior shaping and group nursing with severely retarded patients. In J. Fisher & R. E. Harris (Eds.), *Reinforcement theory in psychological treatment—a symposium*. California Department of Mental Hygiene Research Monograph No. 8, 1966.

Myer, J. S., & Baenninger, R. Some effects of punishment and stress on mouse killing by rats. *Journal of Comparative & Physiological Psychology*, 1966, **62**, 292–297.

Pear, J. J., Moody, J. E., & Persinger, M. A. Lever attacking by rats during free-operant avoidance. *Journal of the Experimental Analysis of Behavior*, 1972, **18**, 517–523.

Powell, D. A., Francis, M. J., Francis, J., & Schneiderman, N. Shock-induced aggression as a function of prior experience with avoidance, fighting, or unavoidable shock. *Journal of the Experimental Analysis of Behavior*, 1972, **18**, 323–332.

Quennel, P. (Ed.) *Mayhew's London. Selections from London Labour and the London Poor*. (1st ed. 1851). London: Spring Books, no date.

Reynolds, G. S., Catania, A. C., & Skinner, B. F. Conditioned and unconditioned aggression in pigeons. *Journal of the Experimental Analysis of Behavior*, 1963, **6**, 73–74.

Schwartz, B., & Williams, D. R. Two different kinds of key peck in the pigeon: some properties of responses maintained by negative and positive response-reinforcer contingencies. *Journal of the Experimental Analysis of Behavior*, 1972, **18**, 201–216.

Segal, E. F. Transformation of polydipsic drinking into operant drinking: a paradigm? *Psychonomic Science*, 1969, **16**, 133–135.

Sereny, G. *The case of Mary Bell*. London: Methuen, 1972.

Sidman, M. Avoidance conditioning with brief shock and no exteroceptive warning signal. *Science*, 1953, **118**, 157–158.

Sidman, M. On the persistance of avoidance behavior. *Journal of Abnormal & Social Psychology*, 1955, **50**, 217–220.

Sidman, M. Some notes on "bursts" in free operant avoidance experiments. *Journal of the Experimental Analysis of Behavior*, 1958, **1**, 167–172.

Sidman, M. *Tactics of scientific research*. New York: Basic Books, 1960.

Skinner, B. F. "Superstition" in the pigeon. *Journal of Experimental Psychology*, 1948, **38**, 168–172.

Thompson, T., & Bloom, W. Aggressive behavior and extinction-induced response-rate increase. *Psychonomic Science*, 1966, **5**, 335–336.

Ulrich, R. Interaction between reflexive fighting and cooperative escape. *Journal of the Experimental Analysis of Behavior*, 1967, **10**, 311–317.

Ulrich, R., Dulaney, S., Kucera, T., & Colasacco, A. Side-effects of aversive control. In R. M. Gilbert & J. D. Keehn (Eds.), *Schedule effects: drugs, drinking and aggression*. Toronto: University of Toronto Press, 1972.

Ulrich, R. E. Johnston, M., Richardson, J., & Wolff, P. C. The operant conditioning of fighting in rats. *Psychological Record*, 1963, **13**, 465–470.

Vernon, W., & Ulrich, R. E. Classical conditioning of pain-elicited aggression. *Science*, 1966, **152**, 668–669.

3

Private Events
in Public Places[1]

Robert L. Schwitzgebel

Claremont Graduate School

Icarus was not a delinquent or a criminal—merely a wayward youth. However, the natural consequence of his deviance was quite severe. The myth blamed his impulsivity or "spirit of exuberance." Dedalus, however, contributed to the tragedy for, although he was flying straight and providing a good role model, he failed to design an adequate sensory feedback system.

Impulsivity has long been claimed to be one defining characteristic of adolescent offenders (Burt, 1930; Michaels, 1959; Quay, 1965; Werthman, 1967). In a frequently cited series of studies by Mischel (1961a, b) and by Mischel and Metzner (1962), delay of reward (e.g., choosing a 10¢ candy bar tomorrow rather than a 5¢ one today) has been found positively correlated with social responsibility, academic achievement, and nondelinquency. Yet it may also be observed that many adolescent offenders will, under specific conditions, engage in very sustained behavior, such as playing a pinball machine, repairing a motorcycle, or gambling.

This apparent inconsistency can be resolved by a rather parsimonious supposition: many behaviors occur in a sequence or "chain." Behavior that is typically defined as "impulsive" occurs when a segment of the chain comes under control of certain *self-generated* consequences rather than more easily observed (and therefore socially common or "expected") *situational* consequences. According

[1] Some of the research reported here was sponsored by National Institute of Mental Health grants MH15838 and MH20315. I apologize for what may seem to be an inconsiderate lack of reference to well-known behavior modification projects with delinquents. I assume readers of this volume will have remedied this limitation; a useful published summary of such projects can be found in Shah (1970).

FIG. 1   Text from J. F. Ormond, *Flight*. New York: Hill & Wang, 1963, preface. (Woodcut courtesty of Deutsches Museum, Munich.)

to Bandura (1969), three regulatory mechanisms can operate to render an individual's behavior practically independent of situational variables:

a. Anticipatory contingencies (e.g., hoping to win money at the horse races)
b. Intrinsic sensory consequences (e.g., hearing the roar and feeling the vibration while tuning a motorcycle)
c. Self-evaluative consequences (e.g., anxiety reactions among males by imagined loss of "reputation" or "masculinity")

The issue of self-control or self-regulation may be particularly critical in natural environments because of the severity of the consequences. In some circumstances, a properly socialized person is expected to demonstrate that his or her behavior is under control of long-term extrinsic (and probably short-term self-generated) consequences, as for example when one refuses a small cash gratuity offered for helping a stranded motorist. In other circumstances, a person may be judged criminal or insane for ignoring short-term extrinsic consequences, as in the case of a person who refuses on religious grounds to be innoculated for a very dangerous communicable disease. A *pattern* of expected response chains and acceptable contingencies is partly specified by the sociolegal rules of a society. Delinquents exceed the parameters in one direction or

---

Dedalus conquered Nature with his inventive spirit. He arranged bird feathers of different sizes in such a way that he began with the smallest feather and kept adding longer and longer ones, so it seemed as if they had grown thus staggered in size. He tied these feathers together with twine and sealed their underside with beeswax. When he had secured them in this way, he gave them an almost imperceptible curvature, until they completely resembled a bird's wings.

Dedalus put the finishing touches to his work, attached the wings to his body, then found his balance between them and rose into the air like a bird. After he returned to earth, he instructed his young son Icarus, for whom he had fashioned a smaller pair of wings.

"Always keep to the middle road, my dear son," he said, "so that, should you fly too low, your pinions will not graze the ocean waves. Weighed down by moisture, they would drag you down to the depths of the sea. Nor must you rise too high into the upper regions, where your plumage might come too near the rays of the sun and catch fire. Always fly between water and sun, in the wake of my own path through the air." Thus speaking, Dedalus fastened the wings to his son's shoulders, but while he did so his old hands trembled and a tear fell on his hand. Then he embraced the boy and gave him a kiss which proved to be his last.

Now both rose up on their wings. The father flew ahead, anxious as a bird who takes its brood from the safety of the nest into the hazards of the air for the very first time. All went well for a while. They passed the isle of Samos on the left, and soon afterward the islands of Delos and Paros. Other coastlines slipped by beneath them. But then the boy Icarus, made confident by the success of his flight, ignored his father's warning and, in a spirit of exuberance, rose up into higher regions. But he soon paid for his foolhardiness. The powerful rays of the sun softened the beeswax that held his pinions together, and before Icarus became aware of it, the wings dissolved and fell away from both his shoulders. The wretched youth still waved and swung his bare arms; but he no longer could catch the air in them, and he plummeted into the sea with terrible suddenness.

another. Kanfer and Karoly (1972) note that therapists are typically concerned with "*increasing* the probability of approach to, or tolerance of, an *immediately aversive* situation in order to achieve a *long-range positive outcome* (e.g., presenting phobic clients with feared objects, or keeping an uninterested student in school); or *decreasing* the probability of approaching an *immediately rewarding* situation in order to avoid *long-term negative* outcomes (e.g., inhibiting the alcoholic's drinking, the smoker's smoking, the obese individual's eating) [p. 408]."

One strategy to alter behavior controlled by an inappropriate pattern of situational and self-generated consequences is to disrupt the pattern by providing novel situational consequences. (Other strategies involve changing the function of stimulus cues or physically preventing the occurrence of the unwanted response.) The situational consequences may be positive or aversive but must be novel as to type, intensity, duration, contingency, etc. "The first step to learning is confusion."

NOVEL CONSEQUENCES

Two classic volumes on delinquency, Aichhorn's (1935) *Wayward Youth* and Eissler's (1949) *Searchlights on Delinquency*, deserve attention by behavior therapists despite the psychoanalytic orientation of the authors. The volumes should be read for what these practitioners say they did—assuming the description is fairly accurate—and for their "praxiological" or prescriptive statements, not for their theoretical justification.[2] Eissler (1949, p. 19) wrote, "It is a general rule of therapy of the delinquent never to act in the way he expects, unceasingly to introduce new and unforeseen elements in order to keep alive his interest in the therapeutic situation." Eissler also recommended the use of money in the initial interview sessions. Aichhorn (1935), Neil (1962), Schmideberg (1949), and Slavson (1956) have described incidents of unexpectedly consequating a delinquent's approach behavior with food.

The practitioner himself may take on secondary reinforcing properties. Referring to the implicit consequences which are often delivered during treatment, Krasner (1962) has termed therapists "social reinforcement machines." The therapists already mentioned, as well as others (e.g., Federn, 1962; Josselyn, 1957; Levenson, 1961), are reputed to be "colorful," "exciting," and "expressive" individuals. There may be a physiological basis for the traditional prescription of unorthodox consequences on a variable schedule. A line of research and evidence suggests that some offenders have relatively high physical thresholds for

---

[2] Technology often *precedes* science, and effective practice does not necessarily require scientifically valid explanatory statements (London, 1972).

arousal (Eysenck, 1964; Franks, 1961; Hare, 1968; Lykken, 1957; Michaels, 1959; Shanmugan & Sundari, 1962). To induce in delinquents an "orienting reflex" (cf. Sokolov, 1963), which may be a prerequisite in the conditioning process, more intense or novel stimuli should be used by therapists.

SHAPING ATTENDANCE BEHAVIORS

A very common behavior of delinquents that is not under control of long-term situational consequences is attendance at prearranged events. Their base-rate attendance at therapy, work, school, or peer group recreation is seldom dependable or prompt. A study by Hamar and Holterman (1965) of behavior disordered adolescents referred to a psychiatric clinic reported that 21 of 54 would-be patients failed to appear and 11 more discontinued after the initial contact. Of 234,000 underprivileged youths invited by letter to visit an employment counselor, only 42,000 appeared for interviews (Gordon, 1965). Of these, fewer than 13,000 were referred to jobs, and fewer than 7000 were hired (some for less than a week). A survey of studies of truancy among delinquents (Tennent, 1971) showed delinquent truancy rates ranging between 5.8 and 98%, whereas non-delinquent adolescent truancy rates ranged between .74 and 10.8%.

The solution to this attendance problem involves, in my experience, a quite simple and straightforward tactic: the therapist should (a) prompt initial attendance by referral or recruitment from streetcorners; (b) liberally, positively, and overtly consequate any attendance behavior on a variable-ratio schedule; (c) shape promptness in the same manner; (d) after the behavior meets criterion approximately ten times, begin to thin out the schedule and/or shift contingency to another target behavior.

The use of variable schedules and the shifting or reinforcement contingencies in a multiple-baseline design creates an atmosphere that one subject has described as a "junior Las Vegas." Unless the offender is arrested, moves from the area, or is using hard drugs, dependable and prompt attendance can be established and maintained at a high rate after 15 to 20 trials (R. L. Schwitzgebel, 1967, 1969). The procedure is demonstrably effective and, by now, quite routine for experienced experimenters. It is as close as we come to establishing a true behavioral technology.[3] Treatment after this point takes a predicable course

---

[3] It is interesting to note that very few APA-insured psychologists have yet been successfully sued for misconduct in practice or research (Gordon, 1970; Hogatt & Dawson Agency, 1968), although cases are presently pending and some successful action in torts is increasingly probable. One reason that plaintiffs have been unsuccessful is that they must show that the defendant–practitioner deviated from "an accepted standard of practice"–a most difficult task at present in view of widely divergent styles of psychotherapy.

(as noted below), but the actual procedure of managing contingencies and consequences becomes much more idiosyncratic and unspecifiable.

In the early sessions, my colleagues and I set the occasion for attendance by making a verbal contract regarding the next appointment time (no more than a 2-day interval). At the end of 2 or 3 weeks, we start to fade this verbal prompting by waiting until the subject is ready to leave. If he mentions nothing, we initiate a discussion about the time of the next meeting. Almost without exception, between the tenth and the fifteenth session, the subject, on opening the door to leave, asks something such as, "Oh, when do you want me to come again?" At that moment, we know that we can begin thinning the schedule of reinforcement for attendance behavior and begin "making demands." A situation has now been established in which there can be a more socially advanced *quid pro quo* relationship.

Because my special contribution to this volume may be related to aspects of working with delinquents in natural social settings, I would like to add a parenthetical note about a problem we have not yet solved. We do not work with female delinquents. The lab has been at various times in a storefront or an old house. We tend to recruit subjects from nearby streetcorners or we accept acquaintances of delinquents already known to us. The first few female subjects (interviewed by a female experimenter) "brought along" their boyfriends who also had police records. This seemed like a convenient recruitment scheme. Usually, however, these boy–girl relationships last only a few months. The girl then acquires a new boyfriend who insists on knowing what she is doing and "protecting" her—possibly from us as well as from the former boyfriend who by this time is a regular lab attendee. Three or four exboyfriends may be involved over a normal 9- to 15-month treatment period. The frequency of fighting and property damage markedly increases. A common subcultural value—with which I do not agree—allows a male to exclude a female from his activities but not the reverse option. If women had the same right of privacy as men, competing males could be excluded with less threat of violence.

PREDICTABILITY OF A FIXED SEQUENCE
OF EMOTIONAL RESPONSES

A long-term series of paid, part-time, tape-recorded interviews of average one-year duration, described elsewhere (R. K. Schwitzgebel, 1964), typically results in a standard sequence of emotional responses. The delinquent, intrigued and confused, appears to regress down a hierarchy from the most probable to the least probable affective responses. Overt behavior generally seems to be under the control of these private affective events. During depression, for example, even usually powerful extrinsic reinforcers, such as money and food, cease to have reinforcing properties. The frequency and duration of emotional responses varies widely from subject to subject, but I have never seen any alteration in the basic sequence. I suspect that this sequence is not peculiar to behavioristically oriented therapy, but I have seen only anecdotal or case-study evidence from the clinical literature.

The five-step sequence is: (a) suspicion, (b) hostility, (c) depression, (d) reorientation, and (e) leveling out. These terms are used in a commonsense way, without the precision of definition that may be preferred, but the referents are not too vague. Suspicion, hostility, and depression are common enough phenomena for some reliable interobserver definition, but "reorientation" and "leveling out" have for us perhaps special denotations. "Reorientation" refers to a period of time during which the subject emits a class of verbal operants traditionally described as "therapeutic insight" or perhaps "religious conversion." The subject weeps, may write poetry, reports more affection toward people, makes promises to improve his behavior, and so forth.

"Leveling out" is the final phase, during which a variety of less intense previous and new behaviors are emitted. Within a week or two of his reorientation experience, the subject may revert to previous behaviors and again exhibit hostility and depression, although for a shorter duration and with less intensity. He may also have another reorientation experience of less intensity. For the first time, he is likely to joke and make humorous statements about his situation and his own behavior. Most importantly, during this time, achievable behavioral goals are cooperatively specified and contracts are formulated relative to social skills, such as acquiring and keeping an outside job, passing a driver's test, returning to school. We gradually thin out consequences by setting longer and longer intervals between interviews.

To summarize, intense affective responses appear to be important, and sometimes controlling, stimuli in the overt behavior of delinquent youth. These stimuli may serve as intrinsic consequences in a chain of antisocial behavior. One question that follows such a supposition is whether affective responses of delinquents and nondelinquents are quantitatively different. Do delinquents "emotionally consequate" common daily events and their own behavior differently than nondelinquents? For example, how many minutes a day does an adolescent feel "happy," "bored," or "fearful" while at his home, school, or hangout? We have made some beginning attempt to answer such questions by gathering base-rate data of affective responses of delinquents and nondelinquents in various social settings.

ELECTROPSYCHOECOLOGY

Although the first systematic collection of time budgets (i.e., what a person does with his time during a given day) began several decades ago (Lundberg, 1934; Sorokin & Berger, 1939), the work of contemporary ecological psychologists

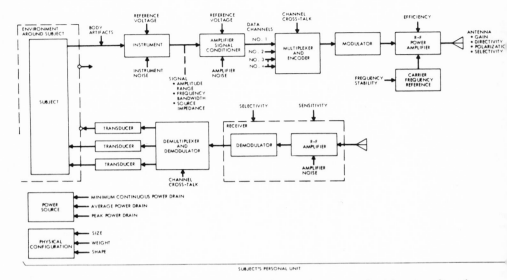

FIG. 2. Diagram of basic parameters of typical transceiver system for telemetry of psycho-environment.

(e.g., Barker, 1963, 1968; Heider, 1959; Tharp & Wetzel, 1969; Wicker, 1972; Willems & Raush, 1969) is methodologically much more sophisticated. Certainly recording and analyzing "streams" or chains of behavior does not suffer from lack of complexity. In principle, however, the inclusion of so-called "private emotional events" does not require any retreat from a rigorous behaviorism. "A private event may be distinguished by its limited accessibility but not, as far as we know, by any special structure or nature" (Skinner, 1953, p. 257). Furthermore, "The line between public and private is not fixed. The boundary shifts with every discovery of a technique for making private events public [p. 282]." The instruments of electrophysiology would seem to be our most obvious tools for trying to make private affective events public—in contrast to, say, pencil and paper tests.

Among the most relevant studies of emotional behavior is a survey of psychiatric hospital patients by Moos (1968). The patients have reported their feelings on predetermined scales (i.e., trusting/suspicious, secure/insecure, involved/uninvolved, sociable/unsociable, friendly/hostile, peaceful/angry) at the time they were in one of six different hospital settings (e.g., individual therapy, alone, lunch). Self-report data of anxiety responses (e.g., heart beating, perspiring) to different social situations cited by Endler and Hunt (1966) confirm the importance of situational factors and suggest that the more threatening the situation, the more response variance is accounted for by the situation than by the private emotional responses. Although the validity of self-reports is notoriously suspect (Doob & Gross, 1971; McCord & McCord, 1961; Weiss & Dawis, 1960), one

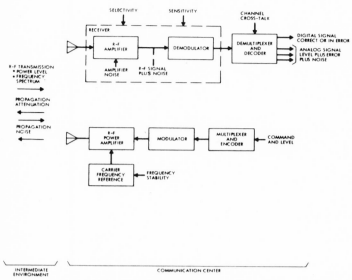

physiological data. A telephone link may replace RF transmission in the intermediate

advantage of studying affective behavior is that autonomic responses can be concurrently recorded.

The choice of the psychophysiological response(s) to record is constrained by a number of factors when behavior is monitored in natural settings. The response should be sensitive to changes that occur in usual social situations, should be capable of being monitored for extended periods of time without embarrassment to the subject, should have temporal characteristics of the same order of magnitude as the overt behavior of interest, and should be subject to minimal confounding by such artifacts as movement. Electrodermal activity and heart rate are the most commonly used measures that seem to meet these criteria. Electrodermal activity (GSR) has some advantage over heart rate because it is more frequently used as an orienting reflex measure, the tranducers are more easily attached, and data reduction is easier.

A study was therefore undertaken to simultaneously monitor for 3 hr/day self-reported affective responses and electrodermal activity of adolescents while at home, at school or work, and during recreation. Eight Caucasian male subjects, between 15 and 21 years of age and with histories of arrest and incarceration, were matched with eight nondelinquent subjects of similar age, race, and social class. A two-channel FM telemetry system (Figure 2) with a telephone link was designed, which permitted oscillograph recording of both GSR and self-reported emotional responses. Subjects sent a coded signal by pressing a small button at the top of their transmitting units (Figure 3). The code consisted of the subject's forced choice in each of three bipolar descrip-

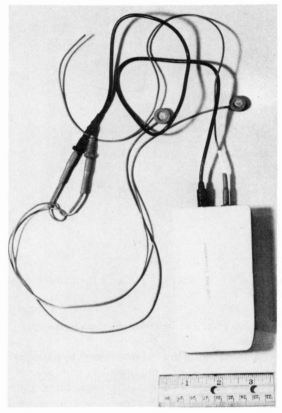

FIG. 3 GSR transmitter worn by the subject. The photograph shows finger electrodes but not the button on top of the unit for sending voluntary coded signals.

tions of emotional states (cf. Arnold, 1945; Sternback, 1962) that presumably corresponded most closely to his feeling at that moment: anger/affection, excitement/boredom, and fear/relaxation.

A time-sampling routine was followed in each of the locations during which the subject sent a coded signal every 15 min. GSR and BSR (basal skin resistance) were continuously recorded during the 3-hr period. Subjects practiced labeling their emotions in order to increase reliability of self-report, and laboratory situations were contrived to elicit each of the affective responses. For example, boredom was induced by asking the subjects to count the number of letters in each word of a long technical manuscript; fear was induced by having a policeman arrive unexpectedly and make general inquiries about stolen property.

The rate (occurrence per hour) of self-reported emotions in different social settings is summarized in Table 1. When forced to choose between anger and affection and between fear and relaxation, adolescents most frequently reported affection and least frequently reported fear. Excitement and boredom had similar rates. Only insignificant differences, if any, exist between delinquent and nondelinquent groups or between settings. Intragroup and intrasetting differences were notable. Individuals showed widely varying but often consistent patterns of reported emotions.

Similarly, neither subject groups nor settings could be differentiated by GSR rates, but individual–setting interaction occasionally accounted for sufficient variance to give a clear correlation between reported emotion and GSR. For example, one delinquent subject gave almost no GSRs when he reported the combined emotions of "affection/excitement/relaxation;" this combination occurred most often at home (while eating), less frequently at recreation, and never at work. In contrast, another delinquent subject, who reported affection/excitement/relaxation while at work, showed the highest rate of GSRs of any subject in a work setting. He showed this high rate of responsivity despite a high BSR, which indicated a low arousal or a nonanxious state. Only one combination of reported emotions, affection/boredom/relaxation, showed a characteristic GSR pattern over all subjects and all settings—i.e., the occurrence of no or only one GSR during the 3 min prior to the subject's report.

The most unexpected finding was the comparatively low frequency of self-reports of anger compared to reports of affection of both delinquents and nondelinquents, particularly in the home setting. One explanation could be that conflicts with parents or siblings did not in fact occur during the monitoring. The most common behavior at home during transmission was watching television (a rather asocial activity) or eating (a response to some degree physiologically antagonistic to anxiety). This observation parallels a finding by Raush, Farbman, and Llewellyn (1960), who reported that overt interactions of preadolescent males were typically friendly where food was available. The time-sampling procedure used may have biased the reports toward a relative calm caused by eating or by relative social isolation.

TABLE 1
Average Occurrence per Hour of Self-Reported
Emotions in Different Social Environments

	Home		Work		Recreation	
	Del.	Nondel.	Del.	Nondel.	Del.	Nondel.
Anger	0.7	1	1	1	1.5	1.3
Affection	3.3	3	3	3	2.5	2.7
Excitement	3	2.3	1.9	2	3	2.3
Boredom	1	1.7	2.1	2	1	1.7
Fear	1	1	0.25	0.7	1	1
Relaxation	3	3	3.75	3.3	3	3

In conclusion, this particular study suggests that delinquents as a group do not differ from nondelinquents in the frequency of certain self-reported affective responses or recorded GSRs. The overt behavioral significance of such private events, if any, must lie in *individualized patterns of affect–situation congruence.*

I would like to add a parenthetical note about practical matters. As paid volunteers, both delinquent and nondelinquent subjects accepted the wearing of the telemetry apparatus in all normal social situations. No equipment was lost or seriously damaged; the contingency for getting paid that day was to return the apparatus in good condition. A "dummy" transmitting unit with electrodes was used in a prerun to permit extinction of anxiety responses elicited by questions from acquaintances.

In addition to the initial cost of telemetry equipment, down time (as high as 50%) and maintenance must be considered. Unless one has a few fixed transmitting locations or a very large budget, one should avoid purchasing any system that does not have the capacity of being coupled directly into a voice-grade telephone line. This arrangement provides flexibility without noticeable decrement in signal quality. If, however, regularly used telephone lines are going to be utilized for research, written release should be obtained in advance to avoid liability because of the inability of the subscriber to send or receive an emergency message.

NEW GAMES: "PSYCHOTECHNOLOGY" AND "NATURALISTIC ETHICS"

At this point I must present here more "program" than achievement. It seems to me that in order to specify contingencies presumably relevant to self-control, a publicly accessible technology that can aid in measuring, recording, prompting, and consequating internal and external events must be developed. Effective and replicable methods of behavior change (e.g., token economies, hypnosis) need not involve chemical, mechanical, or electrical technologies. However, the popularity of instrumentation (e.g., in motion pictures, music, biofeedback) and chemicals (e.g., anesthetics, recreational drugs) suggests that emotional behavior can be powerfully influenced by these technologies.

A predicable major development is the formation of an intellectual craft—possibly termed "psychotechnology" (Schwitzgebel & Schwitzgebel, 1973)—that can systematically explore techniques aimed at the alteration of affective experience. A goal of such an "emotional technology" may be to provide safe tools for self-programmable experiential adventures. Although more humane than previous methods of control, behavior modification (in the sense of conditioning motor behaviors observable with the naked eye) may soon seem crude and dull except perhaps to bureaucrats. I do not intend to derogate significant contributions, but surely it is no sign of progress if the same intellectual games are played in this decade as have been in the past decade or two.

One first step would be the development of a taxonomy of private events and public places. The taxonomy should be susceptible to operational definition and to use by the general public. Like a road map, it should have diverse utility. The study of stimulus configurations in public places relevant to individual behavior (e.g., surveys by architectural and ecological psychologists) can be supplemented by concurrent investigations of private events (cf. Hefferline & Bruno, 1971). Electromechanical instrumentation, such as biofeedback devices, may be able to externalize proprio- and interoceptive events in a way that allows novel cooperation between the subject and his environment. Relaxation training is an obvious beginning. For example, we have found that subjects enjoy playing the following game: A finger electrode of an inexpensive auditory GSR device[4] is attached to one subject; the other finger electrode is attached to a second subject. Five or six subjects then hold hands to complete the circuit and produce a tone that varies with the total resistance of the group. We form two "bioelectronic organisms," of five or six subjects each, that challenge each other to see which one can relax more rapidly or completely under prearranged stress situations. The individual "cells" (i.e., delinquents) of a given "organism" teach each other to relax. They quickly discover that administering aversive consequences, which they typically do at a high rate, is not very effective. It is remarkable how much overt motor behavior of 10 or 12 adolescents can be inhibited for 5- to 10-min intervals by this game.

The "problem" of delinquency suggests part of its own solution when it is analyzed in scientific terms. One important question to ask about any unwanted behavior is "What is 'right' about 'wrong' behavior?"—"right" not in a moral or social sense but in a naturalistic or scientific sense. What stimuli and consequences maintain the behavior? Are artificial or symbolic consequences provided by society congruent with natural or somatic consequences?

In evolution, survival of a species depends in part on the adaptability of mutant forms. Very few mutants prove to be more adaptive than the dominant form; and most mutants live marginally, if at all. Delinquents can be viewed as social mutants. Their pattern of adaptation may generally be self-defeating and therefore socially undesired. "Cops and robbers" is a children's game which when played by teenagers or adults becomes sad and brutish. However, in delinquents may also lie the necessary lack of inhibition to play new somatic and environic games. New technologies should invite human beings to examine, systematically and rigorously, with joy and fear, the sensitive interactions of environmental events and somatic responses and to communicate the results of real-life experiments.

[4]"Lie Detector" Electronic Project Kit #28-128, $12.00, Allied-Radio Shack, 2615 W. 7th Street, Fort Worth, Texas 76107.

Icarus was a wayward youth. Those who would fly need a technology—one somatically sensitive to the life-giving and the life-threatening contingencies of natural environments.

REFERENCES

Aichhorn, A. *Wayward youth*. New York: Viking Press, 1935. (Reprinted New York: Meridian Books, 1955.)

Arnold, M. B. Psychological differentiation of emotional states. *Psychological Review*, 1945, **52**, 35–48.

Bandura, A. *Principles of behavior modification*. New York: Holt, Rinehart & Winston, 1969.

Barker, R. G. (Ed.) *The stream of behavior*. New York: Appleton-Century-Crofts, 1963.

Barker, R. G. *Ecological psychology*. Stanford, California: Stanford University Press, 1968.

Burt, C. *The young delinquent*. New York: Appleton & Co., 1930.

Doob, A. N., & Gross, A. E. Status of a frustrator as an inhibitor of horn-honking responses. In L. W. Schmaltz (Ed.), *Scientific psychology and social concern*. New York: Harper & Row, 1971, Pp. 470–474.

Eissler, K. R. (Ed.) *Searchlights on delinquency*. New York: International Universities Press, 1949.

Endler, N. S., & Hunt, J. McV. Sources of behavioral variance as measured by the S–R inventory of anxiousness. *Psychological Bulletin,* 1966, **65**, 336–436.

Eysenck, H. J. *Crime and personality*. Boston: Houghton-Mifflin, 1964.

Federn, E. The therapeutic personality as illustrated by Paul Federn and August Aichhorn. *Psychiatric Quarterly* (New York State Dept. of Mental Hygiene, Utica), 1962, 1–15.

Franks, C. M. Conditioning and abnormal behavior. In H. J. Eysenck (Ed.), *Handbook of abnormal psychology*. New York: Basic Books, 1961. Pp. 457–489.

Gordon, J. E. Project Cause, the federal anti-poverty program, and some implications of subprofessional training. *American Psychologist*, 1965, **20**, 334–342.

Gordon, R. I. Tort liability in psychological research. *American Psychologist*, 1970, **25**, 190–191.

Hammar, S. L., & Holterman, V. L. Referring adolescents for psychotherapy. *Clinical Pediatrics*, 1965, **4**, 462–467.

Hare, R. D. Autonomic functioning, the orienting response, and psychopathy. *Journal of Abnormal Psychology*, 1968, **73**, 1–24 (Monograph suppl.).

Hefferline, R., & Bruno, L. The psychophysiology of private events. In A. Jacobs & L. Sacks (Eds.), *The psychology of private events*. New York: Academic Press, 1971. Pp. 163–191.

Heider, F. On perception, event structure, and the psychological environment: Selected papers. *Psychological Issues*, 1959, **1**(3), entire issues.

Hoggatt & Dawson Agency, Champaign, Illinois, personal correspondence, 1968.

Josselyn, I. M. Psychotherapy of adolescents at the level of private practice. In B. B. Balser (Ed.), *Psychotherapy of the adolescent*. New York: International Universities Press, 1957.

Kanfer, H. K., & Karoly, P. Self-control: A behavioristic excursion into the lion's den. *Behavior Therapy*, 1972, **3**, 398–416.

Krasner, L. The therapist as a social reinforcement machine. In H. H. Strupp & L. Luborsky (Eds.), *Research in psychotherapy*. Vol. 2. Washington, D.C.: American Psychological Association, 1962.

Levenson, E. A. Jam tomorrow–jam yesterday. *Etc.: Review of Semantics*, 1961, **18**, 167–178.

London, P. The end of ideology in behavior modification. *American Psychologist*, 1972, **27**, 913–920.

Lundberg, G. A. *Leisure: A suburban study*. New York: Columbia University Press, 1934.

Lykken, D. T. A study of anxiety in the sociopathic personality. *Journal of Abnormal & Social Psychology*, 1957, **55**, 6–10.

McCord, J., & McCord, W. Cultural stereotypes and the validity of interviews for research in child development. *Child Development*, 1961, **32**, 171–185.

Michaels, J. J. Character structure and character disorders. In S. Arieti (Ed.), *American handbook of psychiatry*. New York: Basic Books, 1959. Pp. 353–377.

Mischel, W. Preference for delayed reinforcement and social responsibility. *Journal of Abnormal & Social Psychology*, 1961, **62**, 1–7. (a)

Mischel, W. Delay of gratification, need for achievement, and acquiescence in another culture. *Journal of Abnormal & Social Psychology*, 1961, **62**, 543–552. (b)

Mischel, W., & Metzner, R. Preference for delayed reward as a function of age, intelligence, and length of delay interval. *Journal of Abnormal & Social Psychology*, 1962, **64**, 425–431.

Moos, R. H. Situational analysis of a therapeutic community milieu. *Journal of Abnormal Psychology*, 1968, **73**, 49–61.

Neil, A. S. *Summerhill: A radical approach to education*. London: Victor Gollancz, 1962.

Quay, H. C. Psychopathic personality as pathological stimulation-seeking. *American Journal of Psychiatry*, 1965, **122**, 180–183.

Raush, H. L., Farbman, I., & Llewellyn, L. G. Person, setting, and change in social interaction: A normal-control study. *Human Relations*, 1960, **13**, 305–322.

Schmideberg, M. The analytic treatment of major criminals: Therapeutic results and technical problems. In K. Eissler (Ed.), *Searchlights on delinquency*. New York: International Universities Press, 1949.

Schwitzgebel, R. K. *Streetcorner research: An experimental approach to the juvenile delinquent*. Cambridge, Massachusetts: Harvard University Press, 1964.

Schwitzgebel, R. L. Short-term operant conditioning of adolescent offenders on socially relevant variables. *Journal of Abnormal Psychology*, 1967, **72**, 134–142.

Schwitzgebel, R. L. Preliminary socialization for psychotherapy of behavior-disordered adolescents. *Journal of Consulting and Clinical Psychology*, 1969, **33**, 71–77.

Schwitzgebel, R. L., & Schwitzgebel, R. K. (Eds.), *Psychotechnology*. New York: Holt, Rinehart & Winston, 1973.

Shah, S. A. A behavioral approach to out-patient treatment of offenders. In H. C. Rickard (Ed.), *Unique programs in behavior readjustment*. Elmsford, New York: Pergamon Press, 1970. Pp. 223–265.

Shanmugan, T. E., & Sundari, T. A. Difference between delinquent boys and nondelinquent boys in inhibition, disinhibition, and personality traits. *Psychological Studies of Mysore*, 1962, **7**, 64–66 (*Psychological Abstracts*, 1963, **37**, 171, No. 1754).

Skinner, B. F. *Science and human behavior*. New York: Macmillan, 1953.

Slavson, S. R. *The fields of group psychotherapy*. New York: International Universities Press, 1956.

Sokolov, E. N. *Perception and the conditioned reflex*. New York: Macmillan, 1963.

Sorokin, P. A., & Berger, C. Q. *Time-budget of human behavior*. Cambridge, Massachusetts: Harvard University Press, 1939.

Sternback, R. A. Assessing differential autonomic patterns in emotion. *Journal of Psychosomatic Research*, 1962, **6**, 87–91.

Tennent, T. G. School non-attendance and delinquency. *Educational Research*, 1971, **13**, 185–189.

Tharp, R., & Wetzel, R. *Behavioral modification in the natural environment*. New York: Academic Press, 1969.

Weiss, D. J., & Dawis, R. V. An objective validation of factual interview data. *Journal of Applied Psychology*, 1960, **44**, 381–385.

Werthman, C. The function of social definitions in the development of delinquent career. In *Task Force report: Juvenile delinquency and youth crime*. (The President's Commission on Law Enforcement and Administration of Justice), Washington, D.C.: U.S. Government Printing Office, 1967, 155–170.

Wicker, A. W. Processes which mediate behavior-environment congruence: *Behavioral Science*, 1972, **17**, 265–277.

Willems, E. P., & Raush, H. L. (Eds.), *Naturalistic viewpoints in psychological research*. New York: Holt, Rinehart & Winston, 1969.

4
Analysis and Control of Activities in Custodial Human Groups [1]

Benjamin Dominguez
Mario Rueda
Cesar Makhlouf
Armando Rivera

National Autonomous University of Mexico
  and
Preventive City Jail at Villa A, Obregón

Historically, the motives for maintaining people secluded in prison have been to oblige them to compensate society for inadequate behavior; later, these have been to restrain their antisocial impulses, and recently, to rehabilitate them.

There have been no significant changes in the goals of institutions (prisons, reformatories, etc.) created to rehabilitate those who, at some time, have committed infringements considered crimes. In most cases, these institutions have served in such a way that the inmates expect a greater punishment. For a long period of time, punishments implied mutilations, isolation, and at worst, death. Such is still the case in many custodial institutions. Renovation in them is an exception to the rule. At the present time, few specialists believe that custodial institutions are, in fact, achieving those correction and rehabilitation goals that society has assigned to them.

Society continues to use prisons as a means of isolating its most undesirable members, and although this does not make them better citizens, it is still the

[1] The present research is a partial report of the program "Rehabilitacion Integral" which represents a cooperative effort between the Faculty of Psychology of the National University of México and the prison "Villa A. Obregón." Unfortunately it is not possible to mention the names of all the persons that have made this program possible, but we should mention Mario Crosswell, principal of the Prison and the team of psychologists whose main feature has been dedication. Silvia Macotela has been a perservering reviewer of the English version of this paper.

cheapest method and the one with the most immediate results. Isolating subjects displaying behaviors dangerous to the community is, therefore, one of the fundamental arguments to justify the existence of prisons. However, many authorities agree that at least half of the inmates would function better outside the prison (Glasser, 1970; McCorkel & Korn, 1954; Phillips, Phillips, Fixen, & Wolf, 1971; Sánchez, 1971; Street, Vinter, & Penow, 1966).

The great majority of specialists in the field agree that one of the most important aspects that define rehabilitation within a prison is work itself, or a "planned activity" that the inmate performs while he remains in prison. The problem still involves choosing the procedure to modify undesirable behaviors dangerous to the community. Nevertheless, it is clear that punishment is no longer the only option.

At the present time, the options for correcting criminal behavior are liberty or parole, preliberational freedom, open prisons, labor within the prisons, treatment within a community, and substitute homes. Unfortunately, many of these alternatives are only interesting experiments discussed in scientific, specialized journals, and are not applicable on a major scale. Actually, prisons are organized in such a way that they can be handled with few personnel and so that they insure maximum isolation of a considerable number of prisoners.

When an inmate enters a prison, assignment of manual tasks (for example, cleaning the location) that the inmate must perform without receiving remuneration frequently follows. The problem of controlling inmates is solved by using other inmates who are physically stronger and can intervene more directly and immediately than any warden. These characteristics define mainly what Goffman (1961) has termed "total institutions." This concept is crucial for understanding the effects that institutions have on the life and behavior of their members.

The control that a prison exerts on the inmates determines not only the individual's life at the institution, but also his later life and activities on release. In most cases the observed effects are rather undesirable instead of beneficial.

In summary, prisons (as examples of total institutions) are created for the security of wardens, directors, and citizens, without consideration for the security of the inmates. If the known undesirable effects of these total institutions are considered, an alternative may be that such an institution respond primarily to the needs of those who are under its custody.

It can be asserted that scientific methods have merely begun to be applied to the problems described above. In some instances, these problems have been stated in terms of unobservable events, and consequently the results have not been observable either. The fundamental task in this case is to explain how the behavior of the inmates is affected by prison conditions. It is necessarily to bear in mind that everything that happens to the subject while he remains in prison, whether it is planned or not, will affect him inside and later outside the prison.

Recently some principals and persons in charge of prisons have begun to apply some scientific prescriptions in their work. At the present time and beginning from a reform to penal law in Mexico, a unanimously favored but unfortunately scarcely utilized prescription is "penitentiary labor." According to the Twelfth Penal Penitentiary Congress held in La Haya, work should not be considered complementary to the penalty but rather as a method for treating delinquents. Sánchez Galindo (1971) asserts that "work is a necessary element within a penitentiary institution." Today this type of assertion is being made more frequently. Nevertheless, none of them indicates the specific conditions that will produce desirable penitentiary labor as an element of rehabilitation. Some specialists have classified three types of in-prison labor goals: (1) in prison, work can be performed for retribution to society; (2) the production of goods or obtainment of income; and (3) work makes the individual capable of returning to the community.

It has also been pointed out that rehabilitation should have an immediate objective, for example, to educate and to make the individual capable of participating in "profitable" activities, and further on in production, to provide him with a certain amount of money to satisfy his needs inside the prison. Planning and initiating penitentiary labor are in all cases subject to budget conditions in the institution, which are usually tight. This is also subject to fluctuations on the supply and demand of the product being manufactured by the inmates. The lack of appropriate facilities creates long periods of inactivity.

The conditions that prevent the immediate education and activation of the inmate are lack of specialized personnel (technicians), oposition or lack of "will" on the part of the inmate, and organization of activities or daily work. These three problems indicate that the participation of behavioral specialists may be helpful. For a period of 2 years, the program "Integral Rehabilitation" has directed its systematic research endeavour to deal with these problems and implement the stated rehabilitation goals of prisons.

Some efforts have been made to apply behavioral analysis to delinquent behaviors. Meichenbaum, Bowers, and Ross (1968), have presented a series of experiments in which they have used a fundamental technique the elimination (by means of punishment or extinction) of inappropriate behaviors within a specific situation. Cohen, Filizpak and Bis (1968) have illustrated the planning and development of academic skills in partially institutionalized subjects. In this particular case, the objective has been not only to eliminate behaviors but also to create new behaviors that compete with the former.

Burchard (1967) manipulated a wider behavioral category with retarded adolescent delinquents, making reinforcement contingent on the performance of the subjects during academic tasks and on the products of such activity. Phillips *et al.* (1971) demonstrated the possibility of manipulating more complex behaviors, such as cooperation, academic achievement, self- and household care, and complex academic skills. In all of the above reports, the "reinforcers" utilized consisted of adding "something new" to the environment of the subjects.

THE *INTEGRAL REHABILITATION* PROGRAM

One of the main objectives of the "Integral Rehabilitation" is planning a prison absolutely dedicated to the benefit (social, educational, and laboral) of its inmates. However this proposal does not only imply that prisons should be organized in this way. To modify human behavior, instructions contained in one or several decrees are not enough. Empirical research conducted by behavioral scientists constitutes a useful alternative method of confronting the multiple problems of total institutions.

In our case, applying this behavioral analysis approach has been made possible by the use of the recording system developed by Doke and Risley (1972). The "participation" of the subjects in the planned activities of an institution constitutes one of the most important dimensions not only in planning the daily work and activities in an institution but also in assessing on a short- and long-term basis the "goodness" of an institution.

In the first experiment, a procedure was designed to increase participation and performance of educational activities by the inmates in a barely structured situation, such as the free or rest 1-hr period, in which the internees remained in the yard of the prison. In the second experiment work within the workshop was carefully investigated. Two variables were considered in Experiment 2. First, the analysis was centered on the relationships between vocational activity and the effects of introducing a fixed period of rest in the middle of the morning interval (11.00 a.m.). Second, a comparison was made between regular work and a token system having two options to obtain the "luncheon time."

Setting

The prison is a three-story building with 15 dormitories in each story. The medical–dental office, the psychology office, a knitting workshop, and the sanitary facilities are located in one section of the first floor. Around the building there are the blacksmith mosaic, wool and sweater-knitting workshops, and an uncovered 50 × 35 meter yard. The inmates remained in the yard during their free periods, depending on weather conditions.

The population is about 200 people, 65% of whom are an average of less than 22 years old (minimum 18, maximum 50). The same percentage has finished elementary education. Crimes for which they have been imprisoned are distributed as follows: 30%, murder; 35%, robbery; 20%, sexual crimes; and 15%, minor crimes (injury, fighting, etc.). The population has one outstanding characteristic: approximately 90% of the inmates do not have previous crime records, which favors rehabilitation programs.

Procedure

In both experiments, stopwatches, clipboards, manual counters, record sheets, and pencils or pens were used as recording materials. The main type of recording in both experiments was a partial modification of the PLA-CHEK (evaluation of planned activities) used by Doke and Risley (1972). The recording procedure first considered and defined an area of observation. Within it, the procedure consisted of observing at different time intervals the number of persons present and also the number of persons participating in the planned activities of that area. The resulting measure provided data about how many persons participated and for how long, as well as how many did not participate. In all cases two observers recorded the data, and periodically one or two additional independent observers recorded data simultaneously and independently for reliability.

Given the number of subjects (30, 70, and 140) observed an the physical area in which data were obtained, it was necessary to use a variation of the totals reported by the observers comparing data (present and participants) to calculate reliability for these observations.

EXPERIMENT 1

Experiment 1 was carried through with the population remaining in the prison's yard. Observations were made in the rest period between 11:00 a.m. and 1:00 p.m. Before the rest period the inmates had been in the workshops since 8:30 a.m. This free time was given to them on a time-program basis that did not take into consideration the previous activity of the inmate. Observations in the yard during this "free period" permitted the classification of the five activities that occurred in this area, which, in order of frequency of occurrence, were social or recreative, sports, demanded, vocational, and educational. The initial observations allowed the identification of those variables favoring the initiation of these activities and those that did not. In order of importance these were: (a) free and constant availability of materials (balls, magazines, etc.); (b) availability of temporal or physical space, (i.e., arrangement for time and a court); and (c) the inmate's "will" to participate in a given activity (Table 1).

Through these observations, it was also possible to determine the variables involved in maintaining in a continuous and frequent form an activity once begun: (a) variation in the total number of persons present in the observed area (i.e., if there were many or few persons); (b) temporary availability to use materials (i.e., working time per person); (c) variation of the possibility that the inmates

TABLE 1

Conditions Related to the Realization
of Activities in a Prison Courtyard

Activity	Factors to initiate	Factors to carry out	Control psychologists Degree initiated/carried out
Social	c^1, b^1	a^2, c^2, d^2	Low b^{a1} a^2
Sport	c^1, b^1, a^1	a^2, d^2	
Demanded	a^1 $\begin{cases} a^1 \text{ materials} \\ b^1 \text{ space} \\ c^1 \text{ will } S^d \end{cases}$	b^2	Regular b^1, a^2 b^2
Vocational	c^1, a^1	b^2, d^2	High c^1 c^2, d^2
Educational	c^1, a^1 . b^1	d^2, b^2, c^2 . .a^2	

$$\left.\begin{array}{l} a^2 \text{ total population} \\ b^2 \text{ time/person} \\ c^2 \text{ sequence/activity} \\ d^2 \text{ contingencies } S^+ \end{array}\right\}$$

[a]Physical space.

56

themselves could select an activity in each period; and (d) the contingent occurrence of reinforcing events at initiation and termination of an activity.

Five activities were defined on the basis of an "appropriate" use of materials. The "recreative or social activities" were defined in terms of use of such materials as guitars, decks of cards, other games, or simply singing of conversation. "Vocational activities" implied such behaviors as knitting, assembling ballpoint pens, etc. (activities performed in the workshops). "Sporting activities" were, for example, soccer, boxing, and weightlifting; "demanded activities" included those activities required by the wardens or authorities of the institution, for example, standing on a line, roll calling, cleaning up the place, or washing clothes. "Educational activities" implied the use of "academic" material (books, magazines, pens, notebooks, etc.).

All activities differ with respect to the initial control that the experimenters could exert on each performance. Experimenters had no control on the available physical area for a given activity nor on the fluctuations of the total number of persons in a given moment. There was some control over time, duration of an activity (temporary space), availability or existence of materials, and time per person in the use of materials. We found that the conditions on which maximum control could be exerted were *sequence between one activity and another one* and *"will of the inmate" to work*, that is, discriminative properties that participation in an activity could have for an inmate and the reinforcing contingencies that occurred at the beginning or termination of a given activity.

All subjects remaining in the yard during the rest period, whose number was never less than 30 (under 30 not measured) nor greater than 140, constituted the population for Experiment 1.

Procedure

The recording system used was the PLA-CHEK. Two observers surveyed the yard area each 15 min, counting the total number of persons and those participating in the classified activities. In the same interval, various pairs of observers recorded persons present and participating in each of the five activities. When they finished walking around the yard, they wrote down the number of participants in each activity in the recording sheet, comparing them with the other observers. Generally, two observers did the recording, and periodically four observers recorded simultaneously and independently to obtain data for variation ranges.

Inmates themselves carried through 85% of the observations in Experiment 1. The range of variation on the differences from data reported for each pair of observers was never more than two subjects per session.

A multiple-baseline design was used in which all activities were recorded in the same session. During baseline, the following percentages for participation were obtained in each activity: social, 30.4%; vocational, 7%; educational, 10.2%, sports, 4.2%; the demanded activity, because the experimenters could exert no control on it, was not computed. Educational activity was selected as target behavior.

Experimental Periods

The first experimental procedure is depicted in Fig. 1 as Condition 1. The procedure consisted of increasing the number of existing available materials, first in the educational activity, second in sports, and last in social activity. The inmates had at their disposal a limited number of materials, property of the institution, for performing each of the above-mentioned activities (see Fig. 2).

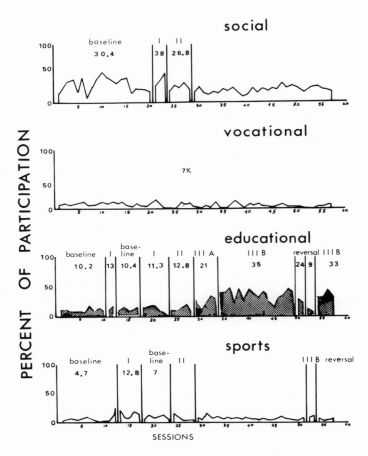

FIG. 1 Percent of inmates' participation in various activities under various experimental conditions.

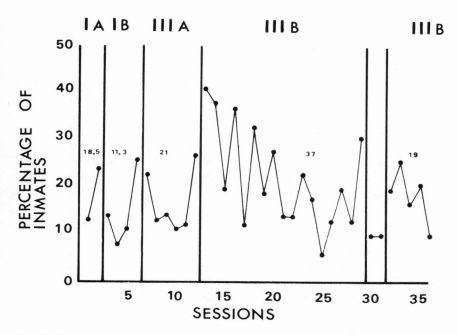

FIG. 2 Percentage of inmates requesting educational materials under various experimental conditions.

The existence and availability of material was publicized in all cases by announcements and posters that were placed in the walls of the yard, or by means of verbal instructions given directly to groups of inmates in the yard.

Experimental Condition II consisted of simultaneously making available materials for the three activities.

Experimental Condition IIIA was applied only to the education activity and consisted of reinforcing by tallymarks on a ticket every 15 min all persons participating in the educational activity.[2] A pair of observers walked across the yard area every 15 min and handed out a ticket to every person participating in the educational activity; in the following 15-min period, those persons who continued participating in that activity received a tally mark on their ticket.

The inmates were informed that the tallymarks obtained would enable them to request keeping the educational, sports, or social materials for 1 or 2 days. After 20 marks their names were entered on a public list of candidates for a "field trip outside the prison." These "field trips" were made in groups of 40 persons. In

---

[2] At the beginning of this period tallymarks were given a 15-min fixed interval, and then they were given on an intermittent one-week basis throughout the duration of the experiment.

this period instructions were given on a written form in posters, or as verbal instructions given over the loudspeakers every 15 min. Inmates were informed about persons present and persons participating in each activity. This was also written on a blackboard in one of the walls of the yard.

An explanation was given to the inmates every 30 min regarding which reinforcing events they could receive with their marks, and every 60 min they were informed about how many were near the 20 marks. Each inmate received an average of three marks per day, or 20 a week.

Experimental Condition IIIB was similar to the previous one, except that the sound system and verbal instructions were not used. In this period only written information in posters was given. These posters also invited the inmates to improve the quality of the reading material.

Reversal

For the educational activity there were two procedures. In the first procedure, the marks were given (noncontingent), irrespective of the response. At the beginning of each rest period, an experimenter handed out the average number of marks that the subjects had obtained in the previous period. He told the inmates that the marks were given for "participating" in the educational activity. The second, reversal, procedure consisted of eliminating reinforcement for the educational activities and sports, with material available for both activities. A follow-up period was carried out a month later, applying this procedure to the educational activity. A series of recordings were obtained under conditions similar to Experimental Condition IIIB. During this period the fundamental variation was frequency of reinforcement, which was 2.5 tally marks (average per session).

It is interesting to note that one of the conditions manipulated by the experimenters during the entire procedure for the educational activity was increasing the availability and number of materials classified as "educational," such as books, magazines, notebooks, and pencils. Many of these materials were owned by the inmates, and a limited number of the materials were handled by the psychologists during Conditions I through IIIB.

Figure 2 depicts the percentage of requested material. To be able to use the materials, the inmate had to request it from the psychologists. This figure also shows the same variations of the entire procedure applied to the educational activities.

Results

The results obtained after the introduction of Experimental Conditions I and II in the three categories, sports, educational, and social, are not very significant, but in all cases a similar effect of these two experimental conditions can be

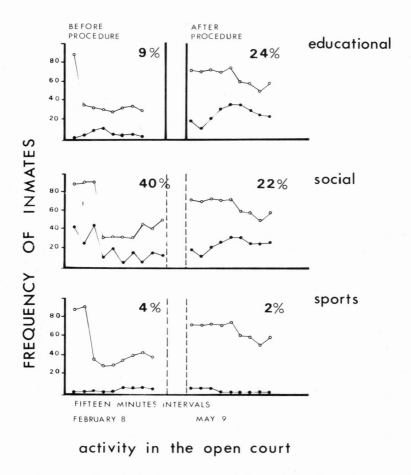

activity in the open court

FIG. 3 Frequencies of activity in the prison court before and after 3 experimental conditions. (○) Total inmates; (●) participating inmates.

observed. The mere availability of the increased materials was not enough to increase activity, and when they were introduced simultaneously into the three activities, the natural trend in sport and social activities in terms of frequency of occurrence was again noticeable.

After the introduction of Experimental Condition IIA for educational activity, there was a twofold increase, 21% compared to the percentage obtained in baseline (10.2%). Condition IIIB yielded 35% (an average over the entire period, which includes 16 continuous sessions). In the first reversal period and noncontingent reinforcement, the percentage decreased from 35% to a 24% average for all sessions in this period. In the second period (reinforcement for sports), the educational activity decreased to conditions lower than baseline, 9%. When Condition IIIB was reintroduced, there again was an increase, to 33%. In the follow-up period (a month later) the educational activity presented an average of 20% per period and the social activity, of higher probability occurrence under original conditions, showed an average of 28.7% per period during six continuous sessions. It is also observed in a fine-grain analysis of each session (Fig. 3), before and after applying the three experimental conditions.

EXPERIMENT 2

Experiment 1 showed that changing from the activities in the workshops to the free activity in the yard had an effect in the participation of the inmates in other activities. It was observed that the activities in the workshops and the activities in the yard essentially were not related. The only relation between the two different types of activities was temporal. This type of situation, which is characterized by the occurrence of regular changes in activities that are made on the basis of nonbehavioral events, for example, passage of time, is known as a "routine," which is, among other things, one of the features of "total institutions" as described by Goffman (1961). These routine sequences within an institution are often demarcated by longer transition periods than those originally planned, with resulting periods of disturbance, occurrence of inadequate behaviors, and boredom inactivity periods. Doke and Risley (1972) have pointed out that labor and recreational activities are easier to observe when conditions for their occurrence are clearly specified. After such observations it was determined that the transition periods had an important effect on performance of activities in the workshop areas. The relationship between periods of transition and other important behaviors was explored.

First, an attempt was made to investigate the relationship between activities in the workshops and activities in the yard. It had been observed that these transition periods sometimes grew to be too long, resulting in periods of inactivity, as pointed out above, and favoring occurrence of inadequate behaviors. A series of informal observations were made before and after the "change period." The variables identified in order of importance were as follows. *Before* the change period the effects were observed mainly in the percentage of those participating in vocational activities in the workshop; *during* the change period, the main variable was "the announcement of change," which was done verbally by a warden inmate; finally *after* the change period, the most important variable was the availability of materials to a switch of activity (in this case the existence of edibles for lunch). These variables are referred to as "variables before, during, and after change." This experiment should be considered as an analysis of the basic components that may affect after the transition periods in the performance of activities of human groups under custody.

Procedures

Subjects were all inmates present in the two workshops. The PLA-CHEK system again was used as the observation procedure. The percentage of persons present and participating was recorded at intervals near to the time of the announcement. The percentage of persons present and participating was recorded every 5 min. In the fifth minute, the observers recorded the total number of persons present in the workshops and the total number of persons participating in the vocational activity.

"Change of activity" was defined as when persons in the fifth minute of observation abandoned the workshop activity and performed another one (e.g., lunch) or when the inmate performed two activities (working and lunch). Observations were made simultaneously in two workshops, and in both the experimental variables were introduced in a sequenced form according to a multiple-baseline design.

There were three conditions. The first consisted in giving tally marks to the inmates contingent upon vocational behavior, in the period from 10:30 to 10:50 a.m. It was simultaneous with the moment in which the announcement for activity change was made.

The second condition (or variable) was a modification in the announcement time. Instead of being made at 10:30 a.m., it was made at 10:40, and the tallymarks were given in the period between 10 and 10:20, contingent on vocational activities.

The third condition consisted of a situation in which no marks were given for any response. The announcement was modified in the sense that the inmates were told that they could have their lunch whenever they wanted between 9:30 and 11:00 a.m. Edibles remained on a table available to all of them.

Setting

The setting included two workshops: assembling and garment knitting. In each of these workshops the average number of working inmates was about 25. This total varied because of the lack of working materials and the arrival of new inmates (see Fig. 4). Data from workshop activity are shown in Fig. 4 to illustrate the variability of attendance per session.

Work within the workshop started in the morning session at 8:00 a.m. and ended at 1:00 p.m., when the inmates prepared themselves for lunch. Initially, in the wool assembling workshop, a rest period of 15 min for lunch was established in the middle of the morning session. This rest period was changed on July 20 to 10:30 in all workshops. The purpose of this change was to reduce the "boredom" that some inmates had expressed over remaining too long in the same area (the inmates reported "that they worked too much"). This 10:30 rest period

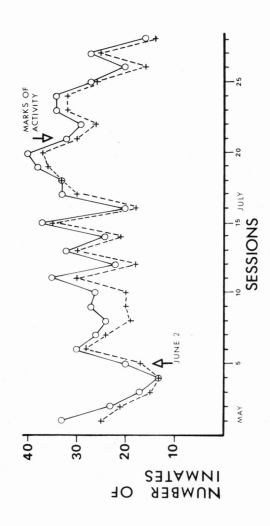

FIG. 4 Average daily numbers of persons present and participating in the planned activity in the waste-wool workshop over 3 months. (○) Inmates in the area; (+) inmates participating in the activity.

began to be used by some inmates not only for a coffee break, but also for taking a walk in the ward or engaging themselves in other activities, such as taking part in a sport, reading a magazine, or talking to another person. It was also observed that from the announcement for rest periods given at 10:30, the inmates began changing activities 20 or 30 min before the anouncement and 20 or 30 min after the announcement. This can be seen in the decrease in the total number of attendants at the workshop as well as in the total number of participants (see Fig. 5).

In both workshops and during the procedure, except for the third condition, every inmate received 20 marks for every 2 weeks of work. These marks could be exchanged each week for a list of reinforcers which included: first, edible reinforcers, such as cookies, soft drinks, canned seafood, or cigarettes; and second, "natural reinforcers," such as making a telephone call to their homes, not using the obligatory uniform, having more than two family visits per week, going out of the workshop in labor hours, obtaining magazines or sports material, and going out of the prison on field trips. These reinforcers were not always available. Reliability in observations was calculated by two observers on the basis of datum variation, from the total number of participants, as well as from the total number of persons present and the total number of persons changing activity in each observation period.

Results

The results of this exploratory study are shown in Fig. 6. These are representative sessions that cover a period of 50 min beginning at 10:30 a.m., the time at

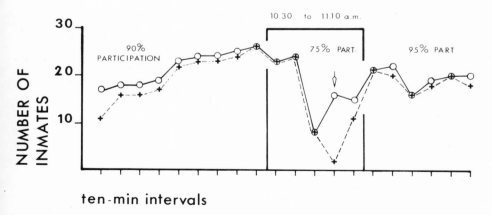

FIG. 5 Activity in the waste-wool workshop over a single session. Activity was switched at 11 a.m. (see arrow) and the effects of this switch on participation is shown. (o) Total inmates in workshop; (+) inmates working.

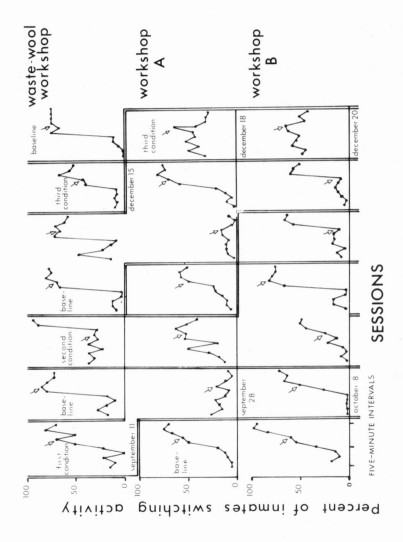

FIG. 6   Percentage of inmates switching activities in various experimental conditions. See text for full explanation.

which, except Condition II, the announcement for change of activity was given.

The first session on the wool-assembling workshop corresponded to the first condition, in which the delivering of tokens in the previous period was affected by delay. When this condition was applied to Workshop A, not only was the change period delayed, but it also seemed to decrease with respect to the baseline data on the same workshop. Each experimental condition was followed by baseline sessions that represented the difficulties that the experimenters had in maintaining in force each of the conditions (this was done for these reasons, and not precisely for methodological purposes). In the second condition for the wool workshop, the delay of the announcement determined that the maximum change did not have to be effective until the three later periods of observation (10:55), which were the maximum periods of activity switching. When this condition was applied in the Workshop B, it had the same affects of delaying and decreasing the number of persons that changed before 10:30 (having all of the changing until 11:10). In the third condition, the edible materials that favored the change of activity (lunch) determined that in the wool workshop the maximum change of activity appeared uniformly after 11:00. This same condition in the case of Workshop A determined that a great number of the inmates changed activity exactly at 11:00 although in this situation the announcement was given at 10:30.

It is important to note that the most uniform effect was in the second condition, in which the announcement, when it was delayed, determined a uniform variation in the number of persons that changed activity before it was made.

FINAL COMMENT

The results of these experiments show the importance of analyzing the effects of custodial institutions on the inmates specifically in terms of an objective evaluation of situational variables (for example, planning of activities). The main objective has been to explore in detail the aspects that may be components of a "harmonious life system." The results also suggest the possibility (Brool, 1969; Doke & Risley, 1972; McCorkel & Korn, 1954; Street et al., 1966) of differentially increasing the participation of groups of inmates in nonidiosincratic activities (educational activities) even though they were given the option of performing the most popular preferred activities, for example, sports or informal lectures. Simple and economical procedures that do not imply human and financial expenditures inconvenient to custodial institutions were used. The results add to the importance and possibility of a "rearrangement of contingencies" focused on the natural aspects of reinforcement in the institution (for example, use of gradual freedom inside and outside the institution as a reinforcer).

The results may be considered in terms of practical and methodological implications. Practical aspects include the problems of the organization of custodial institutions in relation to their daily functions, which are taken for granted (Jewell, 1957; Street *et al.,* 1966). Some specialists have suggested the implementation of functioning programs in custodial institutions (such as the prisons, reform and correctional schools, orphanages, nurseries) that are not always directed toward empirical self-corrective emphasis. In order to have data that enables the authorities of an institution to first select and then decide what should occur and how this affects the behavior of the inmates, it is necessary to have continuous observations.

We have been able to collect casual observations of a function ordinarily attributed to "experience" from some of the directive staff; that is, distribution and supervision of personnel work that mediates between authorities and inmates. Personnel are distributed on the basis of criteria that seldom include the behavior of the inmates in the chosen areas. In most cases, the personnel, which we shall denominate as "mediators," are distributed according to the increase or decrease of inmates in a location (Brool, 1969; Glasser, 1970). In other instances, the labor of the mediators is organized depending on the goals or objectives of the institution, which in fact are custodial, in labors that include maintaining, guarding, ordering, and sanctioning. In rehabilitation the tasks of the mediators are applying treatment, creating an environment of "understanding," etc.

In all of the above-mentioned alternatives, the success for mediating personnel depends on the previous creation of a structured environmental situation that enhances not only the distribution of labor for the mediators, but also the emergence of new functions (maybe of major social implications) and their necessary evaluation and correction. Discussing the implications of creating "harmonious life environments" is not only stimulating but also necessary, especially when a human technology for these purposes is beginning to have experimental support.

From a methodological viewpoint, the results found by Experiments 1 and 2 invite reconsideration of the type of independent variables that researchers have employed, mainly in the area of applied behavioral analysis. These types of variables can be called "social" or "personnel," with a close temporal relation to behavior previously selected. Most representative is the use of social reinforcement as an independent variable. In a custodial institution, selection and systematic application of a reinforcement variable are not always likely, and when achieved, the specification of the behavior on which reinforcement is to impinge often does not complete the requirements of the research filed "with social implications." Often, changes are experimental artifacts in human environments. A possible alternative is the selection and analysis of independent impersonal or noncontingencial variables which in the experiments described here are represented by planning of activities and "organization of transition procedures" within activities in the prison, that favor high percentages of participation by the inmates.

This approach fits better within the outlines specified by Premack (1959) for the environmental arrangement demanded by prisons in which the inmates are already living before the experimenter starts to work, and in which the central point seems to be to specify behavior sequences that favor the inmates recovering their "goods" (being worthy of trust, being able to select what they are to do, etc.) in the institution and later going back to their communities with higher probabilities of continuing their own activities without rejection by the groups in which they belong.

Our main interest has been to deal with some situational aspects in the prison (as an example of a total institution) that integrate environmental variables the effects of which are not so direct or immediate. That is the case for the reinforcement variables that Doke and Risley (1972) have called *"impersonal" variables* and G. Fernández[3] has called *"noncontingent" variables* for example, the proportion of structured and unstructured events that makes up the life of a custodial institution (psychotherapies, vocational therapy, versus being in the yard, walking in the halls, etc.), the proportion of wardens per inmate, the distribution and use of physical areas for performing an activity, the sequence between termination of Activity A and initiation of Activities B or C, and the frequency of interaction between inmates and authorities, and many others. In all cases the proposition has been to deal with these variables as independent variables the effects of which are on the behavior of the inmates.

REFERENCES

Brool, M. Play for hospitalized children. *Young Children,* 1969, 24(4), 219–224.

Burchard, J. D. Systematic socialization: A programed environment of the rehabilitation of antisocial retardates. *Psychological Record,* 1967, 17, 461–476.

Cohen, H., Filizpak, J., & Bis, J. C.A.S.E. project contingencies applicable to special education. In J. Shliev (Ed.), *Research in psychotherapy.* Washington, D.C.: American Psychological Association, 1968. Pp. 34–53.

Doke, L., & Risley, T. The organization of day care environments: Required vs. optional activities. *Journal of Applied Behavior Analysis,* 1972, 5 (4), 405–420.

García, R. S. Panorama sobre el pentenciarismo en México. *Revista de la Secretaría de Gobernación.* Vol. II. No. 9, Mayo-Junio 1973. Pp. 13–27.

Glasser, D. Some notes on urban jails. In D. Glasser (Ed.), *Crime in the city.* New York: Harper & Row, 1970.

Goffman, E. *Asylums.* New York: Doubleday, 1961.

Jewell, D. F. México's Tres Marías Penal Colony. *Journal of Criminal Law, Criminology and Police Science,* 1957, 48, 4.

McCorkel, L. W., & Korn, R. Resocialization within walls. *Annals of the American Academy of Political & Social Science.* 1954, 293, 88–98.

[3] Gustavo Fernández, personal communication, 1973.

Meichenbaum, D., Bowers, K., & Ross, R. Modification of classroom behavior of institution-alized female adolescent offenders. *Behavior Research & Therapy*, 1968, **6**, 343–353.

Miller, K. L., & Miller, A. L. Reinforcing self-help group activities of welfare recipients *Journal of Applied Behavior Analysis*, 1970, **3**, 57–64.

Phillips, E. L., Phillips, E. A., Fixen, D. F., & Wolf, M. M. Achievement Place: Modification of the behaviors of pre-delinquent boys within a token economy. *Journal of Applied Behavior Analysis*, 1971, **4**, 45–59.

Premack, D. Toward empirical behavioral laws: I. Positive reinforcement. *Psychological Review*, 1959, **66**, 219–233.

Sánchez Galindo, A. Adiestramiento y capacitación de reclusos. *Adiestramiento Rapido de Meno de Obra. Revista*, 1971, **1**(2).

Street, D., Vinter, R. D., Penow, C. *Organization for treatment: A comparative study of institutions for delinquents*. New York: The Free Press, 1966.

Sykes, G., M. The prisoner's status as conveyed by the environment. In *The Society of Captives: A study of a maximum security prison*. Princeton, New Jersey: Princeton University Press, 1958.

Wallace, S. *Total institutions*. New York: Transaction, 1971.

5

A Modeling and Informational Approach to Delinquency

Irwin G. Sarason

University of Washington

Research on modeling and observational learning burgeoned impressively during the 1960s. Many of the investigations focused on the fears and social behavior of young children. Experimental variables were manipulated under relatively well-controlled laboratory conditions. In recent years, interest has grown in the therapeutic applications of modeling. Building on laboratory findings, applications have been made in clinical, rehabilitation, and educational settings (Bandura, 1969). This chapter describes a modeling approach to delinquency and reports empirical evidence relative to its short-term and long-term effectiveness in rehabilitating juvenile delinquents. After presenting evidence, I shall describe recent related studies that also bear on the practical implications of modeling research for educational and vocational development.

The possibilities of modeling as a therapeutic vehicle for delinquent and other deviant groups have been pointed out in earlier articles (Sarason, 1968; Sarason & Ganzer, 1969). Results of pilot studies described in these articles have been encouraging in that institutionalized delinquent boys have seemed to become more socially adaptive as a function of observational learning opportunities. This finding is consistent with what is known of the powerful socializing role played by parents. Peterson and Becker (1965) have given a well-delineated picture of some of the negative influences that inadequate parental models can exert on their malleable offspring. Sutherland's concept of differential association is completely consistent with this picture (Sutherland & Cressey, 1966). His concept seems easily translatable into the terms of social learning theory: antisocial values and behaviors of adults and peers come to serve as norms and standards that are imitated by the potential delinquent.

The research described here was aimed at shedding light on the positive effects on delinquents' behavior of opportunities to observe prosocial models. Subjects who were exposed to prosocial modeling were compared with those who were not. Basic to the research was the belief that acceptable social behavior and many deviations from widely accepted norms are explicable in terms of the types of information available to and made salient for individuals. For example, disaffected, angry residents of a community who do not know that they can influence public policy by attending city council meetings do not involve themselves in governmental affairs; college professors who are unaware of society's interest in their reasoned recommendations remain silent; and adolescents who do not believe that they can get things they want through legitimate means may succumb to the temptation to employ antisocial tactics.

I do not contend that all persons armed with information about themselves, the way in which the community functions, and the legitimate avenues to goal attainment will inevitably become paragons of effective prosocial behavior. Psychopaths frequently know full well what is right and what is wrong, but without undue soul searching about means, they elect to behave antisocially so as to achieve their ends. One aim of the work described here has been to shed light on the personal characteristics of youngsters who do and do not make use of information provided by models.

Modeling is not the only or necessarily the best way of conveying information to all groups of people. For example, reinforcement regimens in the form of token economies may be the method of choice for particular groups (e.g., psychopaths). However, for a wide variety of purposes, demonstration in the form of modeled behavior seems to be an effective instructional approach. In order to explore more fully the effectiveness of different ways of presenting information, the experiment to be described includes a condition that provides information about adaptive, prosocial ways of responding to environmental contingencies but that do not use behavioral demonstrations as the medium. Nonmodeled information is provided through a structured discussion format that verbally gives the subjects examples of desirable and undesirable ways of coping with social, educational, and vocational situations.

In order to evaluate our procedures, data were gathered that fell into four categories of dependent measures: (1) self-report and clinical information; (2) behavior ratings made by staff personnel who had daily contact with the subjects; (3) postparole followup data obtained from interviews with the boys; and (4) recidivism rates.

Because the recidivism data were gathered more than two years after administration of the experimental treatments, we regarded them as the "hardest" indices of long-term treatment effects. However, our original expectation was that treatment effects would be more detectable before rather than after parole.

METHOD

Location of Research

The research was carried out at the Cascadia Juvenile Reception–Diagnostic Center in Tacoma, Washington. This is a state institution that receives commitments from Juvenile Court judges. The children at Cascadia are between the ages of 8 and 18 years. The length of stay is approximately 6 weeks for new commitments and 3–4 weeks for parole violators and recommitments. By most standards Cascadia would receive a quite high rating as an institution. Each child is studied diagnostically by a team of psychologists, social workers, teachers, and counselors. Most participate in group therapy programs that are supplemented by individual casework with clinical staff members. There is also a flourishing school program with a self-contained classroom on each cottage of boys or girls. One of the purposes of the scholastic program is to observe and evaluate the students in terms of their academic achievement and potential, their behavior in the classroom, attitudes toward the school program, work habits, and personal characteristics.

The culmination of a child's stay at Cascadia is the Review Board or case staffing that is held prior to his or her parole or transfer to another institution. Staff members working with a child attend the board meeting and present their evaluate findings. The child is also interviewed and a judgment is made about the most appropriate institution to which he or she should be sent. Recommendations about and planning for the child's future are made at the Review Board. Approximately 12% of the children are paroled directly to their home communities.

Subjects

The subjects were 192 male first offenders, drawn from two of Cascadia's cottages. There were 64 subjects in each of the modeling, discussion, and control groups. Half of the subjects in the modeling and discussion groups received televised feedback. However, as most of the long-term results failed to reveal significant group differences caused by this feedback condition, most of the results for the television variable are not be presented here.

The subjects were, at admission, between 15½ and 18 years of age (mean = 16 years, 7 months). The average IQ estimated from the Lorge–Thorndike Nonverbal Intelligence Scale was 95.3. The experimental groups studied were comparable on this measure of intelligence. They were also comparable with regard to the diagnosis made by the Cascadia staff, as well as in terms of the nature and severity of the delinquent activities that led to institutionalization.

Modeling Condition

I (Sarason, 1968) have described the general procedure used in modeling sessions. It emphasized a practical approach to the problems of adolescent boys. Each session was attended by four or five boys and two models. The models used in this study were clinical psychology graduate students interested in working with delinquents and trained to lead the groups. Each modeling session had a particular theme; for example, how to apply for a job, how to resist temptations by peers to engage in antisocial acts, how to take problems to a teacher or parole counselor, and how to pass up immediate gratification in order to lay the groundwork for achieving more significant goals in the future. In each situation, emphasis was placed on the generality of the appropriate behaviors being modeled and their potential usefulness in a variety of situations.

In the first-day orientation for each new group the boys were told:

We think that small groups working together can learn a lot about appropriate ways of doing things by playing different roles and watching others play roles. By role we mean the particular part a person acts or plays in a particular situation, kind of like the parts actors play in a movie scene, only this will be more realistic. These roles will be based on actual situations that many young people have trouble with, like how to control your anger or resist being pressured into doing destructive things by friends. Other roles are directly related to fellows like yourselves who have been in an institution . . . this is like acting, only it is realistic because it involves situations in which you might really find yourselves . . . ."

An example of the topics covered in the modeling sessions is suggested by the "Tackling School Problems" scene.

Scene I: Introduction. Almost everyone has run into some difficulties with at least a few courses in school. Either the teacher doesn't seem to explain things clearly enough, or the course just seems to be too hard, or the subject isn't interesting and seems unimportant to our later lives, or some other problem comes up and interferes with our getting much out of the course. While everyone has experienced these difficulties at one time or another, some people seem to be able to solve school problems better than others. Others just let these problems ride and continue to add up until they are really behind in the course and have a bad attitude toward the course and toward school in general. It is hard for a person to remain interested in school and want to continue going to school when he is getting farther and farther behind and not trying to solve the various school problems as they arise.

One of the best ways of solving school problems is to tackle them as soon as they appear. This should be done by talking over course problems with the teacher. To insure that a talk with the teacher is helpful, the following rules are worthwhile to keep in mind:

1. Don't put off these discussions. Go in as soon as the problem arises. Don't wait until the end of the semester and then walk in just before grades are due and tell the teacher you don't understand anything from the first week on.

2. Have a specific problem in mind. A teacher can only help you when you are able to talk clearly about the things that are giving you trouble.

3. Don't just dump the whole problem in the teacher's lap and expect it to be solved. Follow through on the suggestions he makes to insure that you really understand better what to do.

In the scene today you'll see the right way and the wrong way to talk out a school problem with a teacher. In both scenes a boy is having trouble with math and has come to see his teacher about it. In the first scene Mr. _____ and I will just act out the wrong way. It is too bad, but probably many discussions with teachers turn out to be just as unsuccessful as this one:

Teacher: "Come in, Bob. Did you want to see me?"

Bob: "Yeah. I'm having an awful lot of trouble with your course and I though I'd better come in and see you since we're going to have an exam in a couple of days."

Teacher: "Well, I'll be glad to try and help. What's giving you trouble?"

Bob: (Laughing and shrugging his shoulders) "Well . . . math."

Teacher: (Smiling) "Well, maybe you can pin it down better than that."

Bob: "I don't know. I guess I haven't understood much from the second chapter on."

Teacher: "Well, now Bob, we finished that chapter over 4 weeks ago. If you didn't understand something in Chapter 2, you should have come in then, when you started to have difficulties."

Bob: "Yeah, I guess so, but I thought maybe I'd catch on after a while. But now, I don't know. It seems to be getting worse all the time."

Teacher: "I don't know if I can be much help now. The material in Chapter 9 and in Chapter 10 that I assigned today is pretty much impossible to understand if you didn't get the concepts in the previous chapters. Are you reading the book as we go along in class? Are you up to where the rest of the class is?"

Bob: "Well, no, not really. I just sort of gave up after Chapter 4."

Teacher: "Are you having trouble understanding the book? Does it made sense to you when you read it?"

Bob: "No, I think it's pretty hairy . . . hard to understand. And I haven't understood much of what you've been saying in class lately, either."

Teacher: "Well, I think what we'd better do is to get you so you understand the basic concepts and then try to catch you up with the class. Now, we don't use this book, but it has the same material. Some people find it a little easier to understand. What you should do is try to read the first four chapters in it and try to understand that material and then come in and see me again and we'll talk over any problems you've had with it. Then maybe you can start again in the regular text and read Chapters 5 through 10. I think they'll make better sense to you then. And remember to work a couple of problems at the end of each section that you read. If anything gives you trouble, bring it along with you when you come in to see me."

Bob: "Boy, that's an awful lot of work. I don't know if I'm gonna have time to do that by Friday."

Teacher: "Yes, it's going to take extra effort on your part to catch up. But it's not too bad. You don't have to work all the problems and the new book will go fairly fast, I think. I'll let you skip the exam Friday. You can take a makeup when you get caught up."

Bob: "Well, I didn't expect when I came in here that I'd have *more* work to do. I kind of had some plans lined up for the next few weekends."

Teacher: "Now, Bob, if you're going to catch up and make a passing grade in my class you'll have to sacrifice something. After all, you've let this problem slip too long. You should have come in right away when you first started having trouble."

Scene II.   Scene: The setting of this scene is the same as Scene I.

Teacher: "Come in, Bob. Did you want to see me?"

Bob: "Yeah, I'm having trouble with this section that you assigned yesterday and I thought I'd better come in and see you before I get all messed up."

Teacher: "Well, I'm glad you did. Have you read the section?"

Bob: "Yeah, I read it last night, but I didn't understand it too well. When I went to work these problems here at the end I couldn't get anywhere with them. Could you work through this example problem here? This is where I really got fouled up."

Teacher: "Yes, of course. How have you been doing up to now?"

Bob: "Okay. I thought everything was clear until I ran into this junk."

Teacher: "I'm glad you came in early before you started to really get behind. This is an important section and the material in it is important for the things we'll be studying for the rest of the course. But this section must be much harder to understand than the rest. The author doesn't explain things as well as usual here. I've had about four people come in and ask me for help with this assignment.

Bob: "Really? I thought I was the only one having trouble."

Teacher: "Oh, no. As a matter of fact, it's a good thing that you are all coming in and asking me about it. I had planned to give a quiz on this section tomorrow to see if you are all keeping up with the work. But if some of you are having trouble understanding this section, there's no use testing you on it."

Bob: "Geez, I couldn't pass a test on this stuff."

Teacher: "Also, if you want, you could read these three pages in that other book by Walters. He has a better explanation of what's going on than our textbook."

Bob: "Yeah, okay. I can do that in study hall and get the book back to you right away."

Teacher: "That's fine. Now about this sample problem, let me explain it as I work it on the board."

Following the first day's orientation, which included a short example scene, each subsequent meeting adhered to this format: one of the models began the session by introducing and describing the particular scene to be enacted that day. The introductions for each of the scenes had been memorized by the models. These introductions served to orient the boys to the group's work for the day and to afford them a rationale for the particular scene. After the boys had been briefed concerning specific aspects of the modeling to which they should pay special attention, the models role played the particular scene for the day while the boys observed.

Most of the scenes employed are divided into parts. In some cases the first part depicts an undesirable way of coping with the problem and the second a more desirable way. Following the models' enactment of the situation, one boy is called on to summarize and explain the content and outcome of what had just been observed. The group is not told at the outset which boy will be called on. This procedure helps insure that each boy attends carefully to what is going on in the group. After this, models and boys comment on and discuss the scene briefly. A short break then takes place, during which soft drinks are served and an audio or video role-playing tape is played. After this, the remaining boys enact the situations so that each boy participates in each session. Each meeting ends with final summaries and comments concerning the scene, its most salient aspects, and its generalizability.

In the procedure employed, comments and questions by the models are aimed at sustaining the group's interest in and attention to the scenes being role played. Responses made by the models are brief, specific, and not projective. Lengthy discussion by group members is not encouraged. The models attempt to get the boys thinking about related and similar situations in which the modeled contents of the scene could possibly apply at some point in their lives. An example of this is provided by the "Job Interview" scene, which was followed by an enumeration of the many situations in which boys would be required to make a good impression on somebody in authority.

The modeling sequence consisted of 14 sessions. Pairs of boys in the groups made up and enacted their own scenes during the fifteenth session. These scenes were subsequently role played by the other boys. The boys were informed of this procedure a week in advance, were given adequate time to develop an appropriate scene for the session, and were given the opportunity to use the models as "consultants." This homework assignment aroused the interest of most of the boys, who clearly endeavored to do a good job in the development and presentation of their scenes. Although most of their modeling sessions were elaborations or extensions of aspects of the previously modeled materials, some of the boys produced highly original and relevant situations. The final session, the sixteenth, served as a review and summary of the work conducted during the previous 15 meetings.

Although each boy was urged at the outset to attend the modeling sessions, it was made clear to him that his participation was voluntary. Only 4 subjects decided to forego participation in the study.

Discussion Condition

Every effort was made to keep the sequence and content of the guided discussion group meetings as similar as possible to the modeling sessions. The first day orientation given to discussion group subjects presented the same rationale and purposes as that given to the modeling groups except that all references to role playing were omitted. Boys were told instead that:

> We think that groups working together can help each member of the group learn a lot about what makes him tick, just by talking frankly about the topics. The topics will be real situations that many young people have trouble with, controlling your anger or being pressured into doing destructive things by friends. . . . We use four rules in these groups: (1) one person talks at a time; (2) everyone contributes to the discussion; (3) what goes on here won't be taken outside the group, it will be confidential and not used by the staff; and (4) no ranking. Constructive criticism and comments are good but ranking doesn't help anyone. . . .

An example of how the group discussions are conducted is provided by the "Job Interview" session. One of the leaders introduces the day's topic by commenting on the importance of jobs as a means of getting money for things that we need. He also points out that it is a way of earning something through one's own effort and a means of achieving independence. He comments that getting a job isn't easy and that knowledge and skill are relevant to getting jobs. The job interview is described as a key step in this process. One of the two group leaders then asks the boys what sorts of interviews they have had, what sorts of questions have been asked of them, and how they have handled the situations. Interventions of the group leaders are analagous to those described for the modeling group, questions being raised in order to deal specifically with salient features of the concepts being discussed.

During the fifteenth discussion session the boys were instructed to think up and present topics that they themselves felt should be discussed and to try to develop the reason why these topics were important to them and others. In general, the organization and sophistication of the boys' presentations were not as adequate as they were for the boys in the modeling groups. The discussion topics tended to be vague and to be presented in an excessively rambling fashion.

Both discussion and modeling sessions were arranged to minimize ambiguity and maximize structure. The sixteenth and final session was again a summary conducted as similarly as possible to that for the modeling groups. Although there were differences in the manner in which the modeling and discussion groups were conducted, their content and sequential characteristics seemed comparable.

Dependent Variables

A number of dependent measures were obtained in order to compare the treatment groups. These could be classified as self-report, staff ratings of various behavioral dimensions, clinical variables, followup interview, and recidivism. Some of the measures were obtained only during the initial phase of the research (premeasures), some were obtained on a repeated-measures basis (pre- and postmeasures), and some were available only after subjects had participated in the experiment (postmeasures).

Premeasures only. Shortly after admission to Cascadia all subjects were administered short true–false personality inventories that included Sarason's Test Anxiety Scale (TAS) (Sarason, 1972), the *Pd* scale of the MMPI, Gough's (1957) Impulsivity Scale (Im), and Navran's (1954) Dependency Scale (Dep). The Lorge–Thorndike Nonverbal Intelligence Scale (multilevel edition) was also given at this time.

Repeated measures. Self-report data and staff behavior ratings were obtained along with the premeasures and again just prior to subjects' Review Board meeting. The interval between pre- and posttesting was approximately 5 weeks. These five self-report measures yielded scores on ten variables: (1) Wahler's (1969) Self Description Inventory (SDI), which contains descriptions of favorable (Fa) and unfavorable (Uf) personal characteristics rated on an eight-point scale from "very much like me" to "not at all like me"; (2) the Word Rating Scale (WRS), a series of five semantic differential items similar to an instrument developed by Schwartz and Tangri (1965) and designed to measure different aspects of the self-concept (e.g., "Me as I am now," "Me as my parents see me"); (3) a specially created Goals scale, which required subjects to estimate the likelihood that they would achieve various future goals (e.g., "finish high school"); (4) the Activity Preference Questionnaire (APQ), a forced-choice measure of emotional reactivity developed by Lykken (1957) to discriminate among normal, neurotic, and psychopathic levels of anxiety; and (5) Rotter's (1966) Internalization–Externalization (I–E) scale, a forced-choice measure of the perceived locus of control over the events in one's life.

In addition, cottage counselors completed two kinds of ratings on each subject. The Behavior Rating Scale (BRS) is a shortened version of Tyler and Kelly's (1962) 25-item scale for rating various dimensions of children's behavior. The scale contained ten bipolar behavior descriptions (e.g., "Never hits and pushes–Often hits and pushes"), each rated on a seven-point scale, retained from the original 25 items that had been administered in a preliminary investigation and found to have adequate interrater reliability ($r \geqslant .74$). The second rating scale, the Weekly Behavior Summary (WBS), is a seven-category behavior checklist that describes such areas as peer and staff relationships, work detail performance, personal habits, and general cottage adjustment. The average overall rating agreements among three to seven counselors ranged from 67 to 100%. Subjects' scores were based on the pooled average of the counselors' ratings.

Postmeasures only. The dependent measures obtained at the culmination of the subjects' stay at Cascadia included records of all disciplinary action (e.g., isolations), diagnostic classification, and case disposition. Each case disposition was rank ordered from most favorable (e.g., parole) to least favorable (e.g., higher security institution). Placement in any given institution was objectively rated by clinical staff as reflecting various degrees of maladjustment and need for control. A final measure, frequency and chronicity of preinstitutional delinquent behavior, was based on ratings of case summaries and reports. Interview material and indices of recidivism were gathered during the period of parole.

RESULTS

Pretreatment analyses of variance among the three treatment groups revealed no systematic differences. Comparisons of pre- to postchanges among these groups revealed two significant overall differences. The modeling group showed a reduction in anxiety or emotional reactivity on the APQ that was significantly greater ($p < .05$) than that for the discussion or control groups. Both discussion and modeling groups showed a significantly greater shift toward internalization on the I–E scale ($p < .05$) than did the control group. The difference between modeling and discussion was not significant. Interactions revealed that both nontelevised modeling and discussion groups changed more favorably than did control groups on 11 of the 12 variables employed in the study. This pattern did not appear in comparisons among the televised modeling and discussion groups and the control group. In fact, televised feedback seemed to have a negative effect for the modeling condition. Sarason and Ganzer (1973) have shown that this negative effect is especially associated with high test anxiety.

The variable of case disposition was analyzed by nonparametric comparisons because the range and distribution of the scores suggested that they did not meet the assumptions required for a parametric analysis. Table 1 shows the distribution of placement rating scores of all subjects according to group membership. The eight possible placements were combined and reduced to four categories to permit chi-square comparisons. Categories 1–2 represent favorable case dispositions (e.g., trial parole) and Categories 7–8 represent placement in more structured, higher security institutions that generally receive more severely and chronically delinquent boys. Approximately three times as many boys in the nontelevised modeling groups received favorable placements as compared with other groups ($p < .05$). The number of subjects within the nontelevised modeling group ($n = 14$) is also significantly greater than the number of boys in the televised discussion ($n = 5$) or televised modeling ($n = 4$), and nontelevised discussion ($n = 4$) ($p < .01$). Nontelevised modeling subjects, then, received more favorable case dispositions than have other groups.

Many factors interact to determine the Review Board decision to place any given boy in another institution or to return him directly to his home community. For example, the attitudes of the community toward the boy, the status of his home situation, his behavior and performance while at Cascadia, and other variables are important determiners of case disposition. Because of these factors, it cannot be said with certainty that participation in a modeling group has been the major determiner of the Review Board decision. However, because most boys are comparable across the dimensions measured in this investigation at the

TABLE 1
Comparisons of Placement Ratings for Main Experimental
and Control Groups[a]

Group	Combined placement rating			
	1–2 favorable	3–4	5–6	7–8 unfavorable
Televised modeling	4	9	6	13
Nontelevised modeling	14	7	2	9
Televised discussion	5	8	9	10
Nontelevised discussion	4	11	8	9
Control	19	19	9	27
n:	46	54	34	68

[a]Note that for each of the modeling and discussion groups represented in this table $N = 32$ and for the control group $N = 64$.

time of their admission to Cascadia, it seems reasonable to conclude that the modeling treatment do influence boys' attitudes and behaviors for the better, and that this difference is to some degree reflected in the favorable decisions made by the Review Board. Other things being equal, the cottage attitudes and behavior of boys is a significant determiner of case dispositions. In this regard, it is worth noting that 14 boys have gone from Cascadia directly to a regular parole status. Nine of these boys had participated in modeling groups, all but one of whom had received the nontelevised condition.

The intermediate term data consisted of the behavior rating scales filled out by institution counselors after the subject had spent approximately 4 months in the institution to which they had been sent from Cascadia. Counselors were not told which boys had been in groups while at the diagnostic center. Independent BRS and WBS ratings were obtained from two raters for each subject. It was possible to obtain ratings on 95 of the 128 experimental group boys (74%) and 57 of the 64 control group boys (89%). Boys for whom ratings were incomplete or who had received paroles or early discharges from the institution were not represented in this group. Interrater reliability coefficients between pairs of raters on a sample of 60 boys were $r = .694$ for the WBS and $r = .830$ for the BRS.

Tabular comparisons were made for the behavior rating data on the basis of whether subjects showed positive or no further or negative change from the Cascadia postrating to the subsequent 4-month institution rating. The criterion for determining direction of change was based on one standard deviation from the mean Cascadia postrating. The results of these comparisons are summarized in Table 2.

Significantly more modeling and discussion group boys showed positive as opposed to negative behavior change on the 4-month ratings, whereas control group boys were equally divided ($p < .05$). Approximately 38% of the modeling group and 39% of the discussion group subjects continued to show positive behavior change, whereas 26% of the control group subjects continued to show behavioral improvements. Control group subjects, in addition, were more often rated as behaving more negatively (28.1%) than were experimental group boys.

TABLE 2
Number of Subjects Showing Positive, No, or Negative Rated Behavior
Change from Cascadia Postrating to Subsequent Institution Rating

	n	Positive change	No change	Negative change	% Positive change	% Negative change
Modeling	44	17	23	4	38.6	9.1
Discussion	51	20	23	8	39.2	15.8
Control	57	15	26	16	26.3	28.1

Long-Term Results

Two sources of followup data were available from: (1) personal interviews and readministration of several self-report items, and (2) data on all subjects available through archival records.

Follow-up intereviews. Interviews and self-report data were obtained on 53 subjects subsequent to their discharge from parole. Of this sample, 20 had been in modeling groups, 18 in discussion groups, and 15 had been control group boys. The original aim of the followup evaluation was to collect a considerably larger sample, but this was not possible for several reasons, particularly because the actual parole periods were longer than had been initially estimated (1 year) and because of the geography of the state of Washington. The subjects in the interview followup study were therefore not a random sample of the original 192 boys who participated in the research. The interview sample was biased by (1) earlier parole discharges given to some boys who had participated earlier in the initial phase of the project, (2) the fact that the interviewees were volunteers (however, only seven boys or their parents out of 60 boys who were contacted refused to participate), (3) the fact that most were urban dwellers and, (4) the fact that most were relatively stable in terms of geographic mobility; that is, they remained in the state instead of receiving out of state paroles or joining the military service.

The procedure for contacting, interviewing, and testing the subjects began with a master list of names of all subjects who had participated in the research project. At the time a boy's name was submitted for parole discharge, office personnel notified his parole counselor that the particular boy had been a subject. The counselor subsequently described the followup interview to the boy and his parents during their final meeting. If the boy consented to participate, written parental permission was obtained and the boy's name and address were forwarded to the interviewer. The interviewer was a male social worker who had not previously participated in any phase of the research. He subsequently contacted the boy and an appointment was made for the interview. The interview was structured and it was taperecorded.

Blind ratings were made of interview typescripts in order to determine subjects' evaluations of their experiences during institutionalization and while on parole. Interviews were rated as reflecting positive, neutral, or negative response to these experiences. The ratings are summarized in Table 3. Nonparametric comparisons among the three response categories for each major group revealed that only in the modeling group did the proportions of subjects differ significantly, with 13 of the 19 interviewees indicating an overall positive response to the state's programs for young offenders ($p < .01$). Proportions of subjects in the discussion and control conditions did not differ significantly.

The subjects were also questioned about their involvement in delinquent activities during the time they were on parole. Sixty percent of the discussion

TABLE 3
Combined Global Rating of Responsiveness
to Total Experiences in Institutions
and While on Parole

Group	General responsiveness		
	Positive	Neutral	Negative
Modeling	13	2	4
Discussion	7	6	3
Control	6	4	5
Total:	26	12	12

group subjects admitted to having engaged in further law violations while on parole. The comparable figure for modeling group was 28% and for control group boys was 38%. Most of these delinquent activities could be classified as traffic and curfew violations, running away, and the use of alcohol and drugs. These data must be interpreted with caution because they represent delinquent activities only to the extent that the interviewees admitted to them without coercion. It was interesting and perhaps somewhat surprising that only four of the boys refused to respond to the question.

Another type of followup data was derived from an analysis of experimental subjects' recollections of their previous participation in modeling and discussion groups. The interviewer first asked each subject to recall and describe what he could remember about the procedure, content, and purpose (as had been described by models or group leaders) of the group he had participated in while at Cascadia. Subjects' recall of each of these three aspects of their group participation was rated as adequate or good or as poor. The proportions of subjects falling into these categories for each of the two ratings are summarized in Table 4. A greater proportion of modeling group subjects recalled the content and purpose of the groups than did subjects who had participated in the discussion groups. Although it was expected that recall of the content would be superior for modeling group boys because of the greater specificity and repetition involved in the imitative procedures, their better recall of the purposes of the groups might not have been anticipated because approximately the same amount of time was taken by models or leaders in describing this aspect of the group sessions.

Subjects were also asked to remember as many of the different scenes or topics as they could without prompting from the interviewer. Subjects were considered to have recalled a topic or scene if they were able to adequately describe the concept that had been dealt with and the example used to illustrate that concept (e.g., relating to people in authority—the job problem situation). Fifteen of the

19 modeling group boys (p = .02, binomial test) spontaneously recalled at least two topics, and the mean for the group was 2.5 topics. Seven of the 13 discussion group boys recalled two or more topics, and the group mean was 1.4 topics.

After determining subjects' free recall, the interviewer mentioned each of the remaining topics (e.g., "What do you remember about a problem on the job?") to determine their retention when assisted. Again, recall was considered adequate if the concept or purpose of the topic was verbalized. The modeling group recalled an average of 85% of the content of the group sessions, and the discussion group recalled an average of 57%. An additional effort was made to elicit relevant examples of any applications of the concepts and topics to their subsequent lives. This was done to determine the extent to which boys could make meaningful connections between the topics presented in the group sessions and actual events they had subsequently experienced. Subjects were considered to have applied a topic if they clearly stated that their behavior in the example situation had been a direct function of what had been learned in the group. Sixteen of the 19 modeling group subjects applied at least one topic, seven applied three or more, and the mean was 1.8 applications. Six of the 13 discussion group subjects applied one topic and two had applied three or more, with a mean of 1.1 topics. Only two subjects in the modeling group stated that they had not understood the concepts and topics, whereas six of the discussion group boys had not understood the material. A global rating of the degree to which boys expressed benefit from their previous group participation suggested that at least 12 modeling group boys and four discussion group boys felt that the groups had helped them. Seven boys in each group did not feel that they had derived benefit from their participation.

Recidivism. Recidivism was defined as: (a) the return of a boy to a juvenile institution because of unsatisfactory behavior, (b) conviction in Superior Court

TABLE 4
Interviewees' Recall of Group Participation

Category	Group	Rating Adequate–good	Poor
Recall of group procedure	Modeling	15	4
	Discussion	10	3
Recall of content	Modeling	15	4
	Discussion	5	8
Recall of purpose	Modeling	13	6
	Discussion	7	6

resulting in adult status probation, or (c) confinement in an adult correctional institution. The Office of Research of Washington's Division of Institutions supplied these data as well as complete records of each subjects' movements, such as leaves, escapes, transfers, discharges, and readmissions.

A covariate of recidivism rate is "period at risk." "At risk" refers to the temporal interval after institution release at which statistics on recidivism are obtained. The cumulative recidivism rate for juvenile offenders in the State of Washington ranges from 22 to over 30%, depending on the period at risk and yearly fluctuations in the population. The period at risk for subjects in the present sample has been 18.5 months, which is sufficiently long to warrant confidence in the assumption that the number of recidivists identified closely approximates the maximum number that would eventually occur because an at risk period of 18 months is estimated to identify over 80% of the maximum expected number.

At a point almost 3 years after their arrival at Cascadia, 43 of the 192 boys in the sample, or 22.4%, had become recidivists. There were more recidivists in the control group (n = 22) than in the modeling (n = 12) and discussion (n = 9) groups ($p < .05$, chi-square test). The recidivism rate for the control group (34%) was consistent with the then current cumulative recidivism rate for the male population in the state. Comparisons were made of the proportion of recidivists to nonrecidivists in each of four samples: (1) modeling group; (2) discussion group; (3) control group; and (4) the cumulative Cascadia male population (n = 1242). The z-score comparisons of differences among proportions indicated that fewer modeling ($p < .05$) and discussion ($p < .009$) subjects became recidivists than did controls. Compared to the base rate of recidivism in the population, these differences were highly significant (modeling vs. population, $p < .02$; Discussion versus Population, $p < .001$).

Discussion

Because of the relatively limited scope of our treatments—in terms of duration and content—we were more confident about immediate than continued effects. With the results described above the inevitable question must be raised of what brought them about. Are they explicable in terms of a confounding variable? We do not view this experiment as a perfect one. Indeed, it is unlikely that research conducted in an ongoing clinical setting can be methodologically pure. However, we have failed to uncover biases of sufficient magnitude to account for the findings. The most obvious bias would be preexisting differences among the several groups. As described above, these groups seemed comparable.

One possibility is that the results may be explicable on the basis of the experimental groups receiving extra attention, regardless of the form that attention may take. However, this seems an unlikely explanation for several reasons, the most obvious being posed by the long-term effects. It is difficult to imagine that simply giving attention to boys for a few hours a week over a period of 1 month can bring about the findings I have presented. Furthermore, the Cascadia environment is not the impoverished one in which attention effects are expected to flourish. On the contrary, Cascadia's staff–child ratio is favorable and its residents are rarely idle.

What the modeling and discussion treatments have in common is that they provide personally relevant information to the boys in an interesting and meaningful way. Both treatments are highly structured and lacked "depth." This seems important especially in relation to the discussion format because it limits the free-wheeling conversation typically characteristic of group meetings that rely on verbal transactions. Informal comments by the subjects suggest that they have been impressed with and have responded favorably to the well-ordered, no-nonsense approach of both experimental treatments. Perhaps in psychology's perennial battle (or so it sometimes seems) between behavioristic and depth approaches to the modification of adaptation failures, sight has been lost of an overriding concept, that of information and its transmittal.

Everyone has had the experience of acquiring a new response by virtue of a seemingly minor rephrasing or reordering of relevant elements. The particularly effective teacher frequently is successful because of his or her ability to reduce complex concepts to their most basic elements. Looking at the delinquent from this perspective, perhaps his or her greatest need is for help in (1) pinpointing the specific behaviors needed for adaptation to a complex, industralized society, and (2) incorporating these behaviors into his or her response repertory. Satisfying these needs through psychological introspection or moral entreaties to behave in socially acceptable ways may not be nearly as effective as a straightforward approach to response acquisition. One implication of this possibility is that learning to resist peer pressure to engage in antisocial acts, to attend to relevant information and disregard irrelevant stimuli, and to be considerate of others may be approached in a manner analogous to that used in driver-training courses.

Modeling seems to be an especially intriguing procedure for transmitting information because it makes use of actual demonstrations that facilitate behavior modification. Furthermore, the child's observations of demonstrations within the home are, unhappily, often highly effective; for example, the girl who is anxious because that is how her mother always seems to be, the boy who lies because that is what his father does all the time. Observational opportunities provide an individual with information about the world, how it works, and how to survive in it. Modeling is important developmentally because it provides the child with answers to his questions. The delinquent may act out because he or she has observed significant others do so in solving their problems and achieving gratification. The dropout may withdraw from school because he or she has been deprived of the opportunity to observe models who value and use knowledge acquired in school.

A number of questions are posed by the present investigation. One group of these relates to the factors that brought about these results. I have already pointed to the matter of the similarities and differences between the modeling and discussion formats. For example, they are similar in that they are highly structured, but they differ in their amounts of physical and social activity. A second group of questions relates to the extensions suggested by this study. It is interesting that several attempts have recently been made to increase adaptive behavior through highly structured informational programs similar to the modeling and discussion conditions here. These attempts have been directed toward behavior in a variety of educational and vocational settings, reclaiming high school dropouts, strengthening work-related behaviors in unemployed persons, and providing therapeutic avenues for disturbed individuals (Krumboltz & Thoresen, 1969; Sarason & Ganzer, 1969; Vriend, 1969). What are the desirable personal qualities of an effective model? How similar should a model or discussion leader be to the persons with whom he works (e.g., with regard to age, socioeconomic status, level of adjustment)? To what degree are modeling and discussion effects separable? Further inquiry into these types of questions will advance both theory and practice in these important areas.

Preventing Delinquency

Rehabilitating delinquents is not necessarily the best way of reducing the problem of delinquency. In terms of human values, personal happiness, and money, prevention represents a higher goal than rehabilitation. Whether or not it is reasonable to assign the task to them, the schools are increasingly being asked to play an important role in the prevention of various types of personal and social problems, including delinquent behavior.

One approach to delinquency prevention is through the modification of behavior that accompanies or precedes the commission of delinquent acts. It is well-known that school dropouts are more delinquency prone than are nondropouts, and it would seem reasonable to attack delinquency through an attack on the dropout problem. The dropout problem is, of course, an important one in its own right because of the prices the individual and society pay for his or her inadequate preparation for the world of work.

The dropout has been studied by many investigators in many ways. This is not surprising, considering the scope of the problems posed by large numbers of poorly trained, poorly motivated persons entering the work force. Of the 26 million youths who entered the job market in the United States during the 1960's, over 25% have been school dropouts (Schreiber, 1967). The unemployment rate among dropouts may be three times that of the national average. The research of Hathaway, Reynolds, and Monachesi (1969a, b) has illuminated not only the long-term deleterious outcomes of dropping out of school but also the important sex differences in these outcomes. Not only may there be significant economic disparities between high school dropouts and graduates but, perhaps as important, there may be large disparities in the individual's sense of self-worth and view of him- or herself as a participatory, contributing member of society.

The dropout tends to be someone who comes from a lower socioeconomic background, is older than his or her classmates, does not have even partially crystallized educational and vocational plans, comes from a large family, and frequently has been deprived of one or both parents because of death or separation (Bachman, Green, & Wirtanen, 1972; Schreiber, 1967; Zeller, 1966). Bachman *et al.* (1972) reported a significant positive correlation between rebellious behavior in school and dropping out. They also found that the potential dropout is likely to be lower than average in self-esteem and feelings of personal efficacy. He or she is also likely to be higher in feelings of anxiety over school, tests, and evaluations of his or her ability.

Unfortunately, the dropping out phenomenon has often been treated as a relatively discrete educational problem. An example of this is the effort utilizing mass media to encourage students who are thinking about leaving school to remain in school. Because dropping out is a symptom of other problems, simply urging youngsters to stay in school is unlikely to solve the problem. It seems clear that changing the schools or the attitudes and motivations of a significant group of its students (or both) is needed. Achieving these changes represents a mammoth and highly challenging task. Modeling, the use of reinforcing contingencies, and other behavioral techniques have much to offer as significant components of general educational programs, particularly for disadvantaged youngsters.

What is the role of modeling in efforts to motivate school children along productive lines? I have already described modeling as a medium for information transmittal. A recent study by Harris (1972) provides an illustration of the possibility of integrating modeling methods into school programs.

Harris' subjects were high school students who, using several criteria, appeared to be potential dropouts. They had low grade point averages, came from lower socioeconomic backgrounds, and were either a grade behind or older than their classmates. They also seemed uncertain about their future plans. Most of the students were members of minority groups. Whereas in the research described above all of the subjects participated in both modeling and role playing, Harris used only a modeling paradigm. Her aim was the elevation of aspirations through exposure to achieving models.

Harris' models came from the community in which the school was located and occupied paraprofessional or semiskilled occupations (teacher's aid, bank management trainee, printer's apprentice). All of them entered their occupations without the advantage of a college education. These community models were obtained through recommendations from local agencies, such as the Urban League. The modeling sessions stressed informality. At each one, a guest (community model) would describe his or her work, how he or she got his or her job, his or her present mode of living, the hurdles overcome in achieving his or her present position and the setbacks experienced. Slides were shown of the model as he or she was engaged in the daily work. Refreshments were served and the students were encouraged to ask questions, make comments, and relate what happened at each session to themselves.

The aim of the modeling in Harris' study was to expose potential dropouts to models who were realistic, with whom they might identify, and from whom they might derive inspiration. Harris compared live and filmed models and found no significant differences between these groups. She evaluated her experiment in a number of ways and demonstrated that, when compared with control comparison groups, the students who participated in the modeling program showed increases in their vocational aspirations, improved their school work (that is, they received higher grades), and displayed increased confidence in their ability to shape their own lives. Observational learning therefore resulted in measurable attitudinal and behavioral changes.

Harris plans a followup study to determine the effects of modeling on actual dropping out behavior. Her findings support the use of work–study and apprentice training programs. Vriend's (1969) study, using high performing peer models, has yielded results similar to Harris'. Exposure to realistic role models, together with practical job training, may well mean the difference between the potential dropout being or not being integrated into the socioeconomic system. It should be pointed out that, as with the work on delinquent behavior described above, the number of observational learning sessions is relatively small (six sessions in Harris' work). If such limited experimental programs can yield significant changes, the probability seems reasonably high that more intensive programs can be even more effective.

The spectrum of behavior covered in the studies described in this chapter is a broad one. Similarly, Harris and Vriend have delt with broad categories of behavior. Modeling can also be used in quite focalized ways. For example, Meier (1972) has performed an experiment in which specific components of verbal behavior related to success in job interviews have been studied. Working with high school students, he has found that the opportunity to observe models display adaptive behavior in simulated job interviews has a positive effect on the students' behavior in similar situations. Further research is needed concerning the focus of modeled behavior, as well as the characteristics of the models, whether subjects merely observe models or also themselves engage in role playing, the role of reinforcement (for both model and subject), and the strengths and weaknesses of alternate informational approaches. A given informational program may not be uniformly effective with all stubjects. If that is true, then potential interactions between informational approaches (modeling, reinforcement, psychotherapy) and personal characteristics should be examined.

An important problem that almost certainly will receive increased attention in the years to come concerns the modeling of responses that are usually not overtly observable. Meichenbaum and Goodman (1971) and Sarason and Ganzer (1973) have provided recent examples of empirical approaches to what may be called cognitive modeling; modeling that is aimed at influencing thinking and problem-solving skills of individuals. In cognitive modeling, the individual acquires new sets of self-instructions and more adaptive ways of giving him- or herself directions that lead to action. Cognitive modeling with delinquents may prove especially rewarding if it can be directed to improved capabilities in anticipating future events and delaying gratification.

I should like to conclude on a positive note. Too often, perhaps, attention is directed toward the outcomes of inadequate modeling experiences (psychosis, crime). It is necessary to know where observational learning has gone astray and to know how to help those who have gone astray. However, it is also necessary to know about, and perhaps dramatize a bit, exemplary instances of modeling. Knowledge of exemplary modeling can be acquired through the study of persons who have achieved successes in life that are attributable to observational learning. The ghetto youngster who avoids the pitfalls of temptation, who does not succumb to peer pressure, who does not become a delinquent, and who manages to occupy a useful, satisfying niche in society merits our attention. Glaser and Ross (1970) have described an intriguing study of adult residents of the Watts area of Los Angeles who were exemplary models. They are not James Baldwins, but they are productive, self-supporting members of society. How do these exemplary individuals differ from a matched group characterized by a high crime rate, economic dependence on social agencies, and disturbed interpersonal relationships? Consistently Glaser and Ross note that the exemplary models have themselves been influenced by exemplary models—parents, teachers, and clergymen who have provided models of self-dependence, stability, and self-respect. Knowledge of the effects of planned experimental manipulations in the laboratory is needed. So also are the effects of pivotal events in the world of day-to-day living.

ACKNOWLEDGMENTS

This investigation was supported in part by Research and Demonstration Grant No. RD 2257 P from the Division of Research and Demonstration Grants, Social and Rehabilitation Service, Department of Health, Education, and Welfare. I am indebted to Victor J. Ganzer for his contributions to the research described here. Robert Tropp, William Callahan, Lloyd Bates, Cameron Dightman, Keith Gibson, James Gibbons, Lawrence Castleman, and John Sanguinetti and their colleagues contributed importantly to the conduct of the research. The cooperation and consultation of staff psychologists Ralph Sherfey, Sarah Sloat, Theodore Sterling, and V. M. Tye are gratefully acknowledged. The superintendents and staffs of the juvenile institutions in Washington State contributed ratings and other data necessary for the completion of this research. The following assistants contributed importantly to this research: David Barrett, Peter Carlson, Duane Dahlum, Douglas Denney, Richard Erickson, Robert Howenstine, Robert Kirk, and David Snow.

REFERENCES

Bachman, J. G., Green, S., & Wirtanen, I. *Dropping out—problem or symptom?* Ann Arbor, Mich.: Institute for Social Research, University of Michigan, 1972.

Bandura, A. *Principles of behavior modification.* New York: Holt, Rinehart & Winston, 1969.

Glaser, E. M., & Ross, H. L. *A study of successful persons from seriously disadvantaged backgrounds.* Los Angeles: Human Interaction Research Institute, 1970.

Gough, H. G. *California Psychological Inventory Manual.* Palo Alto: Consulting Psychologists Press, 1957.

Harris, G. An application of observational learning procedures to the modification of educational aspirations of potential high school dropouts. Unpublished doctoral dissertation, University of Washington, Seattle, 1972.

Hathaway, S. R., Reynolds, P. C., & Monachesi, E. D. Follow-up of the later careers and lives of 1,000 boys who dropped out of high school. *Journal of Consulting & Clinical Psychology*, 1969, **33**, 370–380. (a)

Hathaway, S. R., Reynolds, P. C., & Monachesi, E. D. Follow-up of 812 girls 10 years after high school dropout. *Journal of Consulting & Clinical Psychology*, 1969, **33**, 383–390. (b)

Krumboltz, J. D., & Thoresen, C. E. (Eds.) *Behavioral counseling: Cases and techniques.* New York: Holt, Rinehart & Winston, 1969.

Lykken, D. T. A study of anxiety in the sociopathic personality. *Journal of Abnormal & Social Psychology*, 1957, **55**, 6–10.

Meichenbaum, D. H., & Goodman, J. Training impulsive children to talk to themselves: a means of developing self-control. *Journal of Abnormal Psychology*, 1971, **77**, 115–126.

Meier, R. D. The effectiveness of modeling procedures and instructions for teaching verbal employment interview behaviors to high school seniors. Unpublished doctoral dissertation, Columbia University, New York, 1972.

Navran, L. A. A rationally derived MMPI scale to measure dependence. *Journal of Consulting Psychology*, 1954, **18**, 192.

Peterson, D. R., & Becker, W. C. Family interaction and delinquency. In H. C. Quay (Ed.), *Juvenile delinquency: Research and theory*. Princeton, N.J.: Van Nostrand, 1965. Pp. 63–99.

Rotter, J. B. Generalized expectancies for internal versus external control of reinforcement. *Psychological Monographs,* 1966, **80**(609), whole issue.

Sarason, I. G. Verbal learning, modeling, and juvenile delinquency. *American Psychologist*, 1968, **23**, 254–266.

Sarason, I. G. Experimental approaches to test anxiety: Attention and the use of information. In C. D. Spielberger (Ed.), *Anxiety: Current trends in theory and research.* Vol. 2. New York: Academic Press, 1972. Pp. 381–403.

Sarason, I. G., & Ganzer, V. J. Social influence techniques in clinical and community psychology. In C. D. Spielberger (Ed.), *Current topics in clinical and community psychology*. Vol. 1. New York: Academic Press, 1969. Pp. 1–66.

Sarason, I. G., & Ganzer, V. J. Modeling and group discussion in the rehabilitation of juvenile delinquents. *Journal of Counseling Psychology*, 1973, **20**, 442–449.

Schreiber, D. *Profile of the school dropout.* New York: Vantage Books, 1967.

Schwartz, M., & Tongri, S. S. A note on the self-concept as an insulator against delinquency. *American Sociological Review*, 1965, **30**, 922–926.

Sutherland, E. H., & Cressey, D. R. *Principles of criminology.* (7th ed.) Philadelphia: Lippincott, 1966.

Tyler, V. O., Jr., & Kelly, R. F. *Cattell's HSPQ as a predictor of the behavior of institutionalized delinquents.* Psychological Research Report No. 2. Port Townsend, Washington: Fort Worden Diagnostic and Treatment Center, 1962.

Vriend, T. J. High performing inner-city adolescents assist low-performing peers in counseling groups. *Personnel and Guidance Journal,* 1969, 47, 897–904.

Wahler, J. J. *Wahler Self-Description Inventory.* Los Angeles: Western Psychological Services, 1969.

Zeller, R. H. *Lowering the odds on student dropouts.* Englewood Cliffs, New Jersey: Prentice-Hall, 1966.

6

New Strategies
in Community-Based Intervention

John D. Burchard
Paul T. Harig
Ronald B. Miller
Judy Amour

University of Vermont
 and
Burlington Youth Service Bureau

INTRODUCTION

The behavior analyst seeking delinquency prevention or treatment strategies has a fairly broad menu of behavioral techniques from which to sample and a variety of intervention settings within which to work. He or she can choose a very structured institutional site, such as a state training school, or may conduct community-based programs, of which there are several types.

Institutions present the greatest dilemma. Many elegant demonstrations of the law of effect (Thorndike, 1932) have been conducted there. The degree to which environmental control over residents can be obtained and self-care behaviors influenced is quite extensive, and it is not surprising that some corrections authorities have adopted behavioral techniques to manage the ongoing routines in their settings. However, the choice of behavior modification techniques because they offer increased *control* often reflects a limited understanding of the aims of the behavioral approach. When operant psychologists speak of the control of behavior they mean that they are able to understand behavior in terms of its functional relationship with the environmental events which surround it. They do not mean "control" in the repressive sense of the word. Granted that behavioral techniques (especially token economies) have been successful at serving the rule-oriented approach of many correctional facilities, critics have argued that the rather narrow cluster of management targets is of questionable relevance to the broader goal of preparing antisocial youngsters to cope in society. Institutions constitute a very limited environment, with relatively few opportunities to stimulate the demands or stimulus characteristics of the "real" world to which residents ultimately return.

Some problem areas are treated only indirectly within institution behavior modification programs. Often, their structure prevents the occurrence of certain target behaviors that are likely to cause problems in the natural environment. For example, shoplifting or truancy are unlikely events in an institutional setting, yet their absence does not justify the conclusion that a youth has acquired an incompatible behavioral repertoire and that such behavior will not occur in a noninstitutional setting. The dismal pattern of recidivism suggests that institutions have often been more successful in suppressing behavior than in changing it. Behavior modification programs within institutions have shown a relatively poor track record on such issues as the transfer or endurance of skills taught within the institutions to the performance of those skills outside of it. At least one analyst has concluded that as far as the institutional approach is concerned, behavior analysts may be "barking up the wrong treatment tree" (Costello, 1972).

Community-based, or "natural environment," strategies have been gaining rapid popularity because they provide a more direct approach to the problems of antisocial youngsters. Moreover, it is now recognized that the stigma attached to the institutional process may be more damaging to a youth than the events that got him or her there. The main thrust of community-based programs is to minimize the social stigma attached to treatment while maximizing the impact of the youth's regular environment on behavior change. It is thus possible to focus on the actual areas in which the youth is disruptive: truancy from school; maladaptive classroom behaviors; community misconduct; problems with siblings or parents; etc. The power of a community-based approach is that it permits the expression of certain behaviors at a sufficient level for the behavior analyst to determine to what degree they are creating a problem for his or her client, and to what extent subsequent interventions have measurable impact on the client's adjustment.

Three distinct types of behavioral intervention are currently being applied to the problems of youngsters who are aggressive and/or socially disruptive. These include residential programs, or group homes within the youngster's own community; programs that use forms of behavioral contracting involving the youth and significant members of his social environment; and parent-training programs aimed at the behavioral relationship between parents and their children.

The most widely documented residential treatment facility for antisocial youngsters is the Achievement Place project (Phillips, 1968; Phillips, Phillips, Fixsen, & Wolf, 1971; Fixsen, Phillips & Wolf, 1972; Phillips, Phillips, Timbers, Fixsen, & Wolf, 1971). The program is built on a social-learning model that uses a token economy to establish behaviors necessary to bring the youth back into contact with the normal community resources available for developing academic, social, and vocational skills necessary for successful social adjustment.

There are several conspicuous assets to residentail community-based programs, including a smaller treatment population, which facilitates intensive, individualized intervention; closer supervision; considerably more flexibility than found in most institutions; and greater involvement of the youths in developing and carrying out the treatment program (Phillips, Phillips, Fixsen, & Wolf, 1972). However, it is doubtful that all antisocial youth require the degree of structured intervention offered in such facilities. Furthermore, they are a scarce resource, even for youngsters who require some kind of intensive approach. Therefore, the advantages of family-style behavior modification programs must ultimately be weighed against their cost and the practical limits on how many youngsters can be treated there at one time. This generally results in admitting only the most serious cases, the most vulnerable to institutionalization, etc. There still remains a number of youth to be served by nonresidential programs.

The sensitive problem for all behavior modification programs is the issue of generalization of learned behaviors beyond the teaching environment. As illustrated by Wahler (1969), the changes produced by an intervention program cannot always be expected to be maintained in other settings unless there is a systematic effort to program each environment to maintain these changes. This is essentially an elaboration on Ayllon and Azrin's (1968) "relevance of behavior rule": teach only those behaviors that can be maintained in the natural environment unless you are able to modify the natural environment as well. Consequently, the Achievement Place model includes a parent-training component in order to teach parents to maintain behaviors that they may not necessarily be able to teach (Phillips *et al.*, 1972).

A step beyond this strategy is direct intervention totally within the youth's natural environment, making the parent (or teachers) responsible for the modification procedures, under the guidance of a professional whose responsibility is that of educating them in behavioral principles, guiding the application of various techniques, and evaluating the outcomes. Patterson and his associates have contributed extensively to a parent-training technology for intervention in families of unsocialized or aggressive youngsters (Patterson, Cobb, & Ray, 1972) and have written two programmed texts designed to teach behavioral child-rearing procedures (Patterson & Gullion, 1968; Patterson, 1972). Parent-training approaches deal with the issue of generalization by directly modifying the functional relationships within the natural environment that affect deviant child behavior. This eliminates the step required to transfer new behaviors from the therapist's control to that of the home environment. Ideally, the parents learn a class of new responses to problem situations that they can apply as target behaviors arise. Unfortunately, the mobility of older youth limits the effect of the parent-training approach in certain situations. As he or she grows older, his or her natural environment expands and it becomes more likely that problem behaviors will appear outside of the home environment rather than within it. Lying, stealing, fighting, and cheating are often expressed in the community rather than in the home.

A third type of intervention, behavioral contracting, attempts to modify the behavior of youth through the written specification of contingencies between the youth's behavior and reinforcing consequences in his or her natural environment (Stuart, 1971; Tharp & Wetzel, 1969). One advantage of behavioral contracting is the ease with which it can be taught to parents, teachers, probation officers, employers, and others who are in a position to mediate potentially reinforcing consequences. A second is that it can be used to influence a youth's behavior in settings beyond the immediate family.

Nevertheless, a number of factors can impede the successful outcome of a behavioral contract. In a cautionary note, Stuart and Lott (1972) warns that a contract's term appear to be less important variables than those pertaining to the negotiator and suggests that with less stable families there may be more difficulty in achieving success. Another problem, especially with older youths, is that parents do not always control the significant reinforcers in the environment. Many of these—status, certain activities, praise for particular achievements, etc.—are often mediated by the youth's peer group. The contingencies available to the parents of these children are often too weak in comparison to peer-related reinforcers and make successful behavior contracts difficult to accomplish. In such cases, the apparent reward for inappropriate behavior may exceed the available rewards for appropriate behavior.

The senior author of this chapter encountered such a situation while conducting intervention projects with junior high school students to increase their rate of school attendance and improve classroom behaviors. A number of behavior contracts failed, even when attractive sums of money were offered as backup reinforcers. It appeared that the individual contracting approach could not supply these youngsters with powerful enough incentives to modify their behavior but that their peer group was the key to the most powerful reinforcers. With each instance in which the contracting failed the youth was known to roam frequently with specific peers who were not a part of the program. In fact, in many instances either the behavioral target (for example, getting home at 10 p.m. on week nights) or the reinforcing consequence (a trip with the mediator) was incompatible with being with one's peer group.

This conflict with peer groups suggests a modification of the contracting system that is based on the probability of behavior rule: observe what the individual does when the opportunity exists. Those activities that are very probable at a given time will serve as reinforcers (Ayllon & Azrin, 1968). Because youths spend considerable time with their peers (especially those youth who are beyond the control of the school and the home) a more effective contracting program may be one that involves a multitude of peers. Therefore, a new strategy, a large-scale intervention project, has been devised to deal simultaneously with an entire group of youngsters. The program takes the form of a teenage "youth center" conducted biweekly during the evenings at a local junior high school. The center has been developed around a token economy, with points used as the commodity of exchange for special activities, prizes, and refreshments. It is important to note that the project has been conducted on a completely voluntary basis, that is, members have been free to come and go as they please. This is in contrast to most token economies, which have been conducted with captive audiences—within an institution, in a classroom where attendance is manditory, or in a residential placement where there are some holds on the subjects. A unique feature of the Youth Center is the total absence of coercion to participate.

This chapter describes the first, or developmental, phase of the Youth Center program. A second phase, which will incorporate a behavioral contracting system within the token economy program, will be dealt elsewhere in a later paper.

Within phase I there were four primary objectives:

1. To develop and maintain regular attendance in a target population of students (males and females 12–15 years of age) who were having difficulty adjusting to school or the community. An operational definition for selecting this group is presented below.

2. To analyze the natural reinforcing characteristics of certain project areas by determining where the youngsters spent their time when given a free choice among a number of competing activities.

3. To introduce, by means of a point system, a method to increase their time in nonpreferred areas by making access to preferred activities contingent on points earned in those nonpreferred areas, and to conduct a systematic evaluation of this procedure.

4. To evaluate, within this point system, a time-contingent vs. a response-contingent payoff strategy.

In addition to these objectives, there were numerous questions that were pursued on a more descriptive basis. For example:

1. How did youngsters who were attending the project compare with a random sample from the school (controlled for grade and sex) in terms of police contacts, grade point average, and school attendance? This information would tell whether or not a significant proportion of youngsters with "adjustment problems" had been to the project, and whether or not the target population was indeed being served.

2. Among the participants, did youth who were having difficulty adjusting to school or community behave differently during the project than those with no problems?

3. How did all participants rate the experience?

4. What implications did the project have for the future programs?

PROCEDURE

The Setting

The project was located at Lyman C. Hunt School, one of two junior high schools serving the City of Burlington, Vermont. The population of Burlington is approximately 43,000 and Hunt School has an enrollment of about 650 students fairly evenly distributed in grades 7 through 9. The school was chosen because it served an area of the city in which there was a dearth of youth-serving agencies and programs, together with a relatively high rate of troublesome youth behavior. School officials agreed to the use of the facilities from 7:00 to 10:00 p.m. Monday and Wednesday nights throughout the school year. The school cafeteria served as a lounge and coffee house during the evening and the arts and crafts project was located in an adjacent home economics classroom. The school library and gymnasium facilities were also used during the program. These activity areas are described in greater detail below.

Subjects

The target population consisted of junior high school students who were having difficulty adjusting to school or in the community. Difficulty in school adjustment was defined as a mean grade point average that was below C during the previous school year or a record of more than 25 days absent during the previous school year. Data on both of these variables was obtained directly from official school records. Difficulty in community adjustment was defined as more than one previous contact with the police that allegedly involved some form of disruptive or antisocial behavior. This information was obtained from the Juvenile Division of the Burlington Police Department. It should be made clear that neither definition is inclusive of what is generally regarded as "maladaptive." Certainly, a youth could be absent for more than 25 days of school or have multiple police contact and be relatively well-adjusted according to the general connotation of that term. For this reason, it would be inappropriate to label any particular individual on the basis of such criteria. However, such variables do tend to correlate highly with the adjudication of delinquency. On that basis, it seemed desirable to determine how a group of youth with those characteristics would respond to the project.

In order to maximize the chances of obtaining participants from the target population while minimizing the labeling problems mentioned above, membership in the youth center was limited by invitation to a small core of target youth and their friends. This was done by having each of five youths who previously participated in the individual contingency management program (four ninth grade males and one eighth grade male) issue specific invitations to 10–12 of their friends. Then, by allowing those friends to invite additional friends, a "membership" of 91 youths was eventually obtained. This group is hereafter referred to as the experimental group. It should be stressed that although we intended to increase the probability of attracting target-population youngsters by means of selective invitation, membership in the experimental group did not necessarily mean that a participant was, in fact, a "high-risk youngster." Data presented below indicated how many subjects of the experimental group statisfied the criteria of the target population, and how their behavior during the project compared with those who did not.

In order to provide additional perspective on the entire experimental group, it was compared with a random sample of 91 Hunt School students (matched on grade and sex) in terms of school and community adjustment. Table 1 describes the grade and sex distribution for both the Experimental and the random control groups.

Staff

Most of the staff were college students enrolled in an Introductory Behavior Modification class. At the beginning of the semester the students were asked to choose between two alternatives for one-half of their course credit. One alternative was to write a term paper on some controversial topic in the area of behavior modification. The other was to participate in the Hunt School Project on every Monday or Wednesday night from 6:30 to 10:30 p.m. throughout the semester. The students were told not to choose the project if they could not attend every week and that it would probably involve more time than the term paper. They were also warned that once they committed themselves to the project they would lose one letter grade for each unexcused absence. Forty-two students signed up for the project, 20 for Monday nights and 22 for Wednesday nights. Table 2 shows the distribution of major areas and the academic status among the 42 students.

In addition to the Introductory Behavior Modification students, the project also incorporated two "program coordinators" who worked 30 hr/week directing the program.

TABLE 1
Grade and Sex Distribution
of Experimental and Random
Control Groups

| | Grade | | | |
Sex	7	8	9	Totals
Males	6	9	26	41
Females	8	19	23	50
Totals:	14	28	49	91

TABLE 2
Distribution of College Student Staff in Terms
of Major and Academic Status

Major	Total
Psychology	15
Physical therapy	7
Education	6
Political science	3
Nursing	2
Social welfare	2
Home economics	1
Premed	1
Art	1
Speech pathology	1
English	1
Undeclared	2
Total:	42
Academic status	Total
Graduate	1
Senior	11
Junior	15
Sophomore	12
Freshmen	3
Total:	42

The Activity Areas

With one exception, the project operated from 7:00 through 10:00 p.m. on Monday and Wednesday evenings for 12 successive weeks (the Wednesday night before Thanksgiving was canceled for lack of staff). Therefore, there was a total of 23 sessions.

Each night, from 7:00 p.m. through 8:30 p.m., subjects could participate in activities in any one of four areas: the gym, the lounge (game room), the arts and crafts area, and the library. A fifth area was designated "other" and included the hall, the restrooms, the outside area around the school, and any other areas these subjects might have inhabited without our knowledge. There were no conventional classrooms used for the project. The gym (large enough to accommodate two basketball games at once) and the library were used as such by the school. The arts and crafts area was the home economics room and the lounge was the cafeteria during school hours. Listed in Tables 3–6 are the semistructured activities that took place in each area. The numeral 1 following an activity

TABLE 3
Semistructured Gym Activities[a]

Basketball	1
Gymnastic horse	1
Mats	1
Mini trampoline	1
Parallel bars	1
Volley ball	1
Badminton	2
Trampoline	2
Basket toss	2
Obstacle course	2
Jumping	2
Relays	2
Sack races	2

[a]The number one (1) indicates an activity occurring at 15 or more sessions; the number two (2) indicates an activity occurring at three or fewer sessions.

indicates that the activity could have occurred on almost any night. The numeral 2 indicates that the activity could have occurred on only a few nights during the 12 weeks of the project. These less frequent activities were interspersed as evenly as possible throughout the sessions so that participation data would not be unduly biased by an attractive cluster of events in an activity area at any one time.

Staff were assigned to work in specific areas on the basis of their interest and experience. For the most part, they continued to work in that area throughout

TABLE 4
Semistructured Activities Held in Lounge[a]

Card games	1
Board games	1
Checkers	
Clue	
Monopoly	
Smoking	1
Magazines	2
TV and stereo	2

[a]The number one (1) indicates an activity occurring at 15 or more sessions; the number two (2) indicates an activity occurring at three or fewer sessions.

TABLE 5
Semistructured Activities Held in Arts and Crafts[a]

Model cars	1
Electronic kits	1
Filming 8-min movies	1
Cooking	1
Drawing and painting	1
Embroidery	2
Clay modeling	2
Felt and burlap ornaments	2
Macramé	2
Papier maché	2
Toothpick art	2
Mobiles	2
Candle making	2
Christmas decorations	2
Fancy lettering	2

[a]The number one (1) indicates an activity occurring at 15 or more sessions; the number two (2) indicates an activity occurring at three or fewer sessions.

the project. Within an area, the jobs involved the management of the token system (keeping track of points earned and spent) and developing and supervising activities for the subjects. For example, four staff members were assigned to the gym—two to organize activities and two to keep track of subjects entering and leaving the area, administer points, and record what the subjects were doing while they were there.

At 8:30 each night two major program changes took place. First, the lounge was converted into a coffee house where atmosphere was created by the arrange-

TABLE 6
Semistructured Activities Held in Library[a]

Doing homework	1
Writing reports on suggested topics	1
Completing questionnaires concerning project	2
Writing articles for project newsletter	2
Participating in discussion groups	2

[a]The number one (1) indicates an activity occurring at 15 or more sessions; the number two (2) indicates an activity occurring at three or fewer sessions.

ment of small wooden tables, candlelight, and music (stereo, guitarists, or band). Coffee house activity included socializing with peers and staff members, listening to music, dancing, eating, smoking, participating in auctions and raffles, playing a roulette wheel, watching project-made films produced by the arts and crafts group, and other nonspecific events. Second, the home economics room was converted into a store that sold, in exchange for points, sandwiches, french fried potatoes, soft drinks, pastries, potato chips, and candy to members in the coffee house. From 8:30 to 10:00 p.m., therefore, the students could spend their time in either the coffee house (and thereby purchase store items), the gym, or the library.

The Token Economy

The token economy involved a system in which points were earned in the activity areas from 7:00 through 8:30 p.m. (and in the library from 7:00 until 10:00) and spent in the coffee house, store or gym, from 8:30 to 10:00 p.m.

On arrival, each member earned 10 points for entering the Youth Center and requesting a bankbook, within which points earned, points spent, and a balance were recorded. During the earning period a specified number of points were recorded in each subject's bankbook depending on the number of 15-min intervals he remained in the activity area. The amount of points that could be earned per interval varied with the avea. Table 7 indicates the ways subjects could earn points.

It should be noted that throughout most of the project points were administered contingent on the time spent in an area as compared to being contingent on a particular behavior. Although the latter allows many more possibilities for the modification of relevant "target behaviors" the relatively large number of subjects, together with the utilization of an unsophisticated staff, resulted in a decision to operate the first phase of the program mostly on the basis of time-contingent reinforcement. However, during the last 5 weeks (Sessions

TABLE 7
Ways Subjects Could Earn Points

Time contingency	Points
15 min in gym	20
15 min in lounge	20
15 min in arts and crafts	30
15 min on a job	30
Time and response contingency	
Library only	40
Requesting bankbook	
On arrival at project	10

13–24) two different response-contingent points reinforcement schedules were introduced in the library only. Both schedules were contingent on the subject's being in this area for 15 min and his or her writing a specific number of words on a suggested topic.

In addition to the above, during the last 15 sessions any subject could earn 30 points for every 15 min of time assisting staff members in certain jobs. These jobs included helping with the management of the store and coffee house.

Points could be spent in the manner designated in Table 8. They could be spent to admit a member to certain activity areas after 8:30, to purchase store items, and for use in the coffee house or for miscellaneous events which took place within the coffee house or gym.

When the subject spent points the designated staff member would request the subject's bankbook, record the number of points spent, and revise the balance. This was done with a felt-tipped marking pen of a color designating the particular item purchased. At the end of each session, bankbooks were collected at the outside door and *no unspent points could be carried over to another session.*

The subject began each session with the 10 points he received for requesting his bankbook regardless of his behavior in the previous session. A response cost

TABLE 8
Items and Events that Could
Be Purchased with Points

Store items	Points
Donuts and pastry	10
Soft drinks	15
Chocolate bars	10
Cookies	10
Potato chips	10
Sandwiches	25
French fried potatoes	20
Admission to activities	
Coffeehouse	40
Gym	15
Miscellaneous	
Raffle tickets	5
Auction items	5–180
Model cars	200
Pass to leave and reenter school	
after 8:30	10
New bankbook	25
Roulette chips	10

procedure was devised to handle extremely disruptive behavior (fighting, property damage, theft, etc.). However, this system was rarely necessary.

The Data System

Because of the large number of youths participating at the Center and their mobility throughout the evening, care was taken to develop a data collection system that would yield the highest reliability on measures of subject participation. It was decided that a documentation system would be superior to an observer-sampling strategy in assessing the amount of time the youngster spent in the area. The primary dependent variables were recorded as follows:

1. Presence at a session: this was determined by a staff member at the front door who checked the subject's name off of a master list on his or her first entrance into the school.

2. Time spent in specific places: this was determined by a staff member (called a doorman) within each of the four activity areas. The doorman's job was to record on a form (area card) the time that each subject entered or left the area and to enter the appropriate number of points earned on his or her bankbook. These earnings were coded with a felt-tipped marker of a color appropriate to the activity area. Because an area card and bankbook were both marked by the doorman, it was always possible to check a subject's data for discrepancies between earnings and participation, which would reflect forgery. However, the unusual colors of the marking pens and close staff supervision made cheating difficult and it was rarely observed.

3. Points earned and spent during each session: this was recorded on bankbooks, which were turned in as the subject left the project for the evening.

4. Number of words written in the library during the last 15 sessions: staff members kept track of the amount of time each subject was in the library. Also, at the conclusion of each 15 min, the number of written words completed by each student were recorded and the appropriate number of points were administered. Therefore, unlike the other activity areas, during the last half of the project library points were administered as they were earned rather than when the subject was leaving the area.

5. Police contact data: the name of each subject in the experimental group together with the name of each individual in the random control group was submitted (in alphabetical order) to the Juvenile Division of the Burlington Police Department for a blind description of each previously recorded police contact.

6. School data: grade point averages (GPAs) and the number of absent days were recorded from the school's files for each subject for the previous school year.

7. Subjective evaluation by subjects: 3 weeks after the last session, the numbers of the Hunt project were asked to evaluate various aspects of the program on a seven-point scale ranging from "terrible" (number 1) through OK (4) to "great" (7). These were turned in at classes at the school.

Systematic Evaluation of the Point System

In order to evaluate the effectiveness of the point system at the Hunt Project, a sequential comparison was made between nights when point earning and spending was in operation and nights when the youth had free access to events and facilities of the Youth Center. In order to make this analysis, every third night was conducted under a noncontingent point earning schedule. On these evenings, the members obtained 30 points every 15 min through a staff member who operated as "banker," adding the points to the youth's bankbook and indicating the exact time at which the points were given. There were no explicit contingencies in operation on these nights, except periodically appearing before the banker for one's points.

These noncontingent nights permitted us to analyze the natural reinforcing characteristics of the various activity areas, because during these sessions there were no artificial contingencies to bias a youth's choice among competing events.

Finally, it was possible to use these same methods to compare members of the experimental group who differed in their degree of school or community adjustment. We thus investigated possible differences between group members of the target population and the remainder of the project participants.

RESULTS

The Experimental Group as Representatives
of the Target Population

A comparison of the Youth Center participants with a random control group drawn from the Junior High School (and matched on grade and sex) confirmed that the project was attracting youngsters who met the selection criteria of the target population. A chi-square test yielded significant differences on occurrence of previous police contact ($p < .05$ on 1 df) between the experimental and random control groups. Table 9 summarizes the descriptive statistics for both samples.

A total of 26 youngsters drawn randomly from class lists were also a part of the experimental group. These youth accounted for 64% of the police contacts incurred by the random control group and were the only members of the group with more than two previous police contacts.

TABLE 9
Police Contact and School Data
for the Experimental and Control Groups

	Experimental group	Random control group	Also in experimental group
Police contacts			
Total sample	91	91	26
Total police contacts	31 (33%)	11 (12%)	7
1 police contact	13	4	2
2 police contacts	6	2	0
> 2 police contacts	12	5	5
School data			
(eighth and ninth grades only)			
Mean grade point average	3.27	3.72	
Subjects with grade point			
average below 3.0	20	7	4
Mean days absent	14.56	10	
Subjects with > 25 days			
absent	9	4	2

The random control group had a slightly higher mean GPA (where 3.0 = C). However, the experimental group contained more than twice as many youths with grade averages below level C (five times more, discounting youngsters who served in both groups). Similarly, the experimental group members were two to three times more likely to be found on absentee records during the previous school year. The individuals in the experimental group were found to be more similar to the target population, therefore, than were the group of youngsters drawn at random from class lists.

Attendance Rates

Figure 1 depicts the record of Youth Center attendance for the last 18 sessions. The project averaged 55 members per evening because some attended only one night during the week. Attendance ranged between 43 and 67 youths.

Behavior in Activity Area

The percentage of time (between 7 and 8:30 p.m.) spent in the various activity areas is shown by Table 10. The gymnasium was the most popular area and many subjects spent most of their time there. The lounge or game room, the arts and crafts area, and the library were about equally used areas when the data for all nights were taken together. However, a comparison of contingent with

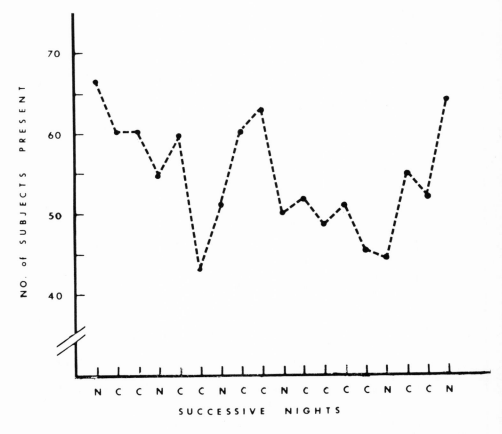

FIG. 1   The number of youth attending the last 18 consecutive sessions of the project (N = 91).

TABLE 10
Percentage of Time All Subjects Present Spent
in Point Earning Areas Across Sessions

	Gym (%)	Lounge (%)	Arts and crafts (%)	Library (%)	Jobs (%)
All sessions	41	18	18	20	3
Noncontingent nights only	43	25	22	7	3
Contingent nights only	38	14	16	26	4

noncontingent nights revealed some interesting differences that demonstrated the power of the point system. Figure 2 depicts the average number of minutes spent in the various activity areas on evenings when point earning was not contingent on performance. This data provides a good estimate of the relative natural preferences for certain activities among competing events. The gym (43%) apparently had more natural reinforcing properties than the school library, which accounted for only 7% of the time spent on these nights. The arts and crafts and lounge area had about the same degree of preference and youths typically spent 15 min or about 24% of their available time in these areas on noncontingent nights. On contingent nights the point system was operating to influence a subject's choice of activity area. The greatest source of earnings on these nights (see Table 7) was the school library, and the average percentage of time there increased from 7% to 26% under the point earning system. Figure 3

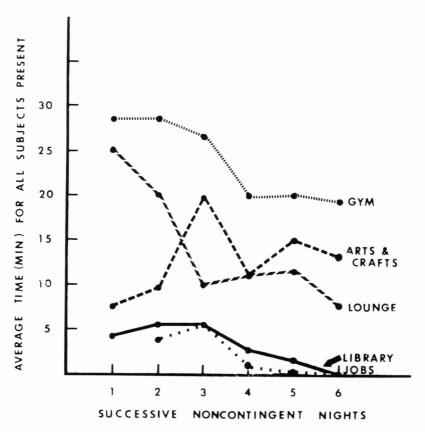

FIG. 2 The average number of minutes all subjects present spent in each point earning area on successive noncontingent sessions ($N = 91$).

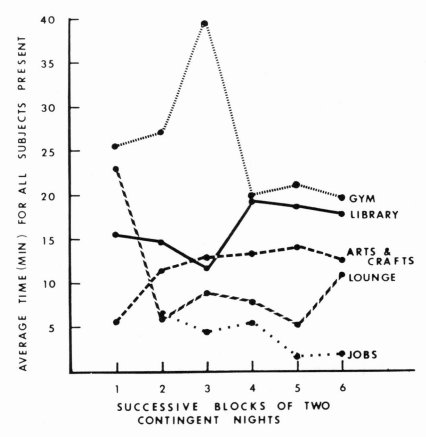

FIG. 3 The average number of minutes all subjects present spent in each point earning area on successive blocks of two contingent nights (N = 91).

illustrates the average amount of time (between 7 and 8:30 p.m.) spent per activity area during the contingent evenings. The library approached the popularity of the gym on these nights.

An examination of Table 10 suggests that during contingent nights the gain in time spent in the library was mostly because of decline in participation in the lounge or arts and crafts area. The gym remained generally stable in amount of use.

That the point system is an effective way to increase the subject's time in nonpreferred areas is illustrated by Fig. 4 which shows for all 91 members over successive nights the average number of minutes spent in the library. Inlibrary participation increased fourfold on contingent nights, and this increase in duration was a regular effect that was systematically replicated on a number of occasions throughout the project.

Another phenomenon observed on noncontingent nights was the staff's subjective report that there was more commotion, more restlessness among the subjects, and more hectic atmosphere than on evenings when point earning was in operation. In order to investigate this more systematically, the average number of minutes spent in various areas was summed across activities to produce a composite view of group participation during the 7:00–8:30 p.m. period. Figure 5 reveals that there was little difference at first between contingent and noncontingent nights, the subjects utilizing most of their 90-min period within an activity area. However, the data confirms the staff's impression that contingent nights were more orderly, because the participation time eventually

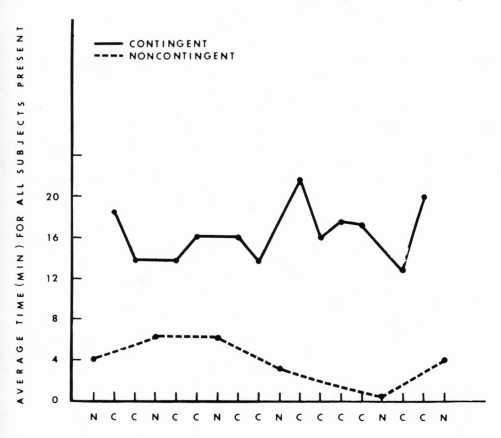

FIG. 4 The average number of minutes all subjects present spent in the library on successive contingent (dashed line) and noncontingent (solid line) nights ($N = 91$).

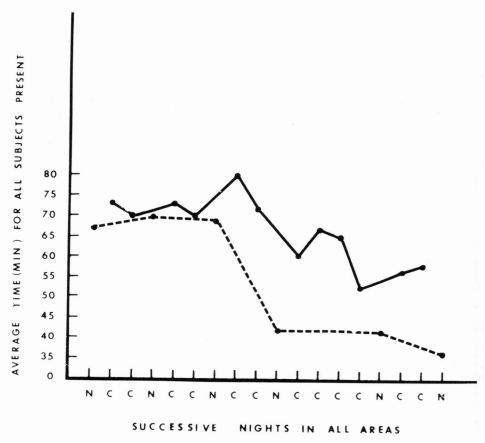

FIG. 5 The average number of minutes all subjects spent in all point earning areas on successive contingent (dashed line) and noncontingent (solid line) nights ($N = 91$).

declined rapidly on noncontingent nights to less than half of the original duration. Time spent in activity areas on contingent nights, in contrast, remained generally the same. The difference in average number of minutes between contingent and noncontingent nights is the average amount of time spent in the bathrooms, outside the building, or loitering in the halls outside of an activity area.

In Phase 1, the time contingency, subjects received 40 points for each 15-min interval they spent within the library. In Phase 2, subjects were not only reuqired to spend 15 min within the library but were expected to work on a composition task in which a specified number of words was required. The data reflected differences between contingent and noncontingent nights. Figure 6 presents data on 27 subjects who are defined as regular participants of the

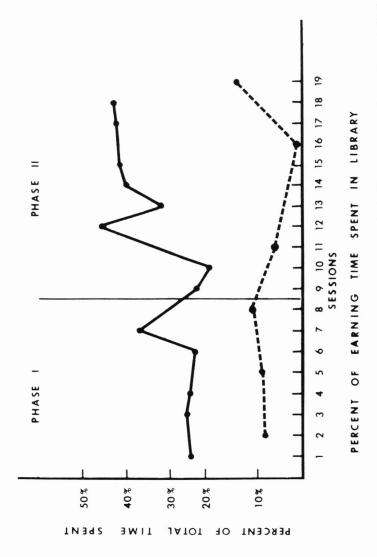

FIG. 6 Percentage of time 27 subjects who missed no more than two sessions spent in the library on consecutive contingent (solid line) and non-contingent (dashed line) nights. During Phase I on contingent nights, points were contingent only on time spent in the library. During Phase II on contingent nights, points were contingent on both a time and a response contingency.

project because each has missed no more than two sessions during the entire project. What was noteworthy about this finding was that the addition of a response contingency had no deleterious effect on the percent of time spent within this activity area. On the contrary, providing a structured task within the activity area appeared to increase the subject's amount of time within it.

Subgroups within the Experimental Population Compared

From the previous discussion it is clear that, although the Hunt School Project tended to attract more youth who were representative of the target group than might be found in a random drawing of the school population, the Youth Center membership was by no means exclusively comprised of "high-risk" or poorly adjusted youth. It was therefore possible to make meaningful comparisons within the experimental group itself to determine whether the target group youths were behaving any differently from the other participants. To accomplish this, a subgroup of 16 subjects was drawn from the experimental group on the basis of their multiple police contacts. A matched control group of program members with no previous police contacts was also selected, matched on grade and sex.

Table 11 describes the percentage in time spent among the activity areas for both subgroups. The outstanding differences were between the gym and the arts and crafts area. In contrast to youths with no police contacts, the target youths spent much more time engaged in physical–motor activities in the gym where there was maximum peer interaction. The nonpolice contact group, however, spent significantly more time in the arts and crafts area, an area with tasks involving considerably more patience and much less motor activity and peer interaction. There were no differences in the use of the lounge or library facilities.

The attendance of both groups is depicted in Fig. 7, a cumulative record of attendance for subjects by group, over the last 18 nights of the project.

TABLE 11
Percentage of Time Spent
in Point Earning Areas Across All Sessions

	Gym (%)	Lounge (%)	Arts and crafts (%)	Library (%)	Jobs (%)
Multiple police contacts (N = 16)	56	13	7	21	3
No police contacts (N = 16)	36	14	26	21	3

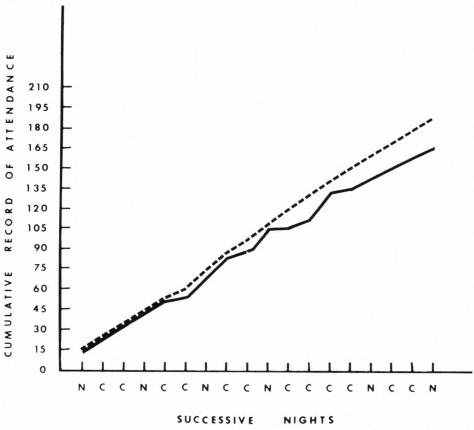

FIG. 7 Cumulative record of attendance of youth with no prior police contacts (solid line, $N = 16$) and youth with more than two prior police contacts (dashed line, $N = 16$).

Although the differences are subtle, the police contact group showed a slightly more steady attendance record than their matched cohorts. This difference is slight, but it confirms that the project not only attracted members of the target group, but that their participation was as steady (if not more) as nontarget members.

Evaluation of Project by Participants

Table 12 presents the results of the attitude survey about the Hunt School Project. Sixty-four subjects who had attended at least five sessions completed the rating scale. The staff members received the highest ratings from the youth, followed by the two backup reinforcers available from the project: the coffee

TABLE 12
Subjective Evaluation of the Project
by 64 Subjects[a]

Areas	Mean	Highest	Lowest
Staff	6.5	7	3
Coffeehouse	6.2	7	1
Gym area	6.2	7	4
Overall project	5.9	7	1
Lounge	5.9	7	3
Hunt students	5.7	7	1
Food	5.7	7	2
Dance	5.6	7	1
Gym show	5.4	7	1
Point system	5.3	7	1
Homemade movies	4.7	7	1
Library	4.7	7	1
Raffles	4.6	7	1
Auctions	4.5	7	1
School	3.2	7	1
Police	2.9	7	1
Xmas vacation	5.5	7	1

[a]19 subjects attended fewer than five sessions and were therefore not asked to fill out this form. Eight subjects did not fill out the form for unknown reasons. Rating scale goes from 1 to 7; 1 = terrible, 4 = OK, 7 = great.

house and the gym area. It is interesting that the point system, although not receiving as high a rating as some other items, was scaled very close to "Christmas vacation," which suggested that the youths did not find it very adversive to function in the token economy. For the most part, the skew in the direction of high ratings among the items is evidence that the overall program was regarded quite favorably by each of the participants.

Discussion

The limitations of current behavior modification approaches for the prevention or treatment of antisocial behavior have been discussed above. Briefly, these include the unsuitability of institutions for teaching relevant community-survival behaviors; the impracticability of large-scale intervention programs utilizing group home or residential behavior modification facilities because of economics and manpower constraints; the shortcomings of parent-training programs when youths have grown beyond family boundaries and are committing inappropriate acts in environments over which the parents have little direct control; and the difficulty in locating adequate reinforcers to back up behavior contracts. A new strategy has been proposed, whereby the natural reinforcing properties of a peer group can be combined with the token economy or point system, exchangeable for material reinforcers, to modify the behavior of high-risk youngsters.

This strategy was implemented in the developmental phase of the Hunt Youth Center project, a behavior modification program organized around a biweekly evening youth center. The objectives of the early research included an empirical test of the program's ability to obtain regular attendance among youths in a target population defined on the basis of poor school or community adjustment, as measured by attendance records and previous contact with local police. Other goals included a descriptive analysis of their natural preferences for various activities, as measured in a free-operant situation; an experimental analysis of the effect of the point system on attendance on nonpreferred activities, such as behavior in the library; a comparison of the differences between subgroups of youngsters who attended the project; and an assessment of the attitudes of the youngsters who participated in the project.

The data confirmed that the program attracted a significant proportion of those youngsters who were representative of the target population. As judged by a sample of these youths, they attended on a steady basis and spent a great deal of time in nonpreferred, constructive activity areas whenever their presence resulted in the administration of points. In the library, youngsters continued to participate instead of playing games and building models for points, even when the performance criterion was raised from time to time and a writing response was added. The point system was also useful in structuring evenings so that youngsters were less likely to roam throughout the halls or wander between activity areas.

What is noteworthy about this project is that it represents one of the first totally voluntary token economies. Until the present, there has usually been an implied form of coercion, in that the subjects have been a captive audience, being offered the opportunity to participate in a token economy program in contrast to an existing program that is maintaining their presence through aversive control. In a school setting, for example, a youth has little choice but to attend or be found truant. In an institution, a resident has little choice but to respond or go without significant privileges. The Hunt project, in contrast, has been maintained under no coercion: the members have been invited but not required to attend; they have not been brought by staff members nor forced to remain within the building. The burden of maintaining their participation within the program has therefore been placed on the staff, who have striven to make the evenings as enjoyable and as reinforcing as possible. The youths have attended, then, not for fear of losing significant privileges but because they have enjoyed attending.

The program, however, was not without problems. The first was the limited access to the center. By restricting the "membership" to youths selected by some of the target subjects and their friends, it was possible to maintain a cohesive, well-balanced (between target and nontarget subjects) peer gropu that did not label itself as "troublemakers," "problem kids," etc. However, there was no way a group of 91 youths that included all of each youth's friends, would be selected. There was also no way to keep all the remaining uninvited youth from expressing curiosity and interest in the program. As a result, on the first night of the project we not only had 82 youths on the inside (this does not coincide with the first data point on Figure 1 because the first five sessions were not used in the data analysis) but 60–70 youth on the outside trying to get in. The outsiders were repeatedly informed that this was an experimental project conducted by the local Youth Service Center and that while we could sympathize with their problem (that is, a dearth of recreational resources in that end of town) all we could do was put their name on a waiting list. Over the next 6 weeks the population of the outsiders steadily approached zero, partly because of the weather (which also approached zero) and partly because 15–20 of the more persistent individuals were eventually invited into the group (but were not included in the data analysis). Fortunately, during those first few nights, when a significant number of youth were being turned away from the center, there was no known property damage or vandalism.

A second problem pertained to the utilization of undergraduate students as staff. Because the students were relatively unscreened and selected on the basis of their "interest," there were five or six students whose primary incentive for participating in the project appeared to be to avoid writing a term paper. Behavioral characteristics of these students included late attendance at staff meetings, missing sessions, and an inability or unwillingness to take initiative and become actively involved in the project. It should be noted, however, that this problem was far outweighed by the positive aspects of using students as staff. This was reflected by the outstanding performance of most students, the students' rating of their experience as "good" on a five-point scale (terrible– poor–fair–good–excellent) and, as previously indicated, the youths' rating of the staff as the most positive characteristic of the project. In general this staffing procedure solved two problems, providing meaningful applied experience for graduate and undergraduate students and operating a rather large applied behavior analysis project on minimal funds. With respect to the latter it should also be mentioned that all of the school facilities were made available at no cost by an understanding school administration that was sensitive to the problems of youth. Although a few teachers expressed concern over the extended use (and occasional misuse) of equipment and some unintentional modifications in their room arrangements, school problems were negligible.

Based on the results presented above, a second phase of research has been initiated to further test the utility of the strategy outlined in this paper. The focus of the token economy has been shifted from behaviors occurring within the center, to behaviors occurring outside the center, in school, and in the community at large.

This has been accomplished by means of behavioral contracts negotiated with the youth by center staff. The contracts include only two parties, the youth and the center. The center agrees to pay specified amounts of points for specified behaviors in school and the community (e.g., being on time to class, looking for a part-time job, increasing classroom effort).

A major objective of Phase II is to analyze the functional relationship between various components of the contracting procedure and specific classroom behaviors. Aspects being investigated include the effects of daily teacher feedback on performance, self-recording behavior, maximal vs. minimal staff attention to performance, and the effects of group vs. individual contracting sessions.

To date, we are encouraged by the willingness of the youth to accept this change in emphasis. Attendance remained good, and over 40 members are working on behavioral contracts. So far, the token system appears to be powerful enough to maintain these efforts.

ACKNOWLEDGMENTS

This study was partially funded by grants from the Department of Health, Education, and Welfare (74-P-05099/1-01) and the Vermont Governor's Commission on Crime Control and Prevention (VA-7259) and by a training fellowship from the National Institute of Mental Health (PHS F01 54814-01). The authors wish to thank Rosemary Downs, Richard Lates, the undergraduate students who participated in the study, the staff at Hunt School, the Juvenile Division of the Burlington Police Department, and Citizens for Quality Life (C-QL) for their cooperation and support during the study.

REFERENCES

Ayllon, T., & Azrin, N. H. *The token economy*. New York: Appleton-Century-Crofts, 1968.

Costello, J., Behavior modification and corrections: current status and future potential. Unpublished review paper, University of California, Santa Barbara, 1972.

Fixsen, D. L., Phillips, E. L., & Wolf, M. M. Achievement Place: the reliability of self-reporting and peer reporting and their effects on behavior. *Journal of Applied Behavioral Analysis*, 1972, 5, 19–33.

Patterson, G. *Families*. Champaign, Ill.: Research Press, 1972.

Patterson, G., Cobb, J., & Ray, R. A social engineering technology for retraining the families of aggressive boys. In H. Adams & L. Unikel (Eds.), *Issues and trends in behavior therapy*. Springfield, Ill.: Charles C Thomas, 1972.

Patterson, G., & Gullion, M. *Living with children: New methods for parents and teachers*. Champaign, Ill.: Research Press, 1968.

Phillips, E. Achievement Place: token reinforcement procedures in a home-style rehabilitation setting for "pre-delinquent" boys. *Journal of Applied Behavior Analysis*, 1968, 1, 213–223.

Phillips, E., Phillips, E., Fixsen, D., & Wolf, M. Achievement Place: modification of the behaviors of pre-delinquent boys within a token economy. *Journal of Applied Behavior Analysis,* 1971, **4,** 45–59.

Phillips, E., Phillips, E., Fixsen, D., & Wolf, M. *The teaching-family handbook.* Lawrence: University of Kansas Press, 1972.

Phillips, E., Phillips, E., Timbers, G., Fixsen, D., & Wolf, M. Achievement Place: Alternative to institutionalization for pre-delinquent youths. Paper presented at American Psychological Association, Washington D.C., 1971.

Stuart, R. Behavioral contracting within the families of delinquents. *Journal of Behavior Therapy & Experimental Psychiatry,* 1971, **2,** 1–11.

Stuart, R., & Lott, L. A. Behavioral contracting with delinquents: a cautionary note. *Journal of Behavior Therapy & Experimental Psychiatry,* 1972, **3,** 161–171.

Tharp, R., & Wetzel, R. *Behavior modification in the natural environment.* New York: Academic Press, 1969.

Thorndike, E. L. Reward and punishment in animal learning. *Comparative Psychological Monographs,* 1932, **8** (39), whole issue.

Wahler, R. Setting generality: some specific and general effects of child behavior therapy. *Journal of Applied Behavior Analysis,* 1969, **2,** 239–246.

7

The Modification of Aggression and Stealing Behavior of Boys in the Home Setting[1]

John B. Reid
Gerald R. Patterson

Oregon Research Institute

The purpose of this chapter is to describe a treatment strategy that has been developed for the modification of predelinquent child behaviors in the natural home setting. The importance of finding effective methods for helping children who demonstrate aggressive–delinquent behavior patterns is obvious, as approximately one-third of all mental health referrals from teachers and parents revolve around problems of delinquency and aggression (Patterson, 1964; Roach, 1958; Rogers, Lilienfeld, & Pasamanick, 1954; Woody, 1969). When these children (often classified as "conduct disorders") are referred to mental health clinics, only a small fraction are offered treatment (Bahm, Chandler, & Eisenberg, 1961). Of those children actually treated, few respond to the traditional individual therapies typically offered (Levitt, 1971).

The picture has been much the same for traditional residential treatment centers; treatment, when it is offered, effects few if any long-term changes in the behaviors of the clients (e.g., Meltzoff & Kornreich, 1970; Teuber & Powers, 1953). Finally, children who have been labeled as "conduct disorders" during childhood do not tend to change for the better if left untreated (e.g., Beach & Laird, 1968; Morris, 1956; Robins, 1966; Westman, Rice, & Bermann, 1967). Therefore, most children who need help with delinquency-related problems are not treated; those who are offered traditional treatment seldom change as a result; and many children are forcibly removed from their homes to residential treatment centers with little, if any, chance of profiting from the experience.

The increasing number of studies failing to show beneficial, observable effects of traditional interview therapy (residential or outpatient) in the treatment of delinquent youngsters is quite consistent with much recent social learning theory. If it is true that social behavior is in large part determined by immediate social consequences, the learning of new ways of talking and thinking about oneself in a psychotherapist's office cannot be expected to have much effect on one's actual social behavior on the streets, at home, or in the ghetto. Redl and Wineman (1952) point up the issue quite clearly in the rather pessimistic epilogue of their classic work, *Controls from Within*:

> . . .our "children who hate" went back into the limbo of "the children that nobody wants." This spectacle of their retraumatization of strengths that had been so painfully, if uncompletely, implanted in their personalities being literally wasted in a battle in a hostile environment, is one that fades slowly, if at all, from our minds [p. 315].

The traditional psychotherapeutic goal to teach the delinquent child to live happily in a destructive social environment appears not only of dubious moral merit but impossible to achieve. If behavioral psychologists are truly to address themselves to the problem of delinquency in children, they must develop methods for changing the structure of the social systems that elicit, shape, reinforce, and maintain delinquent behavior. Instead of a symptomatic treatment (i.e., trying to treat the delinquent child, who is the end product of the system that creates delinquency), a successful solution to the problem of delinquency requires a frontal assault on the homes, neighborhoods, and classrooms in which these behaviors are taught.

Over the past several years, members of our group at the Oregon Research Institute have carried out a series of investigations in an attempt to develop an effective set of techniques for the clinical treatment of delinquent boys in the family and school settings. This chapter is concerned with the findings from work in home settings.

The *assumptions* underlying the development of these techniques are straightforward: (1) behaviors associated with delinquency are social behaviors that are acquired and maintained, in large part, by the process of social reinforcement; (2) the primary locus for the initial development of social behaviors is in the home; and (3) the place to start in the prevention of delinquency is with the pattern of social reinforcement that occurs in the homes of predelinquent children. Because it is assumed that delinquent behavior thrives in any setting in which it is elicited and reinforced, it is not expected that the extinction of delinquent behavior patterns in the home at an early age can eradicate juvenile delinquency. Instead, it is expected that all social systems in which children find themselves must be reprogrammed to extinguish delinquent behaviors, and to support prosocial attempts at survival, if the problem is going to be solved.

The choice of the family as the starting place for our work, and of young children and their parents as our subjects, has been based on three considerations. First, it is assumed that the family represents the simplest naturally occurring social system in which to begin our research. Second, the behavioral repertoires of young children are simpler and easier to understand than those of older subjects. Third, most of the reinforcers relevant to social behaviors of the young child are dispensed in the home.

The families of predelinquents were therefore chosen as the starting point in our attempts to understand and to modify delinquent behaviors by changing environments of social reinforcement. To simplify the problem further, it was decided to work only with children who displayed a particular type of delinquent behavior—social aggression—for the following reasons. First, aggression was a fairly high-rate, highly visible behavior in our subject population; and second, parents almost invariably disliked its high-rate occurrence and were often motivated to change it.

DATA COLLECTION PROCEDURES

The fist step in the research was to develop a set of procedures with which to measure the characteristics of family members in the natural home setting. The following is an overview of the data collection procedures developed for evaluation of this project.

Observation data. An omnibus observation code has been developed (Patterson, Ray, Shaw, & Cobb, 1969; Reid, 1967) to provide a running account of the behaviors of a subject in terms of 29 behavioral codes that are, by definition, mutually exclusive and exhaustive. A list of the behavioral codes is presented in Table 1. As can be seen, 14 of the 29 categories refer to aversive, hostile, or irritating behaviors. In using the code, a trained observer focuses on one family member as subject and records a behavior for that subject each 6 sec as well as any behaviors directed at that subject by other family members in terms of the same 29 categories. One observation for one subject lasts for five consecutive minutes. In any given observation session, each family member is the focus of two such 5-min observations.

From these observation data, the occurrence (rate per minute) for each of the individual behavior codes may be tabulated for each family member, as well as the rates at which other family members react to him or her in terms of the same 29 behavior codes. Because the behavior code permits sequential coding of the behavior of the subject and the reactions of others toward him or her, it has been possible to conduct a variety of functional analyses of the observation data (e.g., Patterson, 1972). It is also possible to combine codes in any manner desired, to produce a frequency or rate at which a class of codes occurred. The best examples of this are the classes, Total Deviant Behavior, which combines the rate per minute of all 14 aversive, hostile, irritating behaviors, and Total Targeted Behaviors, which combines rates per minute of all behaviors modified for a family. In our project, each family is observed for either 6 or 10 baseline

TABLE 1

Prosocial Behavior Categories		
Approval	Laugh	· Receive
Attention	Normative	Self-stimulation
Command	No response	Talk
Compliance	Play	Touching, handling
Indulge	Positive physical contact	Work
Deviant Behavior Categories		
Negative command	High rate (hyperactive)	Negative physical contact
Cry	Humiliate	Tease
Disapproval	Ignore	Whine
Dependency	Noncompliance	Yell
Destructiveness	Negativism	

observation sessions, over a 2-week period, giving us from 60 to 100 min of observational data on every member of each family before intervention. The same format is used in collecting observation data during intervention, termination, and followup for each of the treated families. A large and consistent effort has been made to refine the observation code and to evaluate its reliability (Reid, 1970; Reid & DeMaster, 1972; Taplin & Reid, 1973), stability over time (Reid, 1973), reactivity (Patterson & Harris, 1968; White, 1972), and validity (Patterson & Erickson, 1972).

Parent report data. During the intake interview, and during the course of intervention, the parents construct a list of the child behaviors that have prompted their seeking professional help. These behaviors are, when possible, defined so that they correspond to one or more categories in the observation code. Each time an observation is made in the home, the parents are asked whether their referred child emitted any or all of the behaviors on this list in the last 24 hr. They are not asked to estimate how often the behaviors occurred (as such data have been found to be extremely unreliable), but only whether they have or have not occurred. One of the criterion measures for evaluating the effectiveness of treatment is the daily percentage of these behaviors that occurs during the various phases of treatment.

Parental attitude data. Parental attitudes were assessed in two ways: in the earlier studies a modification of the Becker bipolar adjectives (Patterson, Ray, & Shaw, 1968) was given the parents before and after intervention in an attempt to find out whether the intervention changed the way in which parents perceived their referred children. Later, we changed over to a questionnaire, given after treatment termination, designed to measure the parents' overall perception of the usefulness of treatment (Patterson & Reid, 1973).

Professional time expended on each case. Every minute of professional clinical time spent during intake, intervention, and followup for each case was recorded, providing us with precise data on the amount of time spent on each case.

"Normal" Control Families

For each family admitted to the program, a "normal" family[1] was paid to participate in a baseline observation of the same form and duration as used for the treated families. Each normal family was matched on several demographic variables to a treated family. The data from the normal, matched families made possible a comparison of the two samples in terms of various aspects of social interaction (e.g., Reid & Hendriks, 1973).

Psychometric Measures

Certain more traditional psychometric measures (e.g., MMPI = Minnesota Multiplasic Personality Inventory, WISC = Wechsler Intelligence Scale for Children, WRAT = Wide Range Achievement Test) were given the parents and the children during intake for the purpose of describing our sample to other professionals and because of the possibility that certain personality and intellectual measures might have been related to the behavioral patterns observed in the subject families.

TREATMENT PROCEDURES

The set of treatment procedures to be discussed here evolved gradually through experience in working with several cases between 1965 and 1967 (Patterson & Brodsky, 1966; Patterson, McNeal, Hawkins, & Phelps, 1967; Patterson & Reid, 1970). The families treated during this early period were all referred because they each included at least one boy who was hyperaggressive and out of control. The treatment approach that evolved during this period may be described as follows:

1. An intake evaluation, during which psychometric tests were administered and the referral complaints were thoroughly discussed with the parents and the referred boy
2. A period of approximately 2 weeks of baseline observations in the home by experienced observers, the purpose of which was to establish the base rates of

---

[1] A normal family was one in which there was no evidence of child management problems and for which there was no history of therapeutic contacts with mental health professionals, school counselors, juvenile courts, etc.

aggressive and prosocial child behaviors, against which the effect of treatment would be compared

3. A period during which the parents were given a copy of a programmed textbook describing operant child management procedures (Patterson, 1971; Patterson & Gullion, 1968) on which they had to pass a test for comprehension before further treatment

4. One or more sessions with the parents in the laboratory that were devoted to teaching the parents to carefully define, track, and record targeted deviant and prosocial behaviors

5. A series of sessions during which the parents were taught (at the office) to design and carry out modification programs in their homes (for about one-fourth of the families is was necessary to actually go into the homes to model the procedures directly for the parents)

6. Treatment termination, which occurred when the parents were designing and executing their programs independently and when the observation data showed that the rates of out-of-control referral behaviors had diminished.

Modest success in applying these procedures with these early cases encouraged Patterson and his colleagues to carry out the more systematic treatment studies reported below. These included samples of consecutive referrals and the standardized treatment and assessment as described above.

In the first study (Patterson et al., 1968), five families, each including a hyperaggressive child, were accepted for treatment. Each family was observed for a 2- to 3-week period prior to intervention, during which ten observations were made. The families were then treated in the manner described above. Two observations were made at termination and each month for 6 months thereafter. Followup data on one family were not collected. A mean rate per minute was calculated for each of the behavior categories for the target child. The rates for each of the 14 deviant behavior codes were combined to obtain a rate per minute for total deviant behavior. The same data reduction procedure was employed for termination and followup data. It was found that the rates of deviant behavior for referred children in all families were markedly reduced by termination (range, 62–75% reduction from baseline) and that three of the four families for which followup data were available maintained their gains over the 6-month followup period. An average of 22.8 hr of professional time per family was used in producing these effects.

Thirteen consecutive families referred to Oregon Research Institute in 1969 comprised the sample for the next study (Patterson, Cobb, & Ray, 1973). The cases included problem boys between the ages of 6 and 13 years who displayed extremely aggressive or acting-out behaviors. Most of the families were from lower socioeconomic levels, and five had no resident father. The data collection procedures were the same as in the Patterson et al. (1968) study, except that the systematic parent report of referral behaviors was also collected on each day an observation was conducted. In addition, 2 days of observation data were collected after the fourth and eighth weeks of treatment, at treatment termination, and at monthly intervals for the first 6 months of followup and then bimonthly for the next 6 months.

After the baseline data were collected (including both observation and parent report data), the parents were given a copy of the programmed text to study, were tested on it, and then assigned to a parent group (usually including four sets of parents). The sessions were designed to run about 2 hr each, allowing about one-half hour of didactic instruction with each family. The purpose of the sessions was to teach the parents to observe and collect data in the home, to design and implement modification programs for their referred children, and often to design programs to modify the behavior of their spouses and the siblings of the referred child. The families attended from eight to 12 such weekly sessions. Five of the families required at least one home visit by the therapist during the course of treatment. An average of 25.7 hr of professional time was required to significantly alter the behaviors targeted by the parents.

An analysis of variance (ANOVA) comparing baseline rates of the total deviant behavior with that at termination was highly significant, as was a comparison of the rate of specific referral behaviors from baseline to termination. Although there was a tendency for siblings' total deviant behavior to decrease from baseline to termination, the trend was not statistically reliable. Using a reduction of 30% in the rate of total deviant behavior from baseline to termination as a success criterion, nine of the 13 families treated were categorized as successful. Of the nine families who permitted posttreatment followup observations, eight either maintained termination rates of deviant behavior or showed further reductions. A further criterion measure, an adjective checklist given before and after treatment, indicated that the parents significantly increased their positive feelings toward the children as a function of treatment.

A further study was carried out in an attempt to replicate the 1969 investigation. In this study (Patterson & Reid, 1973), 11 consecutive families were seen and treatment procedures identical to those in the 1969 study were used. The evaluation methodology was different from that used in the previous study in that (a) the observation data were better monitored for reliability; (b) the parent report data were of greater usefulness because the parents generated a list of referral problems that was directly comparable to code categories; (c) the Becker bipolar adjectives were not used in this study; and (d) the parents were given a six-item global parent rating scale after termination of treatment, asking them essentially to rate the effectiveness and quality of treatment in terms of overall family functioning and happiness as well as referral problems. As in the previous study, the amount of professional time expended was recorded for each family.

The results of the study were comparable to those of the 1969 study:

a. The observation data revealed a mean reduction of 64% in the rate of referral targeted behaviors from baseline to termination; a reduction of 50% in the rate of total deviant behaviors; and a statistically unreliable trend for the deviant behavior of siblings to be reduced as a function of treatment.

b. Using a criterion of 30% reduction from baseline, nine of the 11 cases were classified as successful.

c. The parent report data showed that the rate at which parents reported occurrence of referral behaviors during baseline dropped roughly 50% by the termination of treatment (from a mean of 61%/day during baseline to a mean of 34%/day at termination).

d. The global parent report data collected after termination of treatment showed that all parents experienced a high degree of satisfaction with the program, as well as the perception that their children were much improved behaviorally.

e. Mean professional time spent per family was 31.4 hr (range, 9.4–73.1) as compared to a mean of 25.7 hr (range, 5.7–133.0) for the 1969 study.[2]

A complete analysis of follow-up data for the two samples recently completed by Patterson (1974) showed that the reductions of deviant behaviors of our subjects from baseline to termination persisted over a 12-month followup period.

These studies strongly support the contention that a program designed to modify the reinforcers offered by a family (and probably other social systems as well) can result in the reduction of behaviors associated with delinquency. It is also clear, however, that our procedures have not been effecting desired changes in a significant minority of the families treated by these methods; about 30% of the families either have not profitted from or have been made slightly worse by the treatment offered *as measured by the observation data*. This 30% failure rate is quite small, considering the magnitude of the problems of the boys treated; however, because an attempt has been made not to terminate any family until they are improved, the failures are considered serious in that they are cases that simply do not respond to the treatment for one reason or another.

Because something is often learned by analysis of failures, an attempt was made to find out more about the families who did not profit from treatment. The first attempt was informal and involved asking the therapists involved if they had noted any commonalities among the cases categorized as failures. They cited such factors as lower parental cooperation, inability of the parents to be consistent with their children, a tendency for the children to demonstrate low

---

[2] A well-controlled study by Eyberg (1972) essentially reproduced the findings presented here.

rate but highly aversive behaviors, and stealing as a referral problem in cases that were difficult to treat.

This last point—that stealing was involved in unsuccessful cases—led to an analysis by Reid and Hendriks (1973) of the data for all 27 treatment cases, separated into those who were reported to steal at intake ($N = 14$) and those who were not reported to steal ($N = 13$). A matched sample of 27 normal families, for which baseline data were available, was also included in the analysis.

The first analysis compared the stealers and nonstealers in their response to treatment. Comparing the baseline and termination data for the two groups, the following results were found: nonstealers showed a mean reduction of .461 deviant behaviors per minute, whereas the stealers showed a mean reduction of only .171. The difference between these reductions was highly significant ($t = 3.45, df = 22; p < .001$).

Using a success criterion of 33% reduction in the rate of deviant behaviors from baseline, six of the 14 stealers, compared to nine of the 11 nonstealers, were categorized as successes. The intervention procedures were therefore about twice as effective for nonstealers as for stealers in this sample.

With both groups combined, a strong and positive relationship was found between rate of total deviant behavior during baseline and the magnitude of reduction of total deviant behaviors at termination of treatment ($r = +.642, df = 23; p < .001$). The higher the rate of deviant behavior demonstrated by the child, the more likely he was to respond to the social-learning-based treatment offered at Oregon Research Institute.[3]

In an attempt to better understand the differences among stealers, nonstealers, and normals, the baseline data for the entire sample were analyzed. As mentioned previously, from 12 to 20 5-min observations were made of *each* member of all 54 families during the baseline period. The observation code used provided a running narrative account of the behavior of a given subject in terms of 29 categories and all of the reactions of other family members to him in terms of the same categories. Therefore, baseline data were available for each member of each family on the rates per minute for the emission of social behavior in terms of each of the 29 behavior codes. These codes were then combined into two rational categories: positive—friendly and negative—coercive behaviors. From this data pool, it was possible to calculate the mean rate per minute at which these two larger classes of behaviors occurred for each relevant member of each family.

---

[3] An analysis of the parent report data, now underway, suggests that our conclusion that stealers are not helped by the project has been premature. In fact, it appears that if parent report data are used as a success criterion, the stealers are helped as much as the aggressors. It appears that direct observation data may not be valid for use as an outcome measure for children who demonstrate relatively low-rate problem behaviors such as stealing.

Analyses of variance comparing the rates of positive–friendly and negative–coercive behaviors for the three groups of boys revealed fairly reliable between-group differences ($p < .10$ and $p < .05$, respectively). The normal boys, as would be expected, produced the lowest rates of negative behaviors; nonstealers produced the highest rates; and the stealers fell midway between. When the positive behaviors were examined, the normals produced the highest rates, as expected, but the stealers fell below the nonstealers on this dimension. This might suggest that even though stealers appeared to be in less conflict with their families in terms of observable negative–coercive behavior, they were in greater conflict with their families when rate of positive social interaction was used as an index.

Two ANOVAs comparing the rates of positive–friendly and negative–coercive behaviors for the mothers in the three groups revealed significant between-group differences ($p < .05$). In line with the boys' behaviors, the mothers of normal boys produced the lowest rates of negative–coercive behaviors, mothers of nonstealers produced the highest, and the mothers of stealers fell inbetween. In terms of positive–friendly behaviors, the mothers again paralleled their sons: the mothers of normals produced the highest, the mothers of stealers produced the lowest, and the mothers of nonstealers produced an intermediate rate. When the mothers' behaviors were examined, therefore, a curious paradox emerged: if overt negative behavior was a criterion, families of nonstealers appeared most disturbed; if levels of positive social interaction was the measure, families of stealers appeared to be the worst. The same analyses of variance carried out for fathers did not yield significant between-group effects.

The finding that stealers tend to exhibit less deviant behavior than non-stealers is a factor that alone may account for the relative inefficiency with this former group of a program designed to modify high-rate deviant behavior. However, at least two other possibilities exist: first, the stealers may be exhibiting high rates of antisocial behavior, but only outside the home setting; second, stealers may be able to reduce their rates of deviant behavior while the observers or behavior modifiers are present. Although the second alternative is entirely possible and argues against our general model of treatment for this type of client in outpatient settings, it fits neither our clinical impressions nor parent report, nor can its validity be checked with our current data collection technology.

The first alternative (that stealers cause trouble primarily outside the home) does fit our clinical impression, parent report, and the perceptions of neighbors and community agencies. It is a hypothesis that helps to resolve the apparent discrepancy between referral information (i.e., high rates of deviant behavior) and our observation data (i.e., low rates of such behavior). If true, it suggests that the reason the parent-training program produces minimal results is that there is little deviant behavior occurring within the actual home setting on which the parent of the stealer can work. Finally, if it is true that the referred stealer causes little trouble at home, it is possible that the community is more immediately punished by his or her behavior than are the parents. The parents may therefore refer the child for treatment primarily to appease the school counselor or the juvenile authorities. If this is the case, it follows that the parents may be motivated to refer the child but relatively unmotivated to actually work to change him or her. This is in contrast to the parents of nonstealing aggressive children, who are punished daily and at a high rate by their children's behavior. The idea that parents of stealers are relatively unmotivated to change or control their children has gained some measure of support in our subsequent work with stealers and is discussed further in the final section of this report.

Although the fathers' data did not discriminate among the three groups, there was a clear pattern for the mothers and children in the stealer group to exhibit fewer positive social behaviors than those in the other two groups. These findings suggest that stealers and their families are rather distant, having only loose social ties with one another. One possible implication is that the parents of stealers may not have powerful social reinforcers at their command to be systematically and effectively employed within the social-learning treatment paradigm. This low rate of positive (and negative) social exchange gives the picture of a rather boring family climate that may, in fact, serve to motivate the child to seek out his developmental experiences and positive reinforcers in unsupervised, extrafamily settings.

As a result of these analyses and a good deal of discussion among the project staff, it was decided to switch the focus of the research from social aggression to the modification of stealing behavior. The same data collection procedures as previously used were retained, and families were accepted for treatment whose primary referral problem involved at least one child who stole at a high rate (at least one theft per 2 weeks). Thirty-four referrals were made to the project soon after the transition. Only ten of these actually began treatment. The primary reason for the dismal response to our offers of treatment was lack of parental motivation to make the commitments necessary for involvement in the project. The typical pattern was as follows: the parents phoned to request treatment immediately following the child's being apprehended for stealing; they either missed the intake appointment or cancelled it with one of the following explanations—the problem had ceased to exist, one of the parents (usually said to be the father) had refused to cooperate, the parents had reconsidered the incident and now felt that the child was unjustly accused. The message behind these cancellations appears quite clear: the parents were upset at the time the child was apprehended, but after that incident had passed there was little motivated to enter treatment. There was also a marked level of family disorganization characterizing these cases. The children in the families were typically unsupervised for long periods each day and the working schedules of the parents (both mother and father) tended to keep most of them from spending much time with their families.

Our experience with the first ten cases who actually entered treatment further convinced us that the families of stealers presented intervention problems quite different from the families of social aggressors. First, the families developed a pattern of missing appointments with project staff and of failing to carry out the modification procedures suggested. Second, the parents seemed disinclined or unable to monitor or track closely the behavior of their children; third, the parents spent much of their time involved in work and social activities away from the home. The factor most common among the families and perhaps most relevant to treatment was a failure of the parents to identify stealing behavior of their children as theft. The parents had an amazing ability to either ignore actual stealing behavior or to relabel it so that it did not appear deviant. For example, one child came home with a clock that his parents knew was not his. The child told the parents he had found the clock in a tree. More amazing, the parents accepted the story and failed to apply a consequence for the act. This sort of relabeling of stealing as the child finding things, trading for things, or being given things by an unnamed benefactor prevented the parents from recognizing stealing when it occurred and consequating it. One child, during an intake interview, was asked whether he had ever stolen anything. He answered that he had not. When asked whether he found things and brought them home, he answered, "Sure, all the time." After hearing this type of response from all ten families, we came up with the following tentative formulation and intervention strategy for working with the families of stealers.

Recall that in the families of social aggressors, the deviant behavior is highly visible, of high rate, and immediately punishing to the parents. The parents therefore have no trouble identifying the behavior and labeling it when it occurs, and it is so aversive that parents wish to change it. A social-learning behavior management program is therefore highly effective because the parents are able and motivated to track the behaviors carefully when they occur and to apply the immediate consequences that can lead to change. For the families of stealers, however, the picture is quite different. The stealing is not visible (at least if it is done competently); only the report of that behavior is. The parents are free to reinterpret the report of a stealing event in such a way as to make any action on their part unnecessary (e.g., "My child really did not steal that clock, he only found it"). It is also the case that stealing is not a high-rate event, which gives the parents less experience in handling the behavior than is the case for high-rate social aggression. Finally, stealing behavior is seldom aversive to the parents unless it leads to intervention by the juvenile authorities, the school, or the neighbors. At such point that the outside agencies begin to embarrass, coerce, or make demands on the parents because of the child's behavior, the primary motivation of the parents is to rid themselves of the police or school involvement in their family life, not necessarily to deal with the stealing itself. Therefore, the parents may waste their time and energy arguing with the police, teachers, or neighbors over the veridicality of the stealing reports instead of dealing with their child.

To translate this formulation into an intervention strategy, it was decided that before parents of stealers could use the behavior management procedures taught in our program, they needed to learn to label each stealing event as such. If the parents learned to acknowledge the high rate of stealing of the referred child, it was hoped that this awareness would motivate them to actively engage in the intervention program. If this knowledge and acceptance of the high-rate stealing failed to motivate the parents to manage their children, an attempt would be made to use extrinsic reinforcers to increase the participation of the parents in the intervention program (e.g., a parenting salary; preventing the Juvenile Court from taking custody of the child; the therapists' reinforcing of the parenting behavior through daily phone calls). It was assumed that once the parents learned to track and identify all stealing incidents, and once they had the sufficient motivation to do something about it, then the same set of techniques found to be successful with families of social aggressors would be successful in working with the parents of stealers.

The first treatment sessions with the families of stealers therefore involved the defining of stealing as the possession by the child of any object not clearly (in the parents' perception) belonging to him. The parents were instructed that during intervention the child was not to be allowed to offer any explanation as to how he came into possession of such an object. The necessity of tracking and monitoring the referred child's behavior was impressed on the parents and they were given a good deal of training in how to count child behavior and were directed to have a continuous knowledge of the child's whereabouts as a condition of treatment. To insure continued cooperation and effort on the parents' part, the treatment was contingent in nature in that no new steps in intervention were attempted until parents had completed the previous step (and in one case, the parents were given a 60.00 dollars/month parenting salary, contingent on their cooperation with the program). For families who had come to the attention of the juvenile court either before or during the intervention, it was made clear that noncooperation would lead to dismissal from the project and would probably result in the active intervention by the local authorities. As a further reinforcing mechanism, daily phone calls were made to all families at least in the initial phase of treatment.

With the above exceptions, the treatment of stealers was the same as for the previously studied nonstealers (baseline and further observation probes, collection of parent report data, reading the parent book, training in tracking and counting behaviors, and designing and executing modification programs). Because the primary referral problem (stealing) did not lend itself easily to measurement through direct observation by professional observers, a new data collection procedure was added (Jones, 1973). The parents were phoned every day after the initial contact and asked whether any stealing had come to their attention in the previous 24 hr. If any stealing had occurred, a standard set of questions was asked concerning the object stolen: its value, the place where the stealing occurred, whether or not the child was with others when he stole, what the parents did about the act, etc.

PRELIMINARY EVALUATION OF INTERVENTION IN FAMILIES OF CHILDREN WHO STEAL

At this time, there are sufficient data on the first seven families to permit a preliminary evaluation of the effectiveness of the program. Although home observation data have been collected, they are not yet analyzed. The data to be presented here consist of the rate and monetary value of parent-reported stealing events for the target child as a function of intervention.

Family No. 1. The target child in this family was a rather anxious, highly verbal, 12-year-old boy. His mother had been divorced three times, was subject to severe depressive episodes requiring hospitalization approximately once a year, and had been in individual psychotherapy for six years prior to her participation in the project. She discontinued her individual therapy before entering the present program. The boy's stepfather was a warm and friendly person who played little part in the management of the boy and his 15-year-old brother. The intake interview revealed that the target child had a long history of stealing, a preoccupation with women's undergarments (the object of much of the stealing), and an ability to negate his mother's attempts to control him with verbal arguments. He was usually able to talk his way out of reported stealing incidents, and when caught red handed he would successfully present his "neurosis" as the cause for the theft. Intervention with this family was initially quite difficult as they took frequent vacations and were terribly slow both in completing the parent textbook and in initiating recommended modification programs. Both parents were employed, and the father's schedule prevented him from participating in the program. The primary focus of the intervention was to teach the mother to stop arguing with the boy about whether he was or was not guilty of the reported thefts and to consistently use a time-out contingency instead.

As can be seen from Fig. 1, the reported rate of stealing was quite high during baseline but leveled off dramatically after the parents completed the textbook and entered the intervention phase. After each vacation, the parents required help in reinstituting their program for stealing. For example, they required one treatment session during Follow-up 1 that resulted in the total cessation of reported stealing for 18 weeks. The one stealing event in Follow-up 2 occurred while the mother was hospitalized briefly following a suicide attempt. No

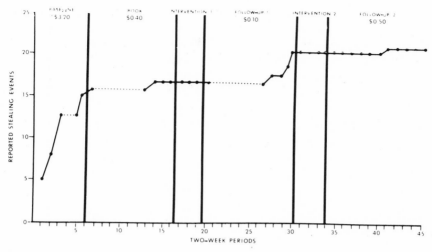

FIG. 1 Cumulative curve for stealing in Family 1. Cash values are the mean monetary values of articles stolen. The dotted sections of the curve indicate the family out of town on vacation.

further treatment contact was made by the project as the mother entered psychiatric treatment for her depression. The mean value of the objects stolen was calculated for each phase of intervention. As can be seen in Fig. 1, the value of the stolen items showed a marked reduction as a function of intervention.

Family No. 2.   The target child in this family was a 10-year-old boy who stole at an incredible rate, beginning at age 5 years. He was first apprehended by the police at the age of 7 years for selling marijuana, and after that for such behaviors as extortion from homosexuals (threatening to tell police that they molested him unless he was given money), car theft, and burglary. He had three brothers and one sister. All three brothers had come into contact with the juvenile court. The mother had been divorced twice, had a number of brief psychotherapeutic contacts before entering the program, and was highly religious. The stepfather was highly resistent to the intervention and stated at the onset that he wanted to have the child committed to an institution. Both the parents were convinced that the child was either genetically damaged or possessed by the devil. They were quite doubtful that the application of contingencies for stealing (which they said they had previously tried to no avail) would alter the boy's stealing behavior. The father was further convinced that the child's purpose for stealing was to break up his marriage.

After intake, baseline observations, and the parents' completion of the textbook, a program is immediately instituted whereby the child would spend 4–8 hr at the local detention facility immediately following reported thefts. After three such occurrences, there was a cessation of reported stealing. At the same time, the parents were taught the tracking, labeling, and consequating skills previously described. Although the child's stealing behavior changed dramatically (see Fig. 2), the parents failed to perceive any meaningful change in his behavior. Fifteen weeks after intervention began, the parents relinquished custody of the child to the youth authority and he was removed from the home. The treatment apparently worked in terms of reducing stealing, but the intervention strategy was too limited in focus to achieve a happy resolution in this case.

Family No. 3. The target child in this family was a 9-year-old boy with a long history of petty theft. Both parents were quite motivated for intervention and very cooperative. There were two other children in the family (an 8-year-old girl and a 7-year-old boy) who demonstrated no significant clinical problems. The intervention was straightforward: the parents read the book and received training in tracking, labeling, and consequating stealing with time out. The cessation of reported stealing was immediate and stable (see Fig. 3).

Family No. 4. The target child in this family was a rather obese, angry, socially unskilled, 13-year-old boy. He had a long history of stealing and fire setting. There were four other children in the family (boys, ages 4, 8, 14, and 15 years), none of whom showed significant problem behaviors. The parents were extremely uncooperative with the project, to the point of not allowing home observations. The father was working full time and attending college. The mother was attending college and was engaged in civic activities. Neither parent supervised the children carefully. The primary task during intervention was to

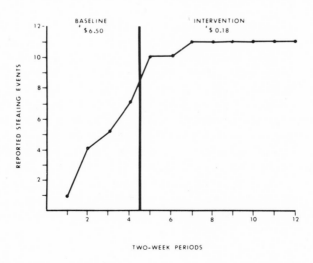

FIG. 2 Cumulative curve for stealing in Family 2. Cash values are the mean monetary values of articles stolen.

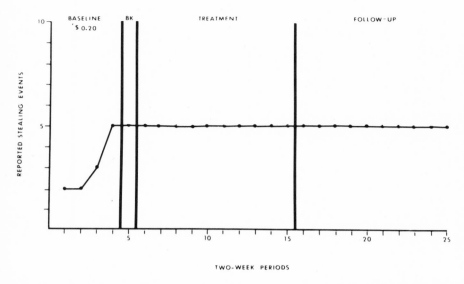

FIG. 3 Cumulative curve for stealing in Family 3. The cash value is the mean monetary value of articles stolen (BK = book).

teach the parents to track the boy's activities. Both parents were quite willing to apply time-out contingent on stealing and fire setting. It took approximately 10 weeks of intervention for the parents to complete the textbook and to partici-pate in the program, at which time the reported stealing stopped (see Fig. 4).

Family No. 5. The target child in this family was a 9-year-old boy who had a twin brother. He had a long history of stealing and running away from home. The parents were cooperative and motivated to work with the project, but they were extremely diffuse in terms of their ability to track, label, and consequate the child consistently. A "salary" of $60.00 per month was made contingent on the parents' recording of data on the child and later for their application of various modification programs. Although the stealing had not stopped com-pletely (see Fig. 5) at the time of this report, one of the two events reported in follow-up was marginal (one involved stealing an empty milk bottle; the other involved his taking another boy's jacket).

Family No. 6. The target child in this family was a 13-year-old girl (the first girl accepted by the project) who had a history of stealing and shoplifting. She was a bright, attractive, and pleasant youngster. The girl's stepmother was working to support her and her two younger sisters and was going to college. The father had left the family as the result of a divorce 3 years before the beginning of treatment. Stealing stopped after the first session of intervention, during which the mother was instructed to simply record (not consequate) each

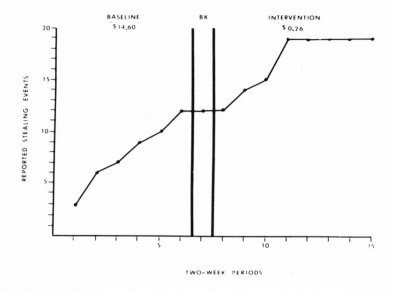

FIG. 4 Cumulative curve for stealing in Family 4. The cash values are the mean monetary values of articles stolen (BK = book).

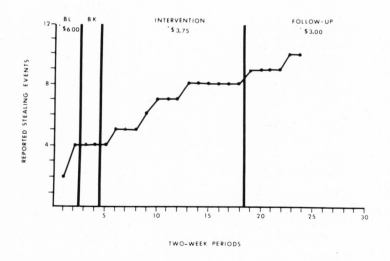

FIG. 5 Cumulative curve for stealing in Family 5. The cash values are the mean monetary values of articles stolen (BL = baseline; BK = book).

stealing event. After three more sessions the child reported she was not stealing anymore in order to please the therapist. It is therefore unclear in this case whether or not the specific intervention technique should be credited with the cessation of stealing (Fig. 6).

Family No. 7. The target child was an 11-year-old boy with a history of reported stealing in the school setting. The parents asked for treatment following a theft at school that aroused the concern of the school principal and the local juvenile authorities. After 3 weeks of baseline data collection, the father phoned to say that he had had several talks with his son over the 3 weeks and the problem of stealing had ceased to exist. This last case is presented to illustrate the more typical reaction of parents who request treatment from the project following a reported stealing event and then withdraw on the grounds that the problem has been "solved" (Fig. 7).

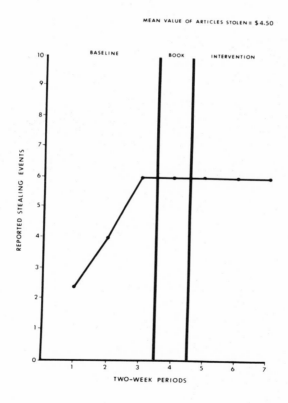

FIG. 6 Cumulative curve for stealing in Family 6. The mean value of articles stolen was $4.50.

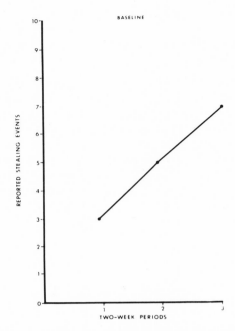

FIG. 7 Cumulative curve for stealing in Family 7. The mean value of articles stolen was $1.75.

CONCLUSIONS

Taken together, the parent report data show that the rate of stealing and the mean value of stolen articles were reduced markedly for all children actually treated in the project. Although observation data and amount of professional time expended have been collected for these new cases, the data have not yet been analyzed. The parent report data presented are not as behavioral as may be preferred, but we have not yet been able to devise a more solid, practical form of data for evaluating theft rate. Because data are collected on reported stealing rather than on the stealing behavior itself, it is certainly the case that some stealing goes undetected. In fact, a cynic may even suggest that our data represent "incompetent stealing" (i.e., only those thefts in which the child has been caught and reported). It can even be argued that our intervention selectively punishes incompetent stealing and that the child's rate of competent stealing (not reported) increases. One check on the accuracy of our data is the rate of referrals to the Juvenile Court, which we are monitoring at present. None of the children seen in this project has been picked up by the police after the beginning of intervention.

It may also be argued that the reporting of parents is inaccurate. Parents, in fact, conceivably may stop reporting thefts for the purpose of terminating treatment. However, we (Patterson and Reid, 1973) have reported a correlation of +.63 between parent reports of rates of aggressive behaviors and rates of those behaviors derived from data collected by our professional observers. What evidence we have suggests that carefully specified parent report data do, in fact, reflect observed behavior quite well. If parents are deceiving us, we should be able to find out by referring to future records at the Juvenile Court.

Combining our preliminary data and impressions with stealers and our previous research with social aggressors, the following conclusions are offered. First, parents of stealers have a harder time recognizing stealing behavior when it occurs than do parents of social aggressors in recognizing aggressive behaviors. Second, once the parents of stealers are taught to recognize and to consequate it, stealing behavior may be modified in the same way as aggressive behavior. Third, we have observed that parents of stealers are harder to motivate than are parents of social aggressors. However, they do respond to the application of extrinsic reinforcement (money, supportive phone calls, and the like). Fourth, these conclusions must remain quite tentative until we have studied more cases and analyzed the observation data and the Juvenile Court records.

To summarize, we feel justified in concluding that we have demonstrated that at least one form of delinquent behavior (social aggression) may be readily and cheaply modified by changing the manner in which it is reinforced in at least one social system (the family). Second, the preliminary data presented here suggest that a relatively minor change in the intervention strategy makes it possible to modify one other form of delinquent behavior (stealing) by making changes in the pattern of reinforcement in the family setting.

Future research in our project is to be directed at demonstrating that aggression and stealing may also be reduced by reprogramming other social settings (e.g., in the classroom—see Patterson, Cobb, & Ray, 1972) and demonstrating that other forms of delinquent behavior (e.g., vandalism, fire setting, truancy) may be modified by reprogramming social systems.

ACKNOWLEDGMENTS

Computing assistance was obtained from Health Sciences Computing Facility, UCLA, sponsored by NIH Grant FR-3. Both writers gratefully acknowledge the financial assistance provided by MH 12972, MH 10822, and MH15985-01. The authors are indebted to R. R. Jones and P. S. Taplin for their advice on earlier drafts of the present chapter.

REFERENCES

Bahm, A. K., Chandler, C., & Eisenberg, L. Diagnostic characteristics related to service on psychiatric clinics for children. Paper presented at the 38th Annual Convention of Orthopsychiatry, Munich, 1961.

Beach, D. R., & Laird, J. D. Follow-up study of children identified early as emotionally disturbed. *Journal of Consulting Clinical Psychology*, 1968, **32**, 369–374.

Eyberg, S. M. An outcome study of child family intervention: Effects of contingency contracting and order of treated problems. Unpublished doctoral dissertation, University of Oregon, 1972.

Jones, R. R. TIROS: "Telephone interview report on stealing." Unpublished assessment device, Oregon Research Institute, 1973.

Levitt, E. E. Research on psychotherapy with children. In A. E. Bergin & S. L. Garfield (Eds.), *Handbook of psychotherapy and behavior change*. New York: Wiley, 1971. Pp. 474–494.

Meltzoff, J., & Kornreich, M. *Research in psychotherapy*. New York: Altherton Press, 1970.

Morris, H. H. Aggressive behavior disorders in children: A follow-up study. *American Journal of Psychiatry*, 1956, **112**, 991–997.

Patterson, G. R. An empirical approach to the classification of disturbed children. *Journal of Clinical Psychology*, 1964, **20**, 326–337.

Patterson, G. R. *Families*. Champaign, Ill.: Research Press, 1971.

Patterson, G. R. Stimulus control: A basis for predicting behavioral events in a natural setting. Invited address presented at the First Texas Conference on Behavior Modification, Houston, Texas, May 1972.

Patterson, G. R. Interventions for boys with conduct problems: multiple settings, treatments and criteria. *Journal of Consulting and Clinical Psychology*, 1974, **42**, 471–481.

Patterson, G. R., & Brodsky, G. A behavior modification programme for a child with multiple problem behaviours. *Journal of Child Psychology & Psychiatry*, 1966, **7**, 277–295.

Patterson, G. R., Cobb, J. A., & Ray, R. S. Direct intervention in the classroom: A set of procedures for the aggressive child. In F. W. Clark, D. R. Evans, & L. A. Hamerlynck (Eds.), *Implementing behavioral programs for schools and clinics*. Champaign, Ill.: Research Press, 1972. Pp. 151–201.

Patterson, G. R., Cobb, J. A., & Ray, R. S. A social engineering technology for retraining the families of aggressive boys. In H. E. Adams & I. P. Unikel (Eds.), *Issues and trends in behavior therapy*. Springfield, Ill.: Charles C Thomas, 1973. Pp. 139–224.

Patterson, G. R., & Erickson, M. Parents' ratings of the aversiveness of categories in the *Zap Code*. Unpublished data analysis, Oregon Research Institute, 1972.

Patterson, G. R., & Gullion, M. E. *Living with children: New methods for parents and teachers*. Champaign, Illinois: Research Press, 1968.

Patterson, G. R., & Harris, A. Some methodological considerations for observational procedures. Paper presented at the 76th meeting of the American Psychological Association, San Francisco, 1968.

Patterson, G. R., McNeal, S., Hawkins, N., & Phelps, R. Reprogramming the social environment. *Journal of Child Psychology & Psychiatry*, 1967, **8**, 181–195.

Patterson, G. R., Ray, R. S., & Shaw, D. A. Direct intervention in families of deviant children. *Oregon Research Institute Research Bulletin*, 1968, 8(9) (whole issue).

Patterson, G. R., Ray, R. S., Shaw, D. A., & Cobb, J. A. Manual for coding of family interactions, 1969. (Available from: ASIS National Auxilliary Publications Service, c/o CMM Information Services, Inc., 909 Third Avenue, New York, N.Y. 10022. Document #01234.)

Patterson, G. R., & Reid, J. B. Reciprocity and coercion: Two facets of social systems. In C. Neuringer & J. Michael (Eds.), *Behavior modification in clinical psychology*. New York: Appleton-Century-Crofts, 1970. Pp. 133–177.

Patterson, G. R., & Reid, J. B. Intervention for families of aggressive boys: A replication study. *Behavior Research & Therapy*, 1973, **11**, 1–12.

Redl, F., & Wineman, D. *Controls from within: Techniques for the treatment of the aggressive child*. Glencoe, Illinois: The Free Press, 1952.

Reid, J. B. Reciprocity in family interaction. Unpublished doctoral dissertation, University of Oregon, 1967.

Reid, J. B. Reliability assessment of observation data: A possible methodological problem. *Child Development*, 1970, **41**, 1143–1150.

Reid, J. B. The temporal stability of observed aggression in children. Unpublished manuscript, Oregon Research Institute, 1973.

Reid, J. B., & DeMaster, B. The efficacy of the spot-check procedure in maintaining the reliability of data collected by observers in quasi-natural settings: Two pilot studies. *Oregon Research Institute Research Bulletin*, 1972, **12**(8) (whole issue).

Reid, J. B., & Hendriks, A. F. C. J. A preliminary analysis of the effectiveness of direct home intervention for treatment of predelinquent boys who steal. In F. W. Clark & L. A. Hamerlynck (Eds.), *Critical issues in research and practice: Proceedings of the Fourth Banff International Conference on Behavior Modification*. Champaign, Illinois: Research Press, 1973. Pp. 209–219.

Roach, J. L. Some social-psychological characteristics of child guidance clinic caseloads. *Journal of Consulting Psychology*, 1958, **22**, 183–186.

Robins, L. N. *Deviant children grown up: A sociological and psychiatric study of sociopathic personality*. Baltimore: Williams & Wilkins, 1966.

Rogers, M., Lilienfeld, A. M., & Pasamanick, B. *Prenatal and parental factors in the development of child behavior disorders*. Baltimore: Johns Hopkins University Press, 1954.

Taplin, P. S., & Reid, J. B. Effects of instructional set and experimental influence on observer reliability. *Child Development*, 1973, **44**, 547–554.

Teuber, H. L., & Powers, E. Evaluating therapy in a delinquency prevention program. *Psychiatric Treatment*, 1953, **21**, 138–147.

Westman, J. C., Rice, D. L., & Bermann, E. Relationship between nursery school behaviors and later school adjustment. *American Journal of Orthopsychiatry*, 1967, **37**, 725–731.

White, G. The effect of observer presence on mother and child behavior. Unpublished doctoral dissertation, University of Oregon, 1972.

Woody, R. H. *Behavioral problem children in the schools*. New York: Appleton-Century-Crofts, 1969.

8

BPLAY—A Community Support System, Phase One[1]

Harold L. Cohen

*School of Architecture
and Environmental Design
State University of New York
at Buffalo*

INTRODUCTION

Two years ago, my colleages and I at IBR designed and initiated a project so large in scope that we were forced to develop new procedures and new modes of operation. Using the basic tenets of operant psychology and behavioral design, we proposed to alter the statistically increasing antisocial behavior of youth defined by the courts, police, and schools as delinquent or predelinquent. We also proposed to deliver the resulting programs into the hands of those same community agencies. By developing a contingency management method of operation, using our funds and personnel as reinforcers, we planned to program this operational shift within 5 years of its inception.

The target laboratory area covers almost half a county and houses over one-quarter of a million people. Our specific target population is approximately 20,000 12–18 year olds presently attending the public schools.

In order to determine what the problem behaviors were, where and when they occurred, and by what age group, and in order to determine whether our behavior modification and general contingency programs were effective when initiated, we needed to establish and maintain a cumulative record of clearly defined behaviors of these target children. We felt we needed to collect at least 1 year's worth of baseline behavior (we collected for 2 years); to design and maintain a consistent behavior collection system; and to establish full cooperation from the community agencies, clients, teachers, and parents. This chapter

---

[1] This chapter is in part selected from a first-year report, soon to be published by the Educational Facility Press of IBR. Its presentation at the Third Symposium on Behavior Modification, January 24, 1973, Mexico City, included slides and charts as well as a short film.

represents a brief report on the procedures and data collected for the behavioral baseline and the community's involvement in Phase 1.

The BPLAY (Behavioral Programs in Learning Activities for Youth) project is a 3-year research program designed to test the effectiveness of behaviorally managed leisure-time activities for adolescents in minimizing juvenile problem behaviors and redirecting adolescent energies into socially acceptable and personally rewarding activities. It is being conducted by the Institute for Behavioral Research, Inc. (IBR), under the sponsorship of the Center for Studies of Crime and Delinquency, National Institute of Mental Health (Grant No. MH19706). BPLAY represents an effort to establish preventive delinquency programs in an urban/suburban community experiencing rapid population growth and associated social problems and dislocations. It is not, however, directed specifically toward children with records of disturbance or delinquency. Instead, it is intended to help all teenagers to handle the problems associated with adolescence and intensified by the physical, social, and economic conditions prevailing in the contemporary scene.

The BPLAY project is an outgrowth of an earlier IBR project called LEAP (Legan and Educational Alternatives to Punishment in Maintaining Law and Order). It is being implemented in a target area defined and studied during LEAP and is employing a data-gathering system initiated during LEAP for an analysis of delinquent behavior in the area.

The research arena is a large section of an urban/suburban region on the periphery of a densely populated metropolitan center on the east coast of the United States. In the past decade, this target area has experienced more than a 50% increase in population, much of it caused by immigration from the inner-city area of the adjacent metropolis. This has resulted in a marked change in the racial composition of some of the neighborhoods and has been attended by increased taxes and a downward shift in employment level. The problems of the public schools in attempting to cope with their greatly increased enrollments have been intensified by disputes over desegregation and busing to achieve racial balance.

Although local government officials, educators, merchants, and residents in the target area are concerned over the upsurge in juvenile crime in recent years, the delinquency problem there is not yet acute—at least, not in comparison to the situation in many other urbanized areas. However, all social indicators point to an abrupt increase in the delinquency rate over the next few years, unless positive action is taken to forestall it.

The purpose of the Institute for Behavioral Research in conducting the BPLAY project is to determine whether, with judicious planning and a limited direct input into the community, it is possible to change the direction of the agencies now dealing with youth problems and stimulate them to seek alternatives to punishment in handling juvenile delinquent behaviors. The project staff is attempting to work through the schools and other community agencies to provide after-school programs intended to attract teenagers to a learning environment and programs during nonschool hours by programming rewards for their attendance and performance. The objectives are to reduce their opportunities for delinquent behaviors, increase their options for socially acceptable and personally rewarding behaviors, and add to their repertoires of useful skills.

Implicit in these formal objectives is another that, although unstated, is requisite to the success of the project: establishing a broad sense of community participation in, and responsibility for, the development of leisure-time activities for adolescents. If the project is to have any lasting effect, it must be planned from the first as a model and a turnkey operation—one that can eventually be funded and administered by the community itself. This objective acts as a constraint on the project, because it necessitates working with and through the community organizations and regulating project efforts to the community pace and scope. It is essential, however, that BPLAY efforts be supportive and additive to other constructive programs for adolescents in the community instead of competitive with them.

Also essential to the success of the project is community acceptance of BPLAY as an educational—recreational resource for all adolescents rather than a program for delinquents. It is true that the research objective of BPLAY is to determine the effect of community-sponsored leisure-time activities for teenagers on the social adaptations of these youngsters, and it is also true that the incidence of delinquent or "problem" behaviors is one measure of this effect. However, the scope of the project is much broader than this. It is intended to offer young people, at a critical period in their lives, healthy outlets for their energies and an adequate repertoire of problem-solving techniques. It is designed to equip them to handle frustration and boredom; to make decisions concerning their actions in full appreciation of the probable consequences of these actions; and to identify positively, although not uncritically, with their communities. These skills are needed by all young people today, regardless of whether they are considered "problem" children on the basis of their behavioral histories. This chapter deals mainly with baseline behavior and methods of establishing community liaison and covers the first year of the project.

Background

The radical technological advances that have taken place in the twentieth century, and particularly since World War II, have precipitated social, economic, and cultural changes with momentous implications for the future. The increased standard of living made possible by technology—including improved diet and medical care—has accelerated population growth. Industrialization and agricultural mechanization have produced concentrations of the population in cities and urbanized areas, particularly along the east and west coasts and in the region of the Great Lakes. Modern methods of transportation have combined with shifting economic pressures to make America a nation of transients, whose mobility contributes to the weakening of family, church, and neighborhood influences. Another factor undermining the stabilizing influence of these traditional agencies is modern communication, which exposes even stay at homes to a wide range of ideas, cultures, and values. Together, all these developments have created a world that, although not necessarily better or worse than the world that existed a generation ago, is certainly vastly different from it.

The impact of contemporary cultural and socioeconomic conditions on today's youth is reflected in reports of turmoil in the schools and in the large and increasing statistics on juvenile delinquency.[2] Both in the schools and in society at large, the traditional means of combating antisocial acts has been punishment of offenders. However, experience has shown that the penalties decreed by law for delinquent behaviors have proved generally ineffective both in deterring delinquency and in rehabilitating offenders.[3] Consequently, concerned government officials, educators, sociologists, and private citizens are seeking viable alternatives to punishment in dealing with the delinquency problems.

One possible approach is for communities to marshal their resources to provide leisure-time environments and activities that attract young people, engage their interest and enthusiasm, and reward them for constructive, socially acceptable behavior. The BPLAY program is designed to implement this approach and test its effectiveness.

Research Arena

The research arena for the BPLAY project is an urban/suburban region on the periphery of a large, densely populated metropolitan center on the east coast of the United States. In this report, the names of locations and agencies are fictionalized but the situation and events are factual. The general target area, a section of Eastco Regional County, is typical of many in the industrialized portions of the country, except that it is more positive and forward looking than most in its approach to its youth problems.

Cooperating with the BPLAY project are the county's school system, police system, civic associations, and merchants. The intent is to attract teenagers into leisure-time activities that are enjoyable and educational for them and that are so scheduled as to be incompatible with loitering in community locations having a high potential for problem behaviors.

[2] The President's Commission on Law Enforcement and Administration of Justice, Task Force on Juvenile Delinquency, *Juvenile Delinquency and Youth Crime*, Washington D.C.: U.S. Government Printing Office, 1967.

[3] The President's Commission on Law Enforcement and Administration of Justice, Task Force on Juvenile Delinquency, *Juvenile Delinquency and Youth Crime*, Washington D.C.: U.S. Government Printing Office, 1967.

BPLAY is conceived essentially as a "seed" project. Implicit in the accomplishment of its objectives is the establishment of a broad sense of community responsibility for, and participation in, the development and implementation of leisure-time activities for adolescents. The BPLAY staff therefore works with and through community personnel, organizations, and institutions and offers its programs to all teenagers, not just to underachievers and disruptive students. The project is designed as a model—one that can eventually be funded and administered by the community itself. This goal places some constraints on the project, because it restricts the pace and scope of the programs and puts a premium on the acceptability of the project to the community at large. It is regarded as essential, however, that the BPLAY efforts be supportive and additive to other constructive programs for adolescents instead of competitive with them. If the project is to be of lasting benefit, the community must be willing and equipped to assume responsibility for the programs when the IBR phase is completed. Therefore, the project has a facilitating role rather than one of prime implementation.

Year One Objectives

The BPLAY project set itself the following objectives for accomplishment during Project Year One:

1. To collect and analyze baseline data on delinquent and predelinquent behaviors in a specified target area
2. To establish a pilot program of after-school activities managed by community personnel trained in behavioral techniques
3. To administer an IBR-developed legal course for adolescents—*Teenagers' Rights and Responsibilities* (TARR)—in selected schools and to monitor the behaviors of TARR students
4. To evaluate the target community in ethnographic terms

THE TARGET AREA AND POPULATION

The target area selected for the BPLAY project is a large, urbanized section of a county in an east coast state. In this report, the county is designated by the fictitious name of Eastco Regional County. It has been chosen as the locale for the project to enable BPLAY to take advantage of the work performed in an earlier IBR pilot project, Legal and Educational Alternatives to Punishment (LEAP). As a result of the LEAP work, BPLAY has had a well-defined area identified for its efforts and has been able to capitalize on contacts already established in the county.

Socioeconomic Characteristics of the Target Area

Eastco Regional County is one of the many areas in the United States that have undergone radical sociological changes in the past two decades. At the end of World War II, it was largely an agricultural region, except for a few suburban towns in the area where it bordered on a large metropolitan center, called "Metrocity." Its inhabitants were predominately white, although with a sizeable black minority occupying chiefly the rural areas. The income level was chiefly middle to lower-middle class, although the rural black population was very poor indeed, and there was a small percentage of upper-income residents, chiefly in the suburban towns. The middle-income blacks also tended to be concentrated in the towns.

Although the sections of the county remote from Metrocity have changed relatively little, the sector near the city has been, in all but the political sense, absorbed as part of the city's metropolitan area. Its population has increased enormously in the last decade—by 50.4% as compared to an average increase of 13.3% nationwide (United States census data). Much of the population increase has been caused by immigration from Metrocity, particularly from its innercity areas. This has changed the racial composition of the section, although whites remain in the majority.

In appearance, this section of the county is almost indistinguishable from that of the adjacent city. It is dominated by high-rise buildings, many of them apartment buildings. In the same period when the population increased by half, the number of multiple-dwelling units increased by 111%. The concurrent increase in one- and two-family dwellings was only 29%. Many high-rise office buildings have also been constructed; These house state, county, and municipal government agencies; a multiplicity of service businesses; and the management of the light industries located in the area. The region has no subway system but its extensive bus system connects with that of Metrocity. It has a number of hotels, motels, and restaurants, and several large shopping centers. In fact, it has become so urbanized that federal agencies dealing with urban problems consider it a city and allocate funds for urban development there.

Among the problems besetting this section as a result of its rapid population expansion are the need for accommodating a greatly increased student population in its schools and the growth in the rate of crime, particularly juvenile delinquency. These problems are heightened by the racial tension that has emerged with the immigration from the Metrocity inner city. Employment levels have dropped and taxation has increased in many areas over the country, and oldtime residents of the section attribute at least a part of this to the black immigrants. The school system, struggling to meet the requirements of its increased student load, has also been engaged with a federal agency in disputes over desegregation, particularly over busing to achieve racial balance. That the children share in the racial antagonisms of the section is evidenced by a serious racial disturbance in one of the senior high schools in the region in the past year.

Although juvenile crime in the area has increased in recent years, the rate of increase has not been greater than in other, similar areas of the country and the total incidence of delinquent acts is less than in many urbanized regions. However, concerned citizens believe that all social indicators point to an increasing rate in the near future unless positive action is taken to combat it.

Four senior and 11 junior high schools are located in this section of the county, which has been chosen as the BPLAY target area. Each of the senior high schools receives students from junior high schools on the basis of designated school boundaries; therefore, each senior high school with its feeder junior high schools forms a student population network. These networks have been the main determinants in defining the actual boundaries of the target area. The Eastco Regional County School Board reports the senior high school enrollment at 9528 and the junior high school enrollment at 10,663, for a total student population of 20,191.

Young people between 12 and 17 years of age, inclusive, who attend or have attended these schools are considered to be members of BPLAY's overall target population.

Definition of Prime Target Area

To implement activities programs within a manageable area and to allow for comparisons with other groupings, the total area of concern was reduced to a prime target area, called "Targetville." This area was defined to coincide with the student population network comprised of one senior high school and its four feeder junior high schools. It was decided that all problem behaviors identified with students from these schools should be considered as originating in Targetville, even if the behavior itself took place outside the community.

Targetville has a population of 14,998 (April 1970 United States Census) and contains 5194 housing units with a median of 5.1 rooms. Although it has shared the population growth of the rest of the overall target section, it is still predominately white. It is the site of the largest of the shopping centers.

The senior high school, which is the one in which the racial disturbance mentioned above occurred, has an enrollment of 2640, and the enrollment in the four junior high schools totals 2913. Two of the junior high schools (to be called by the code names TJHS-1 and TJHS-2) were selected for implementation of the pilot after-school activity programs. These two schools, which together have an enrollment of 1473, form a contiguous neighborhood with good isolating natural boundaries, adjacent to the Targetville Shopping Plaza, a center of juvenile activity in this section of the county.

Once Targetville was selected as the central focus for BPLAY activity in Project Year One, the project opened a local Targetville office to assist in establishing rapport with the community and to facilitate study of the social and political structure of the area.

COLLECTION OF BASELINE DATA

Procedures

Collection of **BPLAY** baseline data began in February 1971, when a supervisor and two collectors were assigned to the staff. Most of the first two months was spent in developing the system: determining what information was available, selecting the variables to be recorded, working out the mechanics of a coding scheme, and establishing intercoder reliability among the data collectors. Because a working relationship had been established with the Eastco Regional County Police Department, the data collection was confined to that agency until the system was clearly defined. Later it was extended to the county's Department of Juvenile Services and to selected schools in the area.

The **LEAP** project provided a valuable pilot study for the early work on the **BPLAY** data collection system. On the advice of a **LEAP** consultant, a system of checklist coding and hand-punched McBee cards had been set up. This system was modified to accomodate the **BPLAY** project. Numerical coding was substituted for checklist coding, and machine-punched **IBM** cards were used in place of hand-punched McBee cards. By the end of March, the definitions, rules, and procedures had been clarified and tested; a data manual describing them had been prepared; and the changeover to mechanical processing was accomplished.

Figure 1 is a flow chart showing the **BPLAY** data collection system as it is now operating. The following items of information are recorded in numerical codes on each problem behavior incident involving a target student:

About the Student

1. Name	5. Home address (block only)
2. Date of birth	6. School
3. Sex	7. Grade in School
4. Race	8. Age at time problem behavior occurred

In data from the schools, the attendance and grade records of the student involved are also recorded.

About the Problem Behavior
1. Description of the problem behavior
2. Date of occurrence
3. Day of week the problem behavior occurred
4. Time of day when the problem behavior occurred
5. Location of the occurrence
6. Whether or not the student was in the company of others when the problem behavior occurred

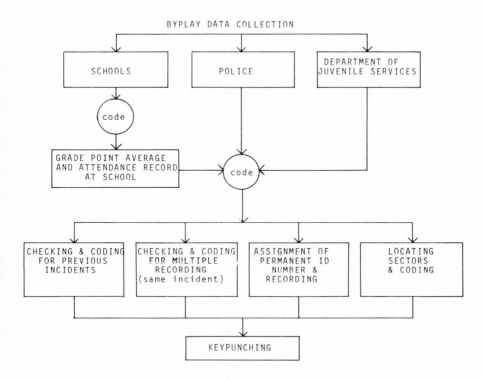

FIG. 1   Flow chart of BPLAY data collection system.

1. The data on the problem behavior incidents are collected at the Police Department, the Department of Juvenile Services, and the target schools
2. The collected information is numerically coded
3. The most recent grades of each student involved are located in the school records and a grade point average is computed
4. The grade point average information is coded on the sheet with the data on the problem behavior from the service agency
5. The coded sheets are brought to the IBR office for in-house processing, which includes:
   a. Checking and coding for previous incidents involving the same student
   b. Checking and coding for multiple recording of the same incident
   c. Assignment and recording of a permanent identification number
   d. Locating the student's home address and the place where the problem behavior occurred on the map and recording the sectors.
6. The completely coded sheets are key punched onto IBM cards.

About the Person Defining the Problem
   1. Who the problem definer is—status of the person
   2. Name of the agency the person represents
   3. Relationship between this person and the student involved
   4. Identity of person contacted about the problem behavior
   5. Whether the problem behavior was harmful to person or property

Police Department Data

Beginning in April 1971, effort was focused on gathering the Police Department data for the year 1970. This was completed by the end of June, and collection of the 1971 data began. As the backlog of data was reduced, the Police records and clerical procedures were examined to identify the optimum timing for the BPLAY data collection. It was determined that if the BPLAY collection were kept one month behind the current date, fewer than 1% of the target cases would be missed.

The Police used two kinds of forms to record incidents: J-1 forms, which are formal youth reports, and J-2 forms, which are field reports. The data collectors code from both of these, scanning the files for BPLAY target students—i.e., youths aged 12 to 17 years inclusive, who attend or last attended one of the 17 target schools. About 200 youth reports and 50 field reports each month involve members of the BPLAY target population. As a data collector can code 25–30 incidents a day, it takes one data collector 8–10 days/month to code the Police Department records.

Department of Juvenile Services Data

The collection of data from the Eastco Regional County Department of Juvenile Services (DJS) began in July. Much of the DJS case load comes directly from the Police Juvenile Office, and these cases are not coded because they would duplicate the Police records. Cases referred from other sources and walk-in cases are coded. On the average, DJS has 25 cases a month involving BPLAY target students.

DJS data are recorded on an intake interview form. Originally, this form did not call for recording the student's school and grade but, at BPLAY request, this information was added. A more serious problem was presented by a number of forms that were only partially completed, although sufficiently for DJS purposes. At first, only 50% of the forms carried all the information needed for the BPLAY research. However, through the cooperation of DJS, this situation was remedied.

The DJS records are filed alphabetically by the student's name, which is convenient for DJS purposes but inconvenient for BPLAY. DJS has therefore given BPLAY access to these records before they are filed. As a return courtesy, the BPLAY collector does the filing. It takes one data collector about 6 hr/week to do the DJS filing and BPLAY coding.

Target School Data

Collection of data from the target schools' disciplinary records presented many problems. Together, the 17 schools generated well over 3000 records a month— and this in spite of the fact that two of the schools were·not even keeping records. The record-keeping procedures varied widely from school to school, as did the criteria for determining which problem behavior incidents were to be recorded. At 15-min coding time per problem incident, data collection from all of the target schools would have been beyond BPLAY's resources. Consequently, it was decided to confine the collection to eight schools—a target senior high school, its four feeder junior high schools, and three control junior high schools. This cut the number of incidents to be coded to about 1000 a month. A staff of two full-time and three part-time data collectors, and a part-time clerk, has proved adequate to handle these eight schools.

Agreement Testing

In establishing the data collection system, a great deal of effort was spent establishing agreement between data collectors. The purposes of this task were to:

1. Establish coder agreement
2. Determine on which variables information was consistently available
3. Clarify category definitions
4. Establish clear rules and procedures for coding
5. Work out an efficient way of processing and handling the data

These goals had been accomplished by the end of March, when the first data were accepted as "good." Prior to that time, a battery of agreement tests was run between coders and the procedures were established. All of the preliminary work was done with police records.

The procedure used to establish intercoder reliability was for two data collectors to code the same cases independently. The coded sheets were then compared to identify items on which there had been disagreement. The data collection supervisor then examined those cases and decided how the items should have been coded. The cases were then discussed with the data collectors and any new rules, procedures, or categories were tested and recorded. On several tests, the supervisor also coded the cases independently of the two collectors to determine whether items coded the same way by the collectors had been coded correctly.

After April 1, 1971, coder agreement remained above 90%. After this desired level of reliability was reached, a system was established to provide an ongoing reliability test. Each collector had one (randomly selected) case coded by another collector daily, and the two records were checked for agreement. The data collection supervisor also checked the coding of the collectors on a regular basis.

A Preliminary Glance at the Baseline Data

In presenting the BPLAY data on juvenile problem behaviors, it is necessary to sound some cautionary notes:

1. These *are* baseline data. They do not reflect any of the BPLAY activities, which were in operation only on a small scale and in preliminary form in Year One.

2. The data cover a time period of 2 years. This is an extremely short time for observing complex phenomena in a large population responding to a multitude of stimuli. Fluctuations in the data may well be attributable merely to chance— or to variations in factors not directly related to the students or behaviors concerned, such as police procedures or public pressures. Care must be taken to avoid premature interpretation of the data. There is much in the information collected to invite speculation but nothing to justify definitive statements at this time.

With these considerations in mind, the following observations (based on the data collected from the Eastco Regional County Police Department) are presented. No school data are included in this chapter.

Student Incidents

The Police Department juvenile records are generated from events (excluding rape and homicide) involving persons under 18 years old. The BPLAY data base is restricted to youths between the ages of 12 and 17, inclusive, who attend, or last attended, one of the 17 target schools and excludes victimized persons. On the basis of a 4% sample (14 days of the year), this restriction results in BPLAY use of 32% of the Police Department records for youths in the indicated age group.

Under the BPLAY procedure for coding the police juvenile records, a single event, if it involves more than one target student, may generate more than one student incident (SI), which is defined as one student involved in an incident. The number of student incidents recorded for 1970 and 1971 is shown in Table 1.

The records for 1970 were inspected to determine how many individual students were involved and how many incidents each student was involved in. The results are shown in Table 2. (The table covers 2985 student incident records; the other seven have been omitted because the records are incomplete.)

TABLE 1
Number of BPLAY
Student Incidents Reported

Type of report	1970	1971	Total
Youth reports (J-1)	2098	2140	4229
Field reports (J-2)	903	1073	1976
Total	2992	3213	6205

TABLE 2
Distribution of Student Incidents Among Students, 1970

Number of students involved in 1 incident	1574
Number of students involved in 2 incidents	328
Number of students involved in 3 incidents	111
Number of students involved in 4 incidents	40
Number of students involved in 5 incidents	18
Number of students involved in 6 incidents	7
Number of students involved in 7 incidents	9
Number of students involved in 8 incidents	4
Number of students involved in 11 incidents	1
Number of students involved in 12 incidents	2
Total number of students involved in incidents	2094

The 2094 students with one or more police contacts during the year represented 9.75 percent of the target population (21,461 students enrolled in the 17 target schools in 1970). Of the students having police contacts, 75.2 percent were involved in only one incident during the year. (See Table 2.)

Table 3 illustrates the need for long-term investigation of such social phenomena as delinquency. It lists the age at which individual students first appear in the BPLAY records of police–student contacts. It cannot be assumed, however, that the figures in the table represent the age at which the students have their first contact with the police, for incidents that may have occurred prior to 1970 are not included and students younger than 12 years are systematically excluded. In 1970, the number of first BPLAY-recorded incidents constituted

TABLE 3
Age at which Individual Students First Appear
in the BPLAY Records of Police–Student Contacts

Age of student at time of 1st incident (years)	1970		1971		2½ months 1972		Totals	
	No.	%	No.	%	No.	%	No.	%
12	113	5.4	115	6.9	15	6.7	243	6.1
13	268	12.8	252	15.2	39	17.3	559	14.1
14	434	20.7	317	19.1	41	18.2	792	19.9
15	451	21.5	351	21.2	40	17.8	842	21.2
16	465	22.2	352	21.2	54	24.0	871	21.9
17	364	17.4	269	16.2	29	12.9	662	16.6
Unknown	–	–	1	0.06	7	3.1	8	0.2
Total	2095	100.0	1657	100.0	225	100.0	3977	100.0

70.3% of all recorded incidents during the year; in 1971, 51.6%; and in the first 2½ months of 1972, 47.6%. The percentage may be expected to decline further as more names are entered in the BPLAY files. Only after several more years of data collection will it be possible to trace the pattern of delinquency for ages between 12 and 17 inclusive by this means.

The number of student incidents recorded on the J-1 reports fluctuates with the day of the week and the season of the year. Figure 2 shows that Fridays and Saturdays account for a disproportionately large number of incidents—and this weekend peak should probably be larger, because many of the incidents recorded on Sunday originate before midnight on Saturday.

Problem Behaviors

The J-1 records of the Eastco Regional County Police Department list "reasons"—that is, the problem behaviors that have been the reason for the police action. Because more than one reason may be listed for any one student

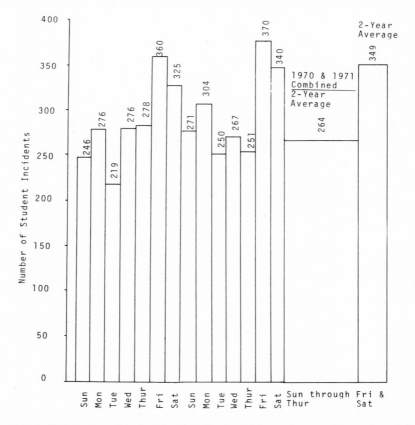

FIG. 2   Distribution of student incidents by day of the week over a 24-month period.

TABLE 4

Comparison of Student Problem Behaviors
in Six General Categories over a 24-Month Period

Behavior	Number
Aggression, person or property oriented	1236
Acquisitive behaviors	1119
Abuse of alcohol and other drugs	620
Behaviors involving motor vehicles	592
Avoidance behaviors	498
All other problem behaviors	440

1. Aggression, person or property oriented: disorderly conduct, vandalism, verbal assault or threat, fighting, use of obscenity

2. Acquisitive behavior: breaking and entering, shoplifting, petty or grand larceny, possession of stolen property, robbery, theft

3. Behavior involving alcohol or other drugs: alcohol, marijuana, solvents, hallucinogens, narcotics, depressants, stimulants: possession, sale, use, other

4. Behavior involving motor vehicles: unauthorized use of, or tampering with, motor vehicles; traffic problems; infraction of minibike laws

5. Avoidance behaviors: runaway, truancy, escapee/AWOL

6. Other behaviors: arson, gambling, improper dress, loitering, parent–child conflict, sex offense, suicide attempt, use or possession of weapon, misuse of telephone, manslaughter, filing a false report, curfew violation, out between 10:30 p.m. and 5:00 a.m., miscellaneous other offenses

incident, the number of problem behaviors is usually larger than the number of student incidents. Table 4 presents the data on problem behaviors for the years 1970 and 1971 grouped into six general behavior categories. Murder and rape are not included, because these are not classified as juvenile offenses.

Seasonal fluctuations in the number of student incidents are marked in the 1970 J-1 data shown in Fig. 3. The number increases abruptly at the beginning of summer (roughly defined as the 6-month period from the beginning of May to the end of October, when daylight savings is in effect). It drops off substantially for the three vacation months (June, July, and August). It may be speculated that the combination of long summer days and daylight savings gives the students more opportunity for getting involved in trouble than they have during the winter months, whereas the interruption of their social patterns during the vacation months may account for the relative decrease in recorded incidents

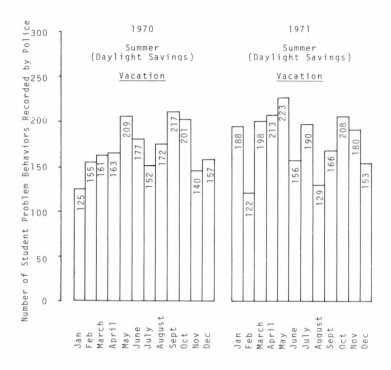

FIG. 3   Distribution of student incidents by month over a 24-month period.

during those months. However, the data for 1971 do not entirely support such an explanation.

In Fig. 4, the average monthly incidence of police–student contacts is compared with respect to school months vs. vacation months, winter months vs. summer months, and summer in-school months vs. summer vacation months. The data do not show any marked difference in the number of incidents in in-school months compared to vacation months or in winter months compared to summer months. There does appear to be a substantial difference between the number of incidents in in-school summer months and the number in summer vacation months. However, it will be necessary to accumulate data for several more years before the seasonal variations can be traced and distinguished from variations caused by other factors.

Figure 5 presents a breakdown of five of the general categories into specific behaviors. (The "all others" category is omitted because the figures for each specific behavior are too small for presentation on this scale.) It may be noted that, whereas the "avoidance behaviors" category was the smallest of the five categories (see Table 4), "runaway" was the single largest specific behavior recorded in any category.

The histogram in Fig. 6 shows a breakdown of the 2-year data for the six general behavior categories into 6-month increments. A notable feature of this chart is the remarkable stability of the figures on problem behaviors involving alcohol and other drugs. To investigate this further, the data on alcohol have been separated from those for other drugs, with the results shown in Figure 7. Note that the figures for alcohol and other drugs appear complementary—that is, when the number of behaviors involving alcohol increases, the number involving other drugs shows a compensatory decrease, and vice versa. The "mirror image" effect created by the contrapuntal fluctuations of the data on behaviors involving alcohol versus those involving other drugs is even more evident in Figure 8, where they are compared by 1-month increments.

It cannot be determined whether this complementary effect is an accidental occurrence peculiar to the 2 years covered by the data, or whether it indicates an

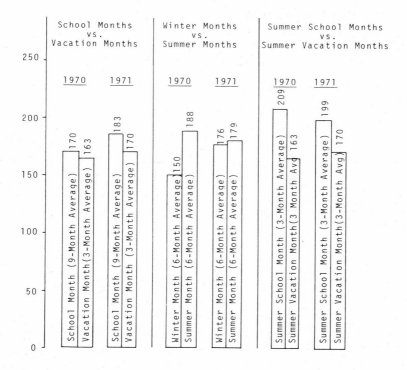

FIG. 4 Average monthly distribution of student incidents over a 24-month period.

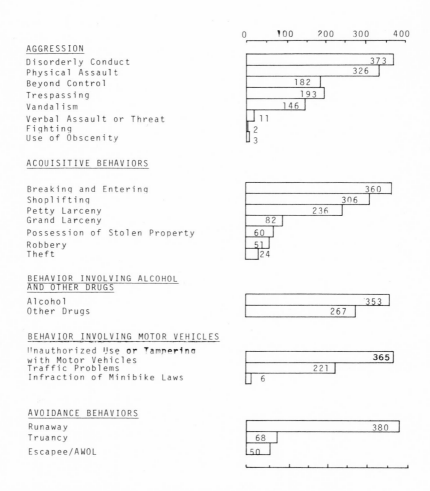

FIG. 5 Breakdown of student problem behaviors in five general categories over a 24-month period.

actual relationship, until data have been collected for a longer period. If the relationship proves real, it will affect future interpretations of the data on the use of psychoactive substances. For instance, an apparent decrease in the behaviors involving alcohol could signify, not an actual improvement, but a shift in the current fad from alcohol to other drugs with abuse potential. Therefore, any meaningful analysis of fluctuations in the use of any one type of drug would have to be made in the context of the incidence of use of the other drugs.

Confidentiality of Data

As is evident from the foregoing material, the BPLAY investigation is concerned solely with the numerical incidence of problem behaviors and their relationship to environmental conditions and events. The sole reason for temporarily recording the identities of the students involved is to eliminate duplications and to gather information on the distribution of behaviors among the student population. However, the identities are recorded in coded form and special precautions are taken to prevent identification of the students, even in the event of loss or

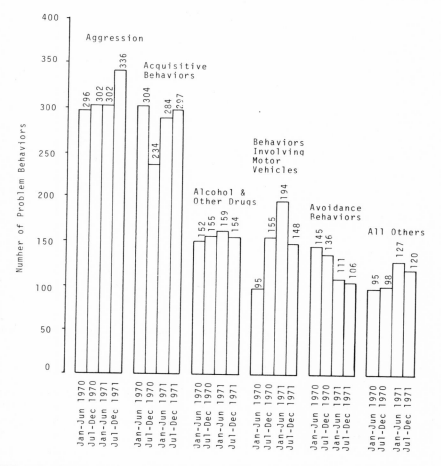

FIG. 6 Breakdown of the 1970–1971 data on problem behaviors into six-month increments.

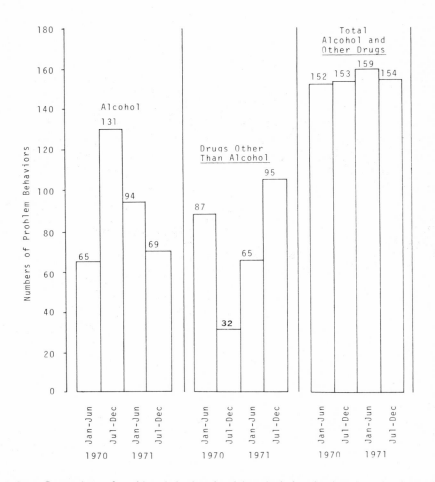

FIG. 7 Comparison of problem behaviors involving alcohol and other drugs by 6-month increments, 1970 and 1971.

theft of some of the materials. The lists of identity codes are kept in locked files separate from the locked files in which the other coded materials are stored. In the case of school data, coding is done at the school and the students are assigned temporary identity codes. The identity code listing is transported separately from the other coded material to the IBR offices, where new identity codes are assigned and the temporary listings are destroyed.

The procedures used have been approved by IBR's Committee for the Protection of Human Subjects, which operates under a general assurance of compliance with the Department of Health, Education, and Welfare policy on the protection of human subjects. The Institute is listed on the DHEW Forty-fifth Cumulative List of institutions whose assurances have been accepted. The procedures also have police and court approval.

CONCLUSION

BPLAY Year One was planned as a pilot year to be devoted to establishing good working relations in the target community, designing and implementing a data collection and analysis system, establishing a behavioral data baseline, conducting a baseline ethnographic evaluation of the community, and initiating and experimenting with both in-school and after-school programs of activities. The results of the year's work regarding community rapport and baseline data are summarized below.

Number of Juvenile Arrests from Target Population,
Aged 12 Through 17 (n = 21,000)

	Total Drug & Alcohol	Alc.	O.D.
Jan-Jun 1970	152	65	87
Jul-Dec 1970	153	121	32
Jan-Jun 1971	159	94	65
Jul-Dec 1971	154	69	85
	618	349	269

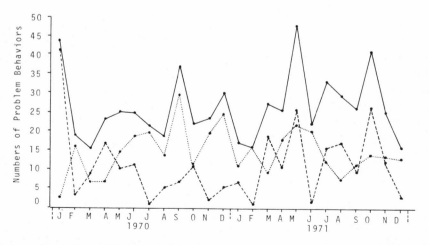

FIG. 8 Comparison of problem behaviors involving alcohol and other drugs by 1-month increments, 1970 and 1971. (— —) total; (• • •) alcohol; (— — —) other drugs.

Rapport with the Target Community

Notable success has been achieved in accomplishing the most difficult and delicate goal of the project—that of establishing good working relations in the target community. The BPLAY project staff members have realized that a certain amount of suspicion always attaches to an "outside" organization coming into a community to "do good" and to "show up," and possibly supplant, local community workers. They were also aware that the situation in Eastco Regional County was exacerbated because of the current conflict between the County and an agency of the Federal Government over school desegregation and busing. Consequently, they moved cautiously, making a low key introduction of the project into the community, working through local people and existing local organizations, and modifying their programs in the light of community reaction. It has been necessary for the BPLAY staff to exercise considerable restraint to do this, because it has involved accepting delays and tolerating ineffective procedures. However, this policy has paid off handsomely.

An extraordinary rapport has been established with the community. The schools have been not only cooperative but actively supportive. They have given BPLAY access to their disciplinary records and in some cases have established reporting procedures to provide the data needed by the project. They have sanctioned the broadcast of BPLAY announcements over their public address systems and have provided separate bulletin boards for display of promotional materials for BPLAY programs. They have permitted nonteacher managers of BPLAY programs to enter the school to meet with the students and make recruiting presentations. On occasion, school administrators have volunteered valuable advice on procedures. Considerable credit for the good relationships established with the school system must be given to a school liaison person supplied to BPLAY by the Eastco Regional County Board of Education.

Eastco Regional County Police have cooperated generously, giving BPLAY access to their records, providing the staff with working space in their facilities, and even adapting some of their reporting procedures to BPLAY needs.

A number of agencies in the community—the Targetville Recreation Council, the State Park and Planning Commission, the Red Cross, the Eastco Regional Plaza Merchant's Association, and others—have worked with BPLAY and accepted the project's techniques and support. BPLAY has helped promote local glass and paper recycling drives.

The first period of BPLAY's activity in the Targetville area has thus insured its acceptance by the community as an innovative and active agent interested in working with adolescents. It is not seen as an "outside" agency but as a resource for the community in providing its young people with constructive leisure-time programs.

Baseline Data Collection

BPLAY's collection of data on youthful problem behaviors in the project target area, although far from complete, has already provided a new perspective on delinquency problems. No equivalent picture of the nature, frequency, and relative seriousness of delinquent and predelinquent behaviors exists for any locality in the United States. The data presented in this chapter are drawn from police records for the years 1970 and 1971. When supplemented by information being gathered from some of the target schools, they throw considerable light on the relationships of youthful problem behaviors to community locations, events, and activity schedules. In addition, the project will make possible joint analysis of quantitative problem behavior information and qualitative problem behavior information and qualitative ethnographic findings. Such an "overview" will provide information valuable in determining the types of new leisure-time activities that will appeal to young people in the area and divert their energies to constructive, socially acceptable behaviors. It will also make it possible to determine how the scheduling of activities influences their popularity and effectiveness.

Finally, the multiprofessional IBR team has become an ongoing agency within the target community. Our new behavior schedules and activities, our training programs, and our insertion of operant research into the community has not yet aborted. It is hoped that the project will be fruitful.

9

The Achievement Place Model: A Community-Based, Family-Style, Behavior Modification Program for Predelinquents

Elery L. Phillips
Montrose M. Wolf
Dean L. Fixsen
Jon S. Bailey

University of Kansas

The predelinquent is a youth who, according to the local juvenile court, is in real danger of being classified as a "delinquent." From the standpoint of contemporary behavior theory, the misdeeds of the predelinquent youth are the result of deficiencies in his behavioral repertoire. His environment has failed to provide sufficient models, instructions, and reinforcement contingencies to allow him to develop a complete set of socially approved behavior. Therefore, prevention of the youth's eventual classification as a "delinquent" requires that he be exposed to an environment that does provide the examples, instructions, and corrective reinforcement contingencies necessary for him to learn the appropriate behaviors. The assumption is that once the appropriate behaviors have been established these behaviors will come into contact with the natural reinforcers that exist for those behaviors in the normal environment and that these natural reinforcers will assume the maintenance of the appropriate repertoire.

This chapter describes the Achievement Place model, a rehabilitative and educational environment designed to overcome the behavioral deficiencies of the predelinquent in his community. Before the program is presented in detail some general features of the program will be briefly introduced.

The Achievement Place model is based on 3 years of research at Achievement Place, a community-based, community-directed, family-style treatment program for six to eight boys between 12 and 16 years of age. Physically, Achievement Place resembles the typical group home. It consists of a large house (3500 ft^2 on each of two floors) with two adults and usually seven adolescent boys. Its similarity to the typical home is only superficial, however, instead of a pair of well-meaning but frequently ill-prepared house parents, the Achievement Place program is carried out by professional teaching parents. The teaching parents are actually teachers (thus teaching parents) in that their explicit purpose is to educate the youths in a variety of social, self-care, academic, and prevocational skill areas. Whereas many group homes only provide supervision, shelter, and food, Achievement Place is also an exceptional educational environment, as we shall describe. In order for the teaching parents to develop the educational environment at Achievement Place, it was necessary for them to become proficient in behavior modification procedures, remedial education techniques, juvenile law, and other areas. The key to the Achievement Place program is the teaching parents and therefore the key to successful replications of the program is the professional training of other prospective teaching parents.

The Achievement Place model is focused on eight major areas of concern. First, the treatment program is *community controlled* and therefore responsive to the unique characteristics of the particular community or neighborhood that it serves. This responsiveness is insured by placing the responsibility for the program in the hands of a local board of directors that is representative of all facets of the community. The board of directors is responsible for the physical facility and all financial matters. Also, the board of directors, in cooperation with the teaching parents, probation officers, teachers, representatives of local church groups, and other interested citizens, select the specific goals of the treatment program. The board of directors is represented as well on the Candidate Selection Committee, which is usually composed of a school official, a juvenile court official, a social worker from the welfare department, and the teaching parents. This committee selects candidates who are most in need of treatment, i.e., are the greatest threats to the community, the school, and their homes. The board of directors is also responsible for periodically evaluating the program and recommending any changes they deem necessary. Therefore, through the board of directors, the community has control of, and responsibility for, the entire program.

Second, the program is *community based*. A boy's problems exist in his community and should be dealt with there, in his school, in his home, and in his peer group. When a boy enters the program, he continues to attend his own school and the teaching parents in cooperation with the boy's teachers can help solve his problems in that school setting. Weekend home visits are encouraged and the teaching parents have frequent discussions with the boy's parents concerning problems that exist and improvements that have been made. Furthermore, Achievement Place provides a new and semipermanent peer group for the boys. Each boy who enters the program comes under the influence of a peer group that has already adopted many of the goals of the program. Both the peers and the teaching parents therefore serve as examples of appropriate behavior. Even after a boy leaves the program he can remain a member of the Achievement Place peer group and can continue to visit the home, eat an occasional meal there, or spend the night. Another advantage of having a community-based program is that the people in the community can see the changes in a boy's behavior as it occurs. This often leads to further improvements in a boy's behavior because the people who used to be critical of him now treat him differently.

Third, the program offers *family-style treatment*. Each facility operates with a set of teaching parents who live in the home 24 hr/day and a "family" of six to eight boys between 12 and 16 years old. The small group allows the teaching parents to interact extensively with each boy and thus to produce a great amount of change in a short period of time. The teaching parents and the boys come to know each other quite well and there is therefore ample opportunity for many social behaviors that occur only in small family groups. One further advantage of a family-style program is that it can be used by communities of any size. Small rural communities may only require one facility because their youth populations are small. Larger urban communities may require many more facilities scattered throughout the community. In larger communities some of the facilities may "specialize" and only take boys or girls who are having a particular type of difficulty in school or in the community. Even in larger communities, however, each family-style, community-based facility can be controlled by the neighborhood or immediate area it serves in order to insure community cooperation and accountability.

Fourth, the program is directed by a pair of *professionally trained teaching parents*. The teaching parents are actually teachers in that their explicit purpose is to educate the youths in the academic, social, and self-help and prevocational skills that make up the curriculum of the educational program at Achievement Place. The professional training (an M.A. program with a specialization for teaching parents) which has aided the teaching parents in educating the youths at Achievement Place includes proficiency in such areas as behavior modification procedures, remedial education techniques, juvenile law, and community relations. Because all aspects of the program are directed by the teaching parents, successful dissemination of the program must include the professional training of other prospective teaching parents.

The fifth major area of the Achievement Place model is emphasis on *individual treatment*. Because no two boys have identical backgrounds or identical problems, the treatment they receive is also individualized. The treatment program and specific behavioral goals for each boy are based entirely on the behaviors that members of his family, his school, his community, and the teaching parents believe should be changed. The motivation system used for all boys is uniquely suited to changing the individual behaviors of the delinquent or dependent— neglected boy.

The sixth emphasis is *supervised self-government*. After a few weeks of training the youths learn the skills that are needed to participate in the semi-self-government of Achievement Place. The youths learn to help make decisions about new rules, rule violations by their peers, and about consequences for those violations. The teaching parents must, of course, retain final responsibility but even so, the youths can make the majority of these decisions themselves with supervision and suggestions from the teaching parents. An important goal of the Achievement Place program is to teach group decision making and the skills of negotiation, compromise, and discussion that can be used by the youths in other family and community settings.

The seventh area is *evaluation*. The treatment program is based on a motivational system that provides constant feedback to the teaching parents concerning the daily progress of each youth. The overall program is also evaluated by routinely following the progress of each youth after he leaves the program and modifications of the program can be made on the basis of particular difficulties a boy has after he leaves the program. In addition, specific procedures for changing a given behavior can be evaluated by the teaching parents by observing the effectiveness of those procedures under specified conditions. Evaluation at all three levels (individual progress, overall program, and specific procedures) is necessary in order to refine the program and improve its efficiency and effectiveness.

The eighth major area of concern is *application*. The overall program and the specific procedures contained within it have been developed to produce desired changes in the goal behaviors and yet to be sufficiently practical to allow application by one set of teaching parents. Too often, researchers have developed programs that can be used only by other similarly trained researchers and not by practitioners who could most benefit others by their use. The research staff has made every attempt to develop procedures that can be effectively used by the professional teaching parents. For example, the teaching parents learn to use the youths themselves as "peer trainers" of each new youth and to enlist the aid of parents and teachers in obtaining information about the day-to-day progress of each boy.

MEASUREMENT AND EVALUATION

The goals of a program based on the Achievement Place model should be carefully defined in terms of observable behavioral objectives. This is very important although it is often difficult to do. Nevertheless, the assumption is that even the most complex behavioral objectives are definable in objective (rather than subjective) terms. If these behaviors can be defined objectively then they can be measured. We can measure the "objectivity" of a behavioral definition directly. Two observers can be presented with the behavioral definition and asked to record the behavior simultaneously and independently. The degree to which these independent observers can agree about the occurrence of the behavior is the degree to which the definition is objective. The technology of observer-measured behavior is well developed (Bijou, Peterson, & Ault, 1968) and has been applied in developing the behavioral objectives of Achievement Place.

We have established the objectivity of a number of the programs' behavioral goals in the areas of academic behavior, social behavior, self-care behavior, and prevocational behavior. We are therefore able to objectively measure and evaluate the individual progress of each boy in the program as well as to evaluate the effectiveness of the specific treatment procedures and the overall program.

SUBJECTS

All youths in Achievement Place have been declared dependent–neglected or delinquent by the County Juvenile Court and committed to the home for an indefinite period of time by the County Department of Social Welfare. With the exception of one youth, all have come from low-income families. For a youth to be considered for placement in Achievement Place, the following guidelines have been established. A youth should be 12–16 years old, not have committed a violent offense (e.g., murder or rape), and not have profound physical or mental handicaps (i.e., the youth's handicap should not be so severe that it would exclude him from public school or require medical assistance beyond that usually provided by Achievement Place). Some of the descriptive terms that have been used in records of parents, teachers, and court officials to describe the youths later committed to Achievement Place, are "aggressive," "inferior attitude," "poor motivation," "general lack of cleanliness," and "low interest." The presenting problems have included truancy, disruptive school behavior, failure in school, stealing, fighting, running away, vandalism, and lack of care and supervision in the home.

Most of the boys who come to Achievement Place are in or have been referred to special education classes. Most of these were soon reinstated in regular classes. Also, most of the candidates have been either suspended or were being considered for suspension from school. Again, all have been reinstated shortly after coming to Achievement Place. Eight of the Achievement Place boys have failed one or more grades before entering the program. None have failed since and, in fact, three boys have advanced an extra grade. The boys have averaged 19.4 days absent for the year prior to coming to Achievement Place. This has decreased substantially to an average of only 1.8 days after the boys have entered the program. In addition, each boy also has improved his grades after entering the program, although the change for some of the boys has been substantially greater than the change for others. Most importantly, however, none of the boys has failed a class after coming to Achievement Place.

For the 12 boys who have graduated from the Achievement Place program, the length of stay has averaged about 10 months and has ranged from 3 to 40 months.

FACILITY

Achievement Place is a two-story frame house that is licensed by the State Board of Health as a group boarding home authorized to care for up to eight boys of junior high to high school age. The first floor consists of a living room, dining room, kitchen, utility room, bathroom, and a separate bedroom, bathroom and study which is the teaching parents' living area. Four bedrooms, two bathrooms, and a recreation room for the boys are located on the second floor. A full basement and a large garage near the house provides space for a workshop, hobby area, and storage.

COST COMPARED TO TRADITIONAL TREATMENT

The cost of an Achievement Place study program is substantial, although it is a great deal less than the cost of traditional programs in large state institutions. For example, in 1970, operating costs were approximately $4000/year for each youth in an Achivment Place style setting that treated six youths. This compares with operating costs of between $8500 and $9000 per boy per year at the Kansas Boys Industrial School, a state institution for about 250 delinquent boys. Initial costs are also much greater for institutional programs. It costs between $20,000 and $30,000 per bed to construct a state institution, whereas it only costs between $6000 and $8000 per bed to purchase and extensively renovate a large older home that already exists in a community. Correction based on the Achievement Place model programs can therefore be expected to cost less than traditional institutional programs.

EDUCATION PROGRAM FOR TEACHING PARENTS

In order to disseminate the overall Achievement Place model treatment program a training program for teaching parents is available to give others the skills that are required for effective application of the model.

The qualification for candidacy is a college degree (preferably in psychology, sociology, or education) or the equivalent experience in a professionally supervised youth-related program.

The training program requires 9 months and results in a masters degree in Human Development or a certificate for noncollege degree holders from the University of Kansas. The curriculum centers on the following topics: behavior modification, remedial education, juvenile law, bookkeeping, nutrition, first aid, and community relations. These topics are discussed in detail in seminars and classes. Practicum experience at an Achievement Place-style training facility is also provided intermittently during this period. The curriculum for the training of professional teaching parents is equivalent to 30 academic hours. Some of these hours, such as those for a thesis, may be acquired while the teaching parents are directing their own treatment home. Close supervision and consultation are also provided during the first several months that the teaching parents are running their own home.

SETTING AND ENVIRONMENT

Daily Routine

On a typical school day the Achievement Place youths arise about 7 a.m. They shower, dress, and clean their bedrooms and bathrooms. Following a breakfast, some of the boys are assigned cleanup duties in the kitchen and others review homework before leaving for the public schools. Unless the youth is engaged in some school or community activity, he is expected to return home within half an hour after school is over. The youths usually have a snack (if they have earned that privilege) after school before beginning preparation of their homework. Once they complete their homework they are free to do as they please until bedtime at 10 p.m., depending, of course, on the privileges they have earned. On weekends some youths have jobs away from home, such as lawn mowing and caring for experimental laboratory animals at the University. Short trips or weekend outings are often planned for all members of the household.

The Motivation System

The motivation system is designed to provide a maximum amount of feedback to a boy when he first enters the program. Then, as the boy's skills and self-control develop, the structured program is faded out and replaced by a more natural set of feedback conditions. The fading of the structure is carried out in three "systems"; the daily point system, the weekly point system, and the merit system.

The motivation program begins by having the goal behaviors followed *immediately* by positive or negative consequences. In order to achieve this a token reinforcement procedure is applied. Some "token" (e.g., metal coin, poker chip, a mark on paper) that can be immediately and rapidly administered is used to bridge the delay between the occurrence of a target behavior and a future, less easily manipulated but more important consequence. At Achievement Place, tokens take the form of points. The youths are given points for appropriate behavior and have points taken for inappropriate behavior. Thus, the points can be "earned" (rewards) or "lost" (fines) immediately. Points are later used to purchase various "privileges" the youths have demonstrated they will work for.

On the *daily point system*, the system under which each new boy begins, the points earned on one day are used to buy privileges for the following day. This system is designed to minimize the delay between earning points and receiving some concrete privilege for doing so.

The *weekly point system* is very similar to the daily point system but points are accumulated over a 7-day period and privileges are purchased weekly rather than daily. On the weekly point system the goal behaviors continue to be followed immediately by points earned or lost but the delay between earning points and receiving privileges is extended from 1 day to 7 days.

In order to delay further consequences of behavior the *merit system* is instituted. Instead of having points immediately follow the goal behaviors, the teaching parents give social feedback to the youth for the appropriate and inappropriate behaviors he engaged in during the day. On the merit system all privileges are free but the youth must maintain an appropriate level of behavior in order to remain on this system.

As a youth progresses through the various systems, therefore, the consequences of the goal behaviors are gradually made more natural and remote. If a youth encounters difficulties on either of the advanced systems he can easily be returned to a more structured system for further training.

The privileges that the youths can buy with their points occur naturally in most homes. Table 1 lists the privileges available at Achievement Place. The "basic" privileges are sold as a package and include the use of tools, telephone, radio, and recreation room and the privilege of going outdoors. The "basics" must be purchased before any other privileges. Any or all of the other privileges can be purchased in any order. The "permission to leave Achievement Place" privilege allows the youth to attend extracurricular activities at school (e.g., sports events), go downtown, visit friends, and go home from Friday evening to Sunday evening. Permission must be obtained from the teaching parents before this privilege can be used. "Bonds" are accumulated by the youths to purchase

TABLE 1
Privileges That Can Be Earned with Points on the
Daily and Weekly Point Systems

	Price in points	
Privileges	Daily system	Weekly system
Basics (hobbies and games)	400	3000
Snacks	150	1000
TV	150	1000
Allowance (per $1)	300	2000
Permission to leave Achievement Place (e.g., home, downtown, sports events)	Not available	3000
Bonds (savings for gifts, special clothing, etc.)	150	1000
Special privileges	Variable	Variable

special items that are not available to them ordinarily. For example, 20 bonds are required to buy striped, bell-bottom trousers or other articles of clothing not usually provided by Achievement Place. The youths can also accumulate bonds to purchase their way out of Achievement Place and back to their natural homes. Sometimes the youths want to do something special. They can discuss this with the teaching parents and a price can be agreed on for the special privilege. The youths can then buy the special privilege whenever a sufficient number of points has been earned.

There is another set of privileges for "one-of-a-kind" opportunities that have no fixed price but are sold to the highest bidder, auction style. One example is the "car privilege," which entitles the purchaser to his choice of seating in the car for a week. Another auctioned privilege is the opportunity for a boy to use the record player for a week.

The prices of most of the privileges are constant from week to week. The economy of the system (the relationship between the total number of points that can be earned and the total cost of all the privileges) is arranged in such a manner that if a youth performs all the tasks expected of him and loses a minimum number of points in fines, he can expect to obtain most of the privileges without performing any extra tasks.

Most of the behaviors that result in points being earned or lost have been made very explicit. The goal behaviors and subcategories of goal behaviors are listed and defined. In addition, listed with each behavior is the approximate number of points that the behavior will earn or lose. Some of the behaviors and their point values are listed in Table 2. (A more detailed list is given in the Specific Behavioral Goals section, below.) There are still a few contingencies that are less formalized but still result in point consequences. For example, the teaching parents do sometimes give or take away points contingent on unusual behaviors they deem appropriate or inappropriate even though these behaviors have not as yet been defined.

Programs Designed to Achieve the Behavioral Goals

When a youth first enters Achievement Place he is placed on a *daily point system*. The youth is given a card on which to record his points and the teaching parents discuss with him the details of the motivation system, the privileges that can be earned, and the goal behaviors. On the first day the youth is given all privileges free. The points he makes and loses on the first day are tallied before bedtime and the difference is used to purchase privileges for the second day. This process is repeated each day thereafter.

The purpose of the daily point system is to minimize the delay between earning points and receiving some concrete privilege for doing so. For some youths, however, even a relatively short delay proves to be too long. These youths do not respond to the point contingencies and do not engage in simple behaviors regardless of the number of points the teaching parents make available

TABLE 2
Some Behaviors and the Number of Points That Can Be Earned or Lost

Behaviors that earn points	Points
Watching news on TV or reading the newspaper	300 per day
Cleaning and maintaining neatness in one's room	500 per day
Keeping one's person neat and clean	500 per day
Reading books	5–10 per page
Aiding teaching parents in various household tasks	20–1000 per task
Doing dishes	500–1000 per meal
Being well dressed for an evening meal	100–500 per meal
Performing homework	500 per day
Obtaining desirable grades on school report cards	500–1000 per grade
Behaviors that lose points	
Failing grades on the report card	500–1000 per grade
Speaking aggressively	20–50 per occurrence
Forgetting to wash hands before meals	100–300 per meal
Arguing	300 per occurrence
Disobeying	100–1000 per occurrence
Being late	10 per minute
Displaying poor manners	50–100 per occurrence
Engaging in poor posture	50–100 per occurrence
Using poor grammar	20–50 per occurrence
Stealing	10,000 per occurrence
Lying	5000 per occurrence
Cheating	1000 per occurrence

for him to do so. They are not yet "hooked" on points. Accordingly, these youths are placed on an item-exchange system that makes the privileges directly contingent on a required number of points (i.e., there is no delay between earning a required number of points and receiving some privilege). The youth starts with no privileges for the day. As soon as he earns a point difference of 400 points (see Table 1) he can buy the basic privileges. Immediately after he earns a cumulative point difference of 550 points he can buy the TV or snack privilege and if his point difference drops below 400 points, he loses the basic privileges. The youth soon learns the connection between earning points and obtaining privileges and is placed back on the daily point system. Under the daily point system the youth therefore acquires a working acquaintance with the point system and its consequences.

The criterion for advancing to the *weekly point system* is a minimum point difference of 1000 points each day for seven consecutive days. Once this criterion is met, the youth accumulates points over a 7-day period and buys privileges on a weekly basis. The direct consequences of behavior (points earned or lost) are still immediate. Although a youth buys privileges for an entire week, he must make a point difference of at least 1000 points each day to engage in those privileges. For example, if a youth makes a point difference of less than 1000 points on Monday, he loses all privileges on Tuesday. If he makes a point difference of at least 1000 points on Tuesday, all his privileges are reinstated on Wednesday. However, a youth with a point difference of less than 1000 can avoid the loss of privileges by volunteering for extra jobs and making a difference of 3000 points between 8 p.m., when points are tallied, and 10 p.m., bedtime. The youths quickly learn that it is much more pleasant to insure a daily point difference of at least 1000 than to lose all privileges for a day or to have to earn 3000 points in 2 hr.

A record of all points earned and lost is made on a 5 × 7 "point card" each youth carries. As shown in Fig. 1, the point card is used to record the number of points made and lost, the code corresponding to the behavior, a short description of the behavior, and the first initial of the person who gave or removed the points. At the end of each day, the earned and lost points are tallied and the difference is recorded on a cumulative weekly point sheet. This record, along with other measures, can be used to evaluate the progress of each youth.

The weekly point system is the "work horse" of the treatment program at Achievement Place. By making points contingent on objectively defined behaviors major changes are effected in all areas of the youth's behavior. Point consequences not only provide immediate, concrete feedback to the youths throughout each day but also provide a means of continuously evaluating each youth's behavior.

Because the world outside Achievement Place does not always provide immediate feedback for appropriate or inappropriate behaviors, the *merit system* has

Points	Code	Description	T-P	Points	Code	Description	T-P
8 0 0	A	News Quiz	E	3 0 0	S	Arguing with Robert	L
1 0 0 0	A	Two pages in Math Book	L	1 0 0	A	Late to start homework	L
3 0 0	S	Helping Lewis with speech	E	5 0 0	M	Failed to clean my bed-room	E
1 0 0 0	M	Wash dinner dishes	E	1 0 0 0	O	Bought manager	L
1 0 0 0	A	Daily Report Card in English	L				
		TOTAL MADE				TOTAL LOST	

FIG. 1   An example of a point card. The codes S, A, M, and O refer to social academic, maintenance, and other behaviors.

been devised. To be advanced to the merit system the youth must accumulate 100 bonds on the weekly point system. Seventy-five bonds can be purchased with points (at a cost of 1000 points each; see Table 1) and at least 25 must be earned on the daily or weekly school report cards, described below.

When a youth advances from the weekly point system to the merit system, he no longer carries a point card as there is no need to earn points. All privileges are given free. The only feedback available is in the form of verbal praise or reprimands when the youth does something right or wrong.

Because points can no longer be used to evaluate the progress of the youth, another method of evaluation must be employed. While on the merit system, the

MERIT SYSTEM EVALUATION SHEET

Name_____   Date_____

	BEHAVIORS	Ave. Freq. Week	M T W T F S S	M T W T F S S	M T W T F S S
SOCIAL	Appropriate language with peers				
	Appropriate language with adults				
	Pouting and sulking				
	Fighting, defiance, and anger				
	Manners and greeting skills				
	Hygiene and neatness				
	Promptness				
	Participation in self-government				
	Limit testing				
	Rowdiness				
CONSTANT MAINTENANCE	Room				
	Bathrooms				
	Constant jobs				
	Weekly jobs				
	Washing dishes				
OTHER MAIN.	Volunteering				
	Quality of work when he volunteers				
ACA.	Social behavior in school				
	Grades in school				
OTHER	Calls or reports by the public				
	Legal offenses				
	Home-visit reports from parents				

FIG. 2 An example of a merit system evaluation sheet.

youth is rated on the presence or absence of critical behaviors on a daily basis. These critical behaviors are important for all youths to have. In addition, there are certain idiosyncratic behavioral goals that are related only to a specific youth. The specific behaviors and the average frequency of these behaviors are determined by going over the last 4 weeks of weekly point system cards in order to make a checklist of certain behaviors he is expected to exhibit. After about 4 weeks of success on the merit system, the youth starts spending more and more time in his natural home with the natural parents helping with the evaluation and correction of the youth's behavior. Figure 2 shows one form used for the evaluation of merit system behaviors.

Specific Behavioral Goals

The aim of the Achievement Place program is to strengthen appropriate behaviors and to weaken inappropriate behaviors. The social, self-care, academic, and prevocational behavioral goals are chosen on the basis of their apparent importance to the youth's success in his current or future environment. These goals are established in consultation with the school, the youth's parents, the juvenile court, and the board of directors.

The lists of goal behaviors presented in Tables 3, 4, and 5 are representative. Each item in these lists, however, is only a label for a larger class of behavior. Each of these labels must be defined by its component behaviors and these described so that two people can agree about their occurrence. For example, the label "manners at meals" listed in Table 3 actually involves at least the following 10 behaviors:

1. Appropriate requests of "pass the _____ please"
2. Appropriate size of portions of food
3. Appropriate size of bites of food
4. Appropriate pace of taking bites of food
5. Appropriate clothes worn
6. Appropriate posture
7. Appropriate use of utensils
8. Inappropriate reaching in front of someone
9. Inappropriate voice level of content of conversation
10. Inappropriate placement of elbows on the table when a guest is present

Although the specific behavior list is not complete, it should convey the primary goals of the Achievement Place program.

One of the characteristics of predelinquents is their lack of social skills. They often react inappropriately to criticism and authority figures possibly because of their inability to communicate effectively. The youth should be able to interact and carry on a conversation with adults and peers (see Table 3).

A lack of personal cleanliness and of helping with chores around their homes are often characteristic of the youths who come to Achievement Place. A

TABLE 3
Social (Interaction) Skills

Increase in:	Decrease in:
Manners at meals	Loud arguing
Manners with guests	Physical fighting
Promptness	Temper tantrums
Cooperation	Insulting remarks
Advice seeking	Rowdiness
Persistance	Obnoxious habits
Correct grammar	Unusual demands
Correct articulation	Negative remarks
Conversational skills	Moodiness
Telephone skills	Aggressive statements
Modesty	Interrupting
Greeting behavior	Nagging
Aiding others	Bragging
Statements of pride	

primary goal at Achievement Place is therefore to improve the youth's personal hygiene and cooperation with routine chores (see Table 4).

One critical test of the effectiveness of the Achievement Place program is how the youth performs in the school, on the job, and in the community. The youth's success in these areas is clearly important to his future (see Table 5).

Procedure Evaluation

In this section are described four experiments that have been designed to evaluate the effectiveness of the motivational system in modifying some selected behaviors; reducing verbal aggressiveness, improving classroom behavior, improv-

TABLE 4
Self-Care Skills

Increase in:	Decrease in:
Cleaning skills	Untidiness
Maintenance skills	Bed wetting
Clothes washing and ironing skills	
Meal preparation	
Meal-serving skills	
Shopping techniques	
Pet care	
Tidiness of personal room	
Tidiness of bathroom	
Folding and hanging clothes	
Skills needed to buy and wear clothes	
Personal hygiene habits	
Dental hygiene	

TABLE 5
Academic, Vocational, and Citizenship Behaviors

Increase in:	Decrease in:
School grades	Classroom rule violations
Attending behavior in school	Forgetfulness
Care of school property	Inattentiveness
Tutoring skills for helping peers	Disruptive behavior
Homework	Gambling (unreasonable
Attendance	betting)
School activities	Lying
Promptness	Stealing
Use of tools and equipment	Cheating
Carpentry, plumbing, and electrical skills	Conning
Repair of small appliances	Wrecklessness
Interviewing skills	Mistreatment of pets
Budgeting and bookkeeping skills	Wastefulness
Participation in self-government	Pollution
Participation in community organizations	Carelessness
Knowledge of current events	
Helpfulness with fellow citizens	
Wise borrowing and lending	
Wise selection of companions	
Practice of safety rules	
Planning ahead	
Following directions	
Care of personal property	
Specific vocational skills (vocational school, college or military service)	

ing personal room cleaning, and improving leadership. These goal behaviors have been selected as examples to reveal the detailed manner in which these behaviors are defined and altered.

AGGRESSIVE STATEMENTS

One behavior pattern that characterized these youths was the "aggressiveness" they exhibited. The terms "aggression" and "aggressiveness" were noted in school records, psychological test reports, court notes, and in general comments from individuals who were familiar with the youths. Inquiry into the nature of the "aggressiveness" revealed it to be inferred almost completely from comments the boys emitted such as "I'll smash the car if it gets in my way" or "I'll kill you."

The following experiment was included in the teaching parents' program to measure and to reduce the aggressive verbal behavior. "Aggressive" phrases were recorded for three boys simultaneously for 3 hr each day (one session) while the youths were engaged in woodworking activities in the basement workshop.

Response Definition

Phrases emitted by the youths were considered to be aggressive if they stated or threatened inappropriate destruction or damage to any object, person, or animal. For example, the statement "Be quiet" was not counted as an aggressive response, while "If you don't shut up, I'll kill you" was recorded as an aggressive statement. Over 70% of the aggressive statements consisted of one of 19 phrases they used repeatedly.

Conditions

The experiment consisted of five successive conditions:

1. *Baseline.* The aggressive statements were just counted. There were no consequences for aggressive statements.

2. *Correction.* The boys were told what kind of statements were considered aggressive and that such statements should not be used. A corrective instruction by one of the teaching parents, such as "That's not the way to talk" or "Stop that kind of talk," was given each time a youth made an aggressive statement. An arbitrary period of approximately 3–5 sec was allowed to elapse after a response (or responses) before the corrective comment was made. This meant that a correction did not follow every aggressive statement; sometimes many responses were emitted before a corrective statement was made. The delay interval was employed in order to increase the probability that the boy had completed his speech episode before correction was administered by the teaching parents.

3. *Fines.* A fine of 20 points was made a consequence for each aggressive response. This condition was introduced unannounced.

4. *No Fines.* Points were no longer contingent on aggressive responses. There were occasional threats to reinstate the fines condition if the rate of responding did not decrease. The threats were worded approximately as follows: "If you boys continue to use that aggressive talk, I will have no other choice but to take away points." These threats were not carried out.

5. *Fines.* This condition was identical to the first fines condition except that fines were 50 points instead of 20. The onset of this condition was announced.

When the rate of aggressive responses during correction is compared with the baseline rate in Fig. 3, it can be seen that correction has reduced the responding of only one boy, whereas fines (20 points per response) have produced an immediate and dramatic decline in each youth's aggressive statements. Aggressive statements gradually returned when fines were no longer levied but were elimi-

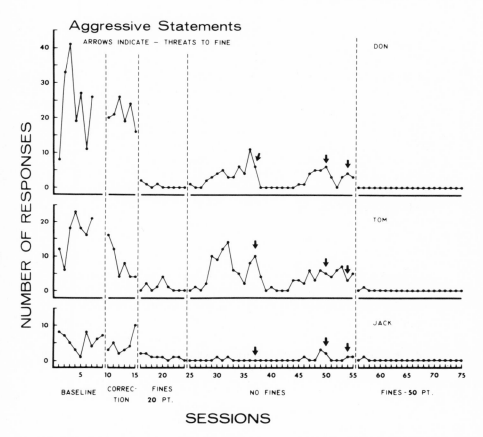

FIG. 3 Number of aggressive statements per 3-hr session for each youth under each condition. Arrows indicate threat to fine (Phillips, 1968).

nated when the fines condition was reinstated. Although the first threat (indicated by the arrows) in the no-fines condition did appear to have a large suppressive effect on the behavior, the last two threats appeared to have much less, possibly because the first threat was not carried out.

Interobserver agreement about the occurrence of aggressive statements was measured during 14 of the 75 sessions and averaged 92%.

Aggressive statements were only partially affected by verbal corrections from the teaching parents. However, fines for aggressive statements almost completely eliminated them. During the no-fines condition the aggressive statements increased, although they were still less than the original baseline rate. Threats during the no-fines condition had only an initial effect. The final fines condition reduced the rate to zero. From the data available, therefore, it is clear that aggressive statements could be affected by contingent points.

CLASSROOM BEHAVIOR

One goal of the academic program is to motivate the youths to obey classroom rules (each teacher has different rules) and attend to assigned materials and the teacher. The following are some of the specific behaviors that are required:

a. Complete homework on time.
b. Complete homework at 75% accuracy or better.
c. Arrive at class and be in seat before the bell rings.
d. Have proper seating posture in class (no sleeping).
e. Have proper dress.
f. Pay attention.
g. Study throughout the period.
h. Have no disruptive behavior.
i. Talk with permission only.
j. Obey classroom rules.

To accomplish the academic goals at Achievement Place, the school program is initiated soon after the youth enters the home. The youth begins by taking a *daily report card* to school each day for *each* class. An example of the daily report card is shown in Fig. 4. The teachers are asked to check whether the youth has done each of the items on the card during the class period. The letter grade in the last two categories is initially set at the level that the youth is

Daily Report Card

Name_____

Class_____

Yes No

☐ ☐ Paid attention and studies the whole period.

☐ ☐ Obeyed the classroom rules.

☐ ☐ Completed homework on time and earned at least _____.

☐ ☐ Earned at least _____ on quiz or exam.

_____   _____
Date   Signature, please use pen

FIG. 4 The daily report card that is completed by each teacher involved with the youths in the school program.

currently performing. After school, the youth takes the cards home to the teaching parents. If the cards are checked "yes" by every teacher in every category, the youth earns 1000 points. If the cards are not marked "yes" in every category, the youth loses 1000 points for each "no" he receives. If the youth does not receive a "no" for an entire week, he then receives a bonus of three bonds toward advancement to the merit system or 2000 points, whichever he chooses.

In addition to the daily report card, each youth takes a *weekly report card*, shown in Fig. 5, to each teacher on Fridays. This provides additional information about the youth's academic performance and no points are contingent on the weekly report card initially. After a youth achieves two consecutive weeks of perfect daily cards, he begins to take the daily cards on an intermittent basis (Tuesday and Friday only). A misbehavior that occurs on a "no card day" is marked by the teacher on the next "card day." Thus, the consequences for academic behavior gradually become more remote. If after 3 weeks of taking the daily report card on an intermittent basis the youth continues to receive a "yes" in every category on every card, the daily report cards are dropped and point consequences are put on the weekly card. The youth loses 1000 points for each "no" on the weekly card and loses 500 points for each category marked "fair." He earns one bond toward advancement to the merit system for each card with every category marked "yes." The consequences for the grade category vary according to the past performance of the youth. If the grade on past weekly cards was a C, the youth would receive 4000 points for an A, 2000 for a B, no points for a C, loss 1000 for a D, and lose 3000 for an F. The rule is that the youth makes 2000 points for each letter grade above his average and loses 1000 points for each grade below his average. After the youth achieves three consecutive weeks of a weekly card with each category marked "yes" and a letter grade at or above his average performance, he begins taking the weekly card on an intermittent basis. Eventually, the only feedback the youth receives is the 9-week report card regularly supplied by the public schools.

An experimental evaluation of the card system was carried out in a special classroom setting. Five boys from Achievement Place worked in math workbooks in a room equipped much as a regular school with desks, a blackboard, pictures on the walls, and a teacher whose role it was to answer questions and grade problems. From an observation booth adjacent to the classroom, observers recorded whether the boys were working in their workbooks or were being disruptive and/or inattentive (according to a set of detailed and reliable response definitions). As shown in Fig. 6, the first 3 days of the summer school the boys were perfect students, working diligently, not talking out or daydreaming. Then they began to "test" the teacher. In a few more days they became less attentive and more disruptive—exhibiting the same behaviors we had observed in their public school classrooms. In fact, they spend about 65% of their time talking,

Dear Teacher:

    Please evaluate for the week just completed ONLY.

                      Thank you.

Did _____ complete an acceptable percentage of his home-work assignment?				
Yes				
Fair				
No				
Was his behavior in class accept-able?				
Yes				
Fair				
No				
According to the amount and quality of his work, how would you grade him? (This is in relation to the class, not in relation to his ability.)				
A				
B				
C				
D				
F				
Has he been attending class every day?				
Yes				
No				
Is he behind in any work?				
Yes				
No				
Teacher's initials (Please use ink)				

Date _____

FIG. 5   The weekly report card that is completed by each teacher involved with the youths in the school program.

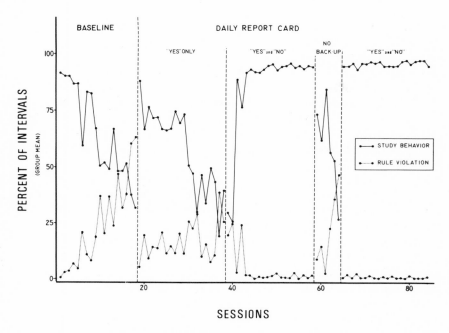

SESSIONS

FIG. 6 Percent of intervals of study behavior (●) and disruptive behavior (▲) in a special classroom (Bailey, Wolf, & Phillips, 1970).

getting out of their seat, looking out the window, and throwing their pencils, and only 35% of their time studying. Interobserver reliability of measures of study behavior and rule-violation behavior averaged 92%.

In the next step of the program, the boys were required by the teaching parents of Achievement Place to carry the daily report card. The boys were told that the teacher would check "yes" or "no" depending on whether a boy had "studied the whole period" and "obeyed the rules." If a boy got a "yes" in each category, he was assured of several privileges for the remainder of the day. However, if a boy got a "no" for one class period, he was told he would lose significant privileges at home for the rest of the day (snacks, TV, permission to go outdoors).

To assure precision in marking the daily report cards, the observers in the booth assigned the report card grades on the basis of the objective data. A 10% level for each behavior was set. That is, more than 10% nonstudy or rule violation led to a boy's being checked "no." As shown in Fig. 6, the report card and the consequences resulted in an immediate improvement in study behavior and a reduction in rule violation behavior of all the boys. They each studied and obeyed the rules better than 90% of the time. After 2 weeks of this superlative behavior the boys were told by the teaching parents that there would no longer be consequences on the daily report cards. After 3 days under this "no-back-up" condition the boys were at almost a 50% level of disruptive behavior and only 25% study behavior. When consequences were placed on the card again, a high level of classroom behavior emerged once more and remained at better than 90% for the remainder of the study.

A similar demonstration of the usefulness of home-based reinforcement has also been carried out in the public schools. Having demonstrated that these youths *can* study 90% of the time and have very few rule violations in a special class, we wanted to see if we could get these same results in a regular public school classroom.

First, we contacted the teacher and had her describe the type of problem behaviors the boys demonstrated in her class. We then worded this into a definition of study behavior and trained on observer to use the code. The observer was then sent daily to sit unobtrusively in the back of the class and to record whether the study behavior occurred or not for each 10 sec of the class period. At the end of each class period the observer computed the percent of the time the youth studied in the class.

As shown in Fig. 7, after several days of observation it was clear that study behavior occurred on the average of 25% of the time. The youth never studied more than 50% on any given day. The boy then began taking the daily report

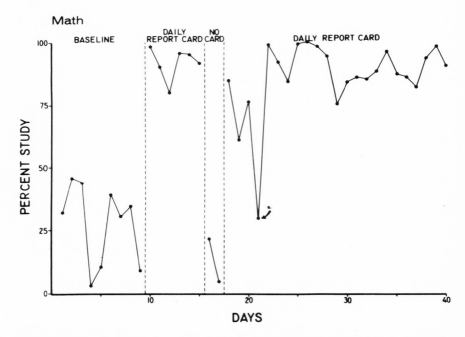

FIG. 7 Percent of intervals of study behavior in a public school mathematics classroom (Bailey, Wolf, & Phillips, 1970).

card. Study behavior suddenly increased to about 90% and remained there for a week. The boy then was told he did not have to take the card and study behavior immediately dropped to a very low level. He then was required to take the card again and study behavior once again incrased. This time, however, he began to "test" the teacher. When study behavior dropped to about 50%, the teacher marked him "no" (see arrow in Fig. 7), and he did not get his privileges for that day. The next day, study behavior was very high and it remained quite high for the rest of the year.

We have replicated this effect of home-based reinforcement on school behavior with several boys at Achievement Place and are convinced that it is a practical and effective system for helping these boys improve in school.

We have also completed an analysis of a fading system to determine its effects on study behavior. When a boy changes from the daily card to the Tuesday/Friday card, his study behavior drops only slightly (e.g., 90–85%). When he is then gradually faded into the weekly card there is an overall small decrement to about 80% study behavior. This is considered quite acceptable because our normative data indicates that a "good" student (suggested by the teacher) studies from 85% to 95% of the time. A rate of 80% study behavior is acceptable and, in most cases, a two- to threefold increase over baseline for these youths.

As can be expected, grades do not improve as dramatically as study behavior, for the youths' academic repertoires are usually quite impoverished. Nevertheless, the grades do gradually improve. In the case described above, the boy's grades improved from C– to B+ over the course of the experiment. Other improvements, from F to D+ or C–, may not appear to be very great but these increases are sufficient to prevent the youth from being placed in special education or being held back a grade.

We also have had reports from the boys that when their study behavior improves, they begin to receive positive social feedback from the teachers and the other students in class.

PERSONAL ROOM CLEANING

Response Definitions

Below is the list of definitions used to measure the cleaning of the boy's rooms. Each of the areas must meet the definition in order for the room to be considered cleaned. Each area was also scored for the number of items that met the definition, up to a maximum. The maximum number of items is described for each area. This detailed response definition is presented as an example of the degree of detail often required for reliable measurement.

1. *Dirty Clothes.* All clothes that are not neatly placed in the wardrobe, dresser, or closet should be in the dirty clothes hamper (in utility room). In

other words, there should be no clothes visible without opening doors or drawers (max. = 13).

2. *Shades and Windows*. Windows should be closed and the shades should be within 3 inches of the middle of the window (max. = 4).

3. *Beds*. No objects on the bedspread. This includes the blankets that may be folded at the bottom of the bed (the blanket should be in the hall closet).

Pillows must be within 6 inches of the head of the bed. The pillow should not deviate more than 6 inches from side to side. This means that the pillows should be centered with a *difference* of less than 6 inches from either side of bed to pillow.

The bedspread must be tucked in under the pillow at least 1 inch, resulting in a line across the bed (pillow line). The pillow line should not deviate more than 3 inches from a straight edge that is 90° to the edge of the bed and is touching the lower edge of the pillow line.

No specification for the condition of the bed above the pillow line is made other than those already given.

No wrinkles greater than 12 × 1 × 1 inches should exist below the pillow line and within the boundaries of the bedspread "cords." The cords of the bedspread are the raised area that runs parallel to the edges of the bedspread about 9 inches from the edges. The cord toward the outside edge of the bed should not deviate more than 1 inch from the cord of the mattress that may be felt throughout the bedclothes.

The bed should be made with two sheets, one pillow with case, no blankets, and the bedspread. None of these objects should be visible except the bedspread when the observer looks below the steel frame that runs around the lower edges of the bed (max. = 20).

4. *Floors*. No objects on the floor other than furniture (bed, wardrobe, desk, chair, dresser), rugs, waste basket, and electric cords. This does not include the closet floors.

Rugs should be straight with the edge of the bed with no more than 2 inches deviation from side to side. They should be within 1 ft of the bed but not under the bed. Of course, this does not count if there is no rug (max. = 15).

5. *Closets*. All clothes in the closet should be on hangers except for hats, shoes, gloves, ties, and belts.

Shoes should be on the closet floor with toes or heels touching some wall and the sides of the shoes touching in two places. Both shoes should be facing the same direction. The only objects that may be on the closet floor are shoes.

All hangers should be in the closets and hanging on the cross bar. There are no requirements as to the condition of the shelves except for those already set forth above (max. = 15).

6. *Doors and Drawers*. All doors should be closed and all drawers should be closed. No more than ½ inch *space*. If clothes are sticking out of doors and drawers, it counts under "dirty clothes," but also counts here if it causes the door

or drawer to be open. Clothes should be stacked neatly in drawers. All personal objects should also be kept neatly in drawers (max. = 4).

7. *Furniture.* All furniture should be within 8 inches of the wall and one end should not deviate from the other more than 3 inches (max. = 4).

8. *Desk.* The desk should be clear of all objects except for a lamp, clock, and tissue box. All of these objects should be within 1 inch of the edge of the desk and must not extend over the edge. The lamp should be in one of the far corners and must be within 1 inch of either edge. The seat of the chair should be under the desk with the back of the chair within ½ inch of the desk (max. = 10).

9. *Surface Tops.* Dresser and wardrobe tops must be clear of all objects (max. = 10).

10. *Baskets.* Baskets should be free of all objects (max. = 5).

Interobserver agreement of bedroom cleaning as defined above averaged 99%. The reinforcement contingency involved points being earned for each time completed when the overall score was 80% or above. Points were lost for each uncompleted item when the overall score was below 80%.

Results

The first points condition in Fig. 8 shows the almost perfect level of tidiness of the rooms for all of the boys. At this point the contingency had been in effect

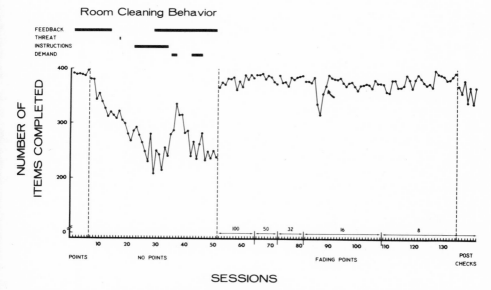

FIG. 8 Number of items completed each day (100 possible for each youth) for all youths under each condition (Phillips, Phillips, Fixsen, & Wolf, 1971).

for 2 months. As can be seen, the boys met about 90% of the criteria. When the contingency was removed the number of items completed fell drastically. The effects of a number of variables were probed during the reversal (no points) period. Feedback was given during the first points condition and was continued during the beginning of the reversal period. The feedback consisted of a diagram of the rooms and indicated the exact nature of the items that did not meet criteria. As can be seen in Fig. 8, neither discontinuing nor reinstating this feedback procedure during the reversal stage appeared to have any effect. When the points condition was reinstated, without the feedback, there did not seem to be any loss of control. Apparently, although precise feedback may have been functional in the beginning, it clearly no longer was.

Several other probes were made during the reversal period: *instructions* that they clean their rooms and a *threat* to reinstate the point contingency if they did not clean their rooms produced no change in the youths' room cleaning behavior. *Demands* that they "get up and clean their rooms *now*" resulted in the boys going to their rooms and engaging in apparent room straightening behavior. The first group of threats also produced an increase in appropriate behavior. However, after the original threats were not backed up, the remaining threats had almost no effect on the room cleanliness measure.

In the third phase, when the point contingency was reinstated, the room cleaning behavior immediately increased. The contingency was then slowly withdrawn. During the fading points condition the percentage of days when the contingency occurred was reduced from 100% to 50%, then to 32%, to 16%, and finally to 8%. Although the points were given on a variable and intermittent schedule during the fading points condition, the cleanliness of the bedrooms was measured every day.

When the intermittent contingency was first introduced, an "adjusting consequence" was added in order to avoid reducing both the frequency and magnitude of points at the same time. Under the "adjusting consequence" the potential number of points that could be earned or lost accumulated each day the contingency did not occur. Thus, if the contingency was finally applied after 5 days, five times as many points would be earned or lost than if the contingency had occurred on successive days. This "adjusting consequence" was discontinued at the arrow in Fig. 8 and a fixed number of points occurred as the consequence for each intermittent contingency thereafter with no loss of control. The value of this new consequence was equal to a week's accumulation under the adjusting consequence.

During the postchecks condition the behavior was measured for almost 1 year and the behavior did not drop below 80%.

One question often asked is whether there is any way to maintain certain behaviors without continued application of points. This study demonstrates one method of fading the point consequences. Point rewards and fines were faded from 100% to 8% of the time with no reduction of effectiveness. Later (post-check) we found that the behavior maintained for over a year at an acceptable level.

LEADERSHIP

The manager is one of the boys who purchases the privilege of being manager and of administering points to his peers. His duties consist of seeing that a specified list of tasks, such as taking showers and cleaning the bathrooms, yard, and basement, are accomplished each day. The manager has the authority to give and take points depending on the quality of the job completed. In turn, the manager earns or loses points according to whether the tasks are accomplished or not and, whenever possible, as a function of the quality of work.

Following is a sample list of tasks that the manager oversees each day:

1. Have the boys up on time.
2. Have the boys brush their teeth.
3. Insure that all the dirty clothes are in the clothes hamper.
4. Have someone help set the table.
5. Have the bathroom cleaned each morning.
6. Check to see whether everyone has done his homework.
7. Make sure the windows are closed before going to bed.
8. Make sure the doors are locked before going to bed.
9. Check to see that everyone takes a shower.
10. Have all the boys in bed on time.

Fines and Rewards

The manager earns points for each task completed. Some tasks are worth more than others but overall he makes approximately 1500 points a day. The manager in turn can pay approximately 1500 points or remove 1500 points from the boys working for him in order to get the job completed.

Modification

The example used to evaluate the effectiveness of the managership is bathroom cleaning. Following are samples of the specific criteria required for reliable measurement of bathroom cleanliness:

1. *Sink*. Should be able to pass the "white glove test" (a Kleenex tissue is used). No objects should be on the sink other than the soap and soap dish. No water should be on the sink.

2. *Towels*. There should be one towel and one washcloth per hanger. No edge of a towel should extend beyond another edge of the same towel by more than 2 inches.

3. *Floor*. There should be no objects greater than ¼ × ¼ × ¼ inches and not enough dirt or dust to cover an area of ¼ × ¼ × ¼ inches. If rugs are required, they should be centered under the sink (less than 6 inches deviation from one side to the other) within 1 ft of the wall (the wall edge of the rug should not be closer than 10 inches and not further than 14 inches away from the wall).

Procedures and Results

Sixteen cleaning tasks (similar to the ones above) in the bathroom involving the sinks, stools, floors, etc. were scored as accomplished or not accomplished. The bathrooms were scored every day between 12:00 and 12:30 p.m., except in the baseline condition, where recording was done as soon as the boys reported that the cleaning had been completed (usually before noon). Consequences, if there were any, were levied immediately after inspection.

Conditions

The experiment was conducted with six successive conditions.

1. *Baseline*. The baseline condition consisted of instructing all the boys to clean the bathrooms. No consequences were given for their behavior other than the instruction that they clean the bathrooms again if fewer than four of the tasks had been accomplished.

2. *Manager*. During the manager condition one boy was given the responsibility for cleaning the bathrooms daily. He picked the individual, or individuals, to clean the bathrooms each day and then paid or fined the workers (20 points lost or gained per task) according to the quality of their work as judged by him. Later, when the bathrooms were checked by the teaching parents, the manager received or lost points (20 points per task). The manager earned points only if 75% or more of the tasks were completed. The privilege of being manager was auctioned to the highest bidder each week.

3. *Group*. The group condition consisted of all boys being responsible for cleaning the bathrooms and subject to the same fines. There was no manager. The boys were fined when less than 75% of the 16 tasks were completed. The amount of fines varied from 20 to 300 points.

4. *Manager*. This condition was identical to the first manager condition.

5. *Group*. Identical to the first group condition except that the fines were 100 points.

6. *Manager*. Identical to the first and second manager conditions.

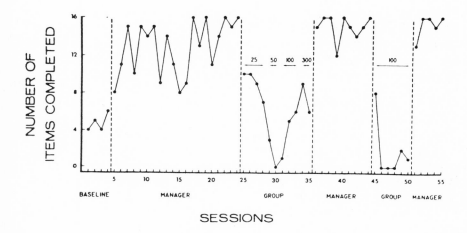

FIG. 9 Bathroom cleaning behavior, manager system vs. group contingency, showing number of tasks accomplished per session for each condition. The numerals above the arrows indicate the possible number of points that can be lost or gained for the sessions indicated by the horizontal arrows (Phillips, 1968).

As shown in Figure 9, the point consequences levied by the manager under the manager condition were more effective than the fines administered by the teaching parents under the group condition, even when the value of the fines under the group condition were greater than those administered by the manager. The greater effectiveness of the manager condition may have been the result of the differential contingencies for each boy administered by the manager.

Table 6 shows the average number of points lost per boy each day under each condition. Table 6 shows clearly that the managership was not purchased

TABLE 6
Average Number of Points Lost per Session by the Workers and
Manager under Each Condition[a]

	Baseline	First manager	First group	Second manager	Second group	Third manager
Worker	0	18	73	13	100	0
Manager	0	64	–	20	–	15

[a]From Phillips (1968).

because it was possible to earn a large number of points as a manager. The manager consistently lost more points than the workers he supervised. Item-by-item interobserver agreement about the accomplishment of the bathroom cleaning tasks for 20 sessions ranged from 83% to 100% agreement and averaged 97%.

As can be seen in Figure 9, under the baseline condition, when the boys were simply instructed to clean the bathrooms, very few of the items were completed. When the manager condition was put in for the first time, it took about 2 weeks for an acceptable level of bathroom cleanliness to occur. The manager condition was then discontinued and point contingencies were placed on the entire group. As can be seen, various point values that were applied did not produce the level of tidiness that the managership accomplished.

Other detailed descriptions of procedures that have been found to be effective in modifying social, academic, self-help, prevocational and self-government behaviors at Achievement Place have been described in reports by Phillips (1968), Bailey, Wolf, & Phillips (1970), Phillips, Phillips, Fixsen, & Wolf (1971), Braukmann, Maloney, Fixsen, Phillips, & Wolf (1971), Timbers, Phillips, Fixsen, & Wolf (1971), Bailey, Timbers, Phillips, & Wolf (1972), Fixsen, Phillips, & Wolf (1972), Fixsen, Wolf, & Phillips (1972), Phillips, Wolf, & Fixsen (1972), Wolf, Phillips, & Fixsen (1972), and Wolf & Risley (1971).

PROGRAM EVALUATION

The preliminary results of the Achievement Place program indicate that the individual behavior modification procedures are effective in correcting a number of social, academic, self-care, prevocational, and family living behavior problems. However, evaluation of the overall effectiveness of the Achievement Place program is just in the preliminary stages, and it will be a few years before we will have enough followup data for a meaningful evaluation of the effects of the overall program. Our plan is to compare the adjustment of the Achievement Place graduates with that of two comparison groups consisting of boys who have been placed on probation and boys who have been sent to the state reformatory. We will compare these boys on school performance, police contacts, court records, and employment.

CONCLUSION

The Achievement Place program has used an applied behavioral science approach to the development of community treatment for predelinquents. The goal has been to devise and evaluate a practical treatment program that is effective in reducing delinquent and predelinquent behavior. The approach we have taken has been to informally try various procedures until one seems to work and then to experimentally evaluate this procedure to determine its measurable effectiveness. We feel that this commitment to an applied research approach is the way to the solution to many of the important problems of our society.

Although the program continues to be refined and expanded to include more goal behaviors, the Achievement Place model represents, at the present time, a seemingly effective and practical alternative to placing youths in institutions. Because probation is relatively inexpensive and does not require removing the youth from his home, most youths should be placed on probation before more drastic treatments are attempted. Those youths whose unlawful behavior continues can next be removed from their natural homes and placed in a family-style treatment program such as Achievement Place. Although the youth no longer lives at his natural home he can still remain in contact with his parents, his friends, his school, and community while professional treatment is being carried out. Only when all community resources have been exhausted should a youth have his ties with his home and community severed by placing him in a reformatory or mental hospital, for the potentially harmful effects of institutionalization have been well documented.

Although this sequence reflects the philosophy of most juvenile courts, many communities have limited resources and juvenile judges are too often faced with the choice of placing a youth on probation for the third or fourth time or committing the youth to a state institution outside the community. The development of such community-based resources as Achievement Place can provide the court with an important alternative to institutionalization.

ACKNOWLEDGMENTS

The development of the treatment program and the research reported in this chapter were supported by grant MH16609 from the National Institute of Mental Health (Center for Studies of Crime and Delinquency) and by grant HD03144 from the National Institute of Child Health and Human Development to the Department of Human Development and Bureau of Child Research, University of Kansas. At earlier version of this report was presented at the Delinquency Prevention Conference, Santa Barbara, California. A great debt of appreciation is owed to the Board of Directors of Achievement Place, the Douglas County Department of Social Welfare, the Douglas County Juvenile Court, and the citizens of Lawrence, Kansas for their untiring cooperation and support of the research and development of the Achievement Place treatment program. Further information about the Achievement Place program can be obtained by writing the authors, Bureau of Child Research, 211 Haworth, University of Kansas, Lawrence, Kansas, 66044.

REFERENCES

Bailey, J. S., Wolf, M. M., & Phillips, E. L. Home-based reinforcement and the modification of pre-delinquents' classroom behavior. *Journal of Applied Behavior Analysis*, 1970, 3, 223–233.

Bailey, J. S., Timbers, G. D., Phillips, E. L., & Wolf, M. M. Modification of articulation errors of pre-delinquents by their peers. *Journal of Applied Behavior Analysis*, 1972,

Bijou, S. W., Peterson, R. F., & Ault, M. H. A method to integrate descriptive and experimental field studies at the level of data and empirical concepts. *Journal of Applied Behavior Analysis*, 1968, 1, 175–191.

Braukmann, C. J., Maloney, D. M., Fixsen, D. L., Phillips, E. L., & Wolf, M. M. An analysis of the effects of training on interview skills. Paper presented at the American Psychological Association, Washington, D.C., September, 1971.

Fixsen, D. L., Phillips, E. L., & Wolf, M. M. Achievement Place: The reliability of self-reporting and peer-reporting and their effects on behavior. *Journal of Applied Behavior Analysis*, 1972,

Fixsen, D. L., Wolf, M. M., & Phillips, E. L. Achievement Place: Experiments in self-government with pre-delinquents. *Journal of Applied Behavior Analysis*, 1972, in press.

Phillips, E. L. Achievement Place: Token reinforcement procedures in a home-style rehabilitation setting for "pre-delinquent" boys. *Journal of Applied Behavior Analysis*, 1968, 1, 213–223.

Phillips, E. L., Phillips, E. A., Fixsen, D. L., & Wolf, M. M. Achievement Place: Modification of the behaviors of pre-delinquent boys within a token economy. *Journal of Applied Behavior Analysis*, 1971, 4, 45–59.

Phillips, E. L., Wolf, M. M., & Fixsen, D. L. An experimental analysis of governmental systems at Achievement Place. *Journal of Applied Behavior Analysis*, 1973,

Timbers, G. D., Phillips, E. L., Fixsen, D. L., & Wolf, M. M. Modification of the verbal interaction behavior of a pre-delinquent youth. Paper presented at the American Psychological Association, Washington, D.C., September, 1971.

Wolf, M. M., Phillips, E. L., & Fixsen, D. L. The teaching-family: A new model for the treatment of deviant child behavior in the community. In S. W. Bijou & E. L. Ribes (Eds.), *First symposium on behavior modification in Mexico*. Academic Press, 1973.

Wolf, M. M., & Risley, T. R. Reinforcement: Applied research. In R. Glaser (Ed.), *The Nature of Reinforcement*. Columbus, Ohio: Charles E. Merrill Books, 1971, 310–325.

10
Social Learning Analysis of Aggression

Albert Bandura

Stanford University

Psychological explanations of aggression have been largely concerned with individual injurious acts that are aversively motivated. In most of these accounts aggression is not only attributed to a narrow set of instigators but the purposes it presumably serves are limited. Inflicting injury and destruction is considered to be satisfying in its own right and therefore the major aim of aggressive behavior. Because aggression has many determinants and serves diverse purposes, theoretical formulations couched in terms of frustrating instigators and injurious aims have limited explanatory power (Bandura, 1973). Social learning provides a general theory intended to be sufficiently broad in scope to encompass conditions governing all facets of aggression, whether individual or collective, personally or institutionally sanctioned.

For purposes of the present discussion, aggression is defined as behavior that results in personal injury and in destruction of property. The injury may take the forms of psychological devaluation and degradation as well as physical harm. Although injury is the major defining property of aggression, it also entails social labeling processes that determine which injurious acts are likely to be judged aggressive. Destructive behavior may be labeled aggressive or not depending on subjective judgments of whether it is intentional or accidental. The same act is judged differently depending, among other factors, on the sex, age, socioeconomic level, and ethnic background of the performer. Value orientations of the labelers also affect the way in which particular activities are interpreted in everyday life.

People ordinarily do not aggress in conspicuous direct ways that carry high risks of retaliation. Instead, they tend to hurt others in ways that diffuse or obscure responsibility for detrimental actions to protect against counterattack. The injurious consequences of major social concern are often caused remotely, circuitously, and impersonally. Thus, for example, individuals who endorse social practices known to have deleterious physical and psychological effects on others are, in their view, exercising democratic prerogatives, but to the victims who must endure the harmful consequences they are behaving aggressively. Social scientists have examined direct assaultive behavior in minute detail but remote circuitous acts, which produce widespread injurious consequences, are seldom considered in analyses of aggression.

Disputes over the labeling of aggressive acts assume special significance in the case of collective behavior. How coercive protest is characterized partly determines the countermeasures employed, which can have far-reaching effects. Social labeling of collective challenges as lawlessness prompts coercive countercontrol, whereas if they are designated as warranted protests against inequitable or grievous practices, efforts are more likely to be directed toward effecting social reforms.

A related issue concerns the use of a double standard in judging dissident and institutionally sanctioned aggression. Social agencies are entrusted with considerable coercive power designed to protect the citizenry. Those whose social and economic interests are well served by the system applaud coercive enforcement practices to maintain social control. In contrast, dissenters who seek social change through collective pressure regard coercive countermeasures by control agents as aggressive acts more intent on preserving the status quo than on impartially protecting the welfare of all segments of society. When the dispensers of unwarranted aggression are sanctioned authorities, their injurious behavior is minimized as vigorous pursuit of duty, but if freelancing individuals do it, they are apt to be judged as acting violently. In areas of social conflict, one person's violence is another person's social righteousness. Even a brief review of social labeling processes suggests that a comprehensive analysis of aggression requires a broader perspective than is usually found in psychological approaches to the problem.

A complete theory of aggression must explain how aggressive patterns are developed, what provokes people to behave aggressively, and what maintains their aggressive actions. The determinants of these three separable aspects of functioning are summarized in Fig. 1 and discussed more fully in the remainder of this chapter.

ACQUISITION OF AGGRESSIVE MODES
OF BEHAVIOR

People are not born with preformed repertoires of aggressive behavior. They must learn them in one way or another. Some of the elementary forms of aggression can be perfected with minimal guidance, but most aggressive activities—whether they be dueling with switchblade knives, sparring with opponents,

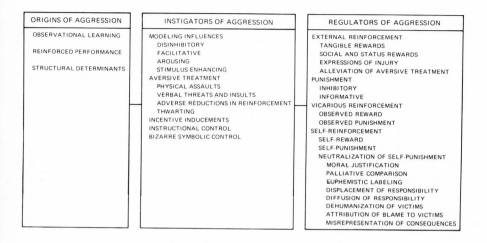

FIG. 1 Schematic outline of the origins, instigators, and reinforcers of aggression in social learning theory.

military combat, or vengeful ridicule—entail intricate skills that require extensive learning. People can acquire aggressive styles of conduct either by observing aggressive models or from direct combat experience.

New modes of behavior are not fashioned solely through experience, either of a direct or of an observational sort. Biological structure, which is determined by genetic and hormonal factors, obviously sets limits on the types of aggressive responses that can be perfected. Biological determination of aggression varies across species, however. Animals must rely on their biological equipment for combat successes. In contrast, people's capacity to use destructive weapons and the organized power of numbers has greatly reduced his dependence on physical characteristics for aggressive attainments.

Observational Learning

Most of the behaviors that people display are learned observationally, either deliberately or inadvertently, through the influence of example. By observing the actions of others one forms an idea of how the behavior can be performed, and on later occasions the representation serves as a guide for action. Laboratory research has been mainly concerned with observational learning of specific aggressive actions. However, models can teach more general lessons as well. From observing the behavior of others one can learn general strategies that provide guides for actions that go well beyond the particular modeled examples (Bandura, 1973).

Exposure to aggressive models does not automatically insure observational learning for several reasons. First, some people do not gain much from example because they fail to observe the essential features of the model's behavior. Second, persons cannot be much influenced by observation of a model's behavior if they have no memory of it. Past modeling influences achieve some degree of permanence if they are represented in memory in images, words, or some other symbolic form (Bandura, Grusec, & Menlove, 1966). Mental rehearsal is another means of retaining what has been learned observationally. Evidence for the stabilizing effects of covert rehearsal appears frequently in naturalistic reports. Assassins in some of the mass slayings originally got the idea from descriptive accounts of a mass killing. The incident remains salient in their thinking long after it has been forgotten by others, and it is repeatedly revivified and elaborated in thought until, under appropriate instigating conditions, it serves as the basis for an analogous murderous action (*New York Times*, 1966). Even though symbolic representations of modeled activities are developed and retained, behavioral enactment may be impeded because the individual does not have the physical capabilities or the means with which to carry out the necessary aggressive activities.

Social learning theory distinguishes between acquisition of behaviors that have destructive and injurious potential and factors that determine whether a person will perform what he has learned. This distinction is important because not all the things learned are enacted. People can acquire, retain, and possess the capability to act aggressively, but the learning may rarely be expressed if the behavior has no functional value for them or if it is negatively sanctioned. Should appropriate inducements arise in the future, individuals may put into practice what they have learned (Bandura, 1965; Madsen, 1968). In predicting the occurrence of aggression, the concern should be more with predisposing conditions than with predisposed individuals. Given that aggressive modes of conduct have been learned, social circumstances largely determine whether and when they will be performed.

In a modern society there are three major sources of aggressive behavior that are drawn on to varying degrees. These different modeling influences are discussed next.

Familial influences. One prominent source is the aggression modeled and reinforced by family members. Investigators who have studied the familial determinants of antisocial aggression report a much higher incidence of familial aggressive modeling for delinquent than for nondelinquent boys (Glueck & Glueck, 1950; McCord, McCord, & Zola, 1959). That familial violence breeds violent styles of conduct is further shown by similarities in child abuse practices across several generations (Silver, Dublin, & Lourie, 1969).

Most assaultive youngsters, however, do not have criminally violent parents. In middle-class families that produce violence-prone offspring, parental aggressive modeling usually takes less blatant forms. Parents of such children favor aggressive solutions to problems, although their actions rarely extend to unlawful performances (Bandura, 1960; Bandura & Walters, 1959). It is in the context of disciplinary activities that children are furnished with vivid parental examples of how to influence the behavior of others. Parents who favor coercive methods have children who tend to use similar aggressive tactics in controlling the behavior of their peers (Hoffman, 1960). There is evidence also that otherwise conforming parents often foster aggressive modes of response by modeling aggressive orientations in word and attitude rather than in deed (Johnson & Szurek, 1952).

Subcultural influences. Although familial influences play a major role in setting the direction of social development, the family is embedded in a network of other social systems. The subculture in which people reside and with which they have repeated contact provides a second important source of aggression. Not surprisingly, the highest rates of aggressive behavior are found in environments where aggressive models abound and where aggressiveness is regarded as a highly valued attribute (Short, 1968; Wolfgang & Ferracuti, 1967). In these aggressive subcultures status is gained primarily through fighting prowess. Consequently, good aggressors are the prestigious models on whom members pattern their behavior.

The preceding discussion has been concerned with subcultural training in aggressive styles of conduct that are disavowed by the larger society. Most societies maintain elaborate social agencies to which they officially assign aggression-training functions. These include military enterprises with their many supporting subsystems. Military establishments can, within a relatively short period, transform people who have been taught to deplore killing as morally reprehensible into skilled combatants who feel little compunction and even a sense of pride in taking human life. Such radical personal changes have more profound implications for accounts of aggression than the actions of assaultive individuals or youthful groups residing in dismal neighborhoods.

The task of converting socialized men into proficient combatants is not achieved by altering personality structures, drives, or traits. It is accomplished by assigning a high moral purpose to warfare and intensive training in the intricate combat techniques. Training proceeds by demonstration and repeated practice of attacks against simulated targets until proficiency is attained. Throughout this process recruits are subjected to obedience tests and firmly disciplined for noncompliance.

Soldiers are returned to civilian life without putting them through a resocialization process designed to instill aggression restraints or to restore commitment to the dignity of human life. Nevertheless, the great majority promptly revert to their civilian self-evaluative and reinforcement systems and behave in considerate, peaceful ways. Achievement of such marked shifts in destructive behavior through moral sanctions without greatly changing the person provides the most striking testimony that the determinants of human aggression are best sought in social practices.

Symbolic modeling. Much social learning occurs through casual or directed observation of real-life models. However, styles of behavior can be conveyed through pictures and words as well as through action. Comparative studies, in fact, show that response patterns portrayed either pictorially or verbally can be learned observationally about as well as those presented through social demonstration (Bandura & Mischel, 1965; Bandura, Ross, & Ross, 1963a).

The third source of aggressive behavior is the symbolic modeling provided by the mass media, especially television because of its prevalence and vivid portrayal of events. The advent of television has greatly expanded the range of models available to the growing child. Whereas their predecessors, especially those in middle-class homes, had limited opportunity to observe brutal aggression, the modern child has witnessed innumerable stabbings, beatings, stompings, stranglings, muggings, and less graphic but equally destructive forms of cruelty before he has reached kindergarten age. Both children and adults, regardless of their backgrounds, thus have unlimited opportunities to learn from televised modeling aggressive coping styles and the whole gamut of felonious behavior within the comfort of their homes. Controlled field studies have shown that exposure to televised violence increases interpersonal aggressiveness (Friedrich & Stein, 1973; Leyens *et al.,* 1975; Parke *et al.,* 1975; Steuer, Applefield & Smith, 1971). It is not uncommon for people experiencing appropriate inducements to pattern criminal activities after ingenious styles portrayed in the mass media (Bandura, 1973).

The influence of symbolic modeling is most striking in the shaping and spread of collective aggression. Social contagion of new styles and tactics of aggression conforms to a pattern that characterizes the transitory changes of most other types of contagious activities: new behavior is initiated by a salient example; it spreads at a rapidly accelerating rate; after it has been widely adopted it is discarded, often in favor of a new form that follows a similar course.

Modeled solutions to problems that achieve some measure of success are not only widely adopted by people facing similar difficulties but tend to spread to other troublesome areas as well. The civil rights movement, which itself was modeled after Gandhi's crusades of nonviolent resistance, in turn provided the example for other protest campaigns aimed at eliminating injustices and undesired social practices. The model of collective protest as a means of forcing social reforms spread to the antiwar movement and to disadvantaged groups, including Chicanos, Indians, homosexuals, and women.

The turbulent sixties provide numerous additional illustrations of the rapid contagion of the style of collective aggression. The campus protest movement at Berkeley served as the model for the sit-in method of protest in universities throughout the country. The peaceful sit in was supplanted by progressively more violent forms, graduating to combative disruptions of university functions, and eventually to mobile trashing of buildings. Following a New York rally in which construction workers beat up antiwar demonstrators, assaults on students by hardhatters spread nationwide.

Airline hijacking provides another striking example of the rapid rise and decline of modeled aggression. Air piracy was unheard of in the United States until a commerical airliner was hijacked to Havana in 1961. Prior to this incident there was a rash of hijackings of Cuban airliners to Miami. These incidents were followed by a wave of hijackings, both in the United States and abroad, reaching its height in 1969 when a total of 87 airplanes was pirated. Thereafter, hijackings declined in the United States but continued to spread to other countries so that international air piracy became relatively common (Fig. 2). News of an inventive hijacker who successfully parachuted from an airliner with a large bundle of extorted money temporarily revived a declining phenomenon in the United States as others became inspired by his successful example (*San Francisco Chronicle*, 1971).

In Brazil a new form of political collective bargaining was devised when a United States ambassador was abducted and later freed in exchange for political

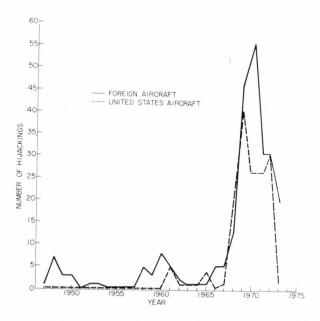

FIG. 2 Incidence of hijackings over a span of 25 years. The rise in foreign hijackings during the 1949–1950 period occurred in Slavic countries at the time of the Hungarian uprising, and the second flareup in 1958–1961 included almost entirely Cuban hijackings to Miami. A sudden widespread diffusion of hijackings occurred in 1969–1970 involving airliners from a total of 55 different countries.

prisoners. This practice quickly spread across Latin America as other consular and ambassadorial envoys were kidnapped in Argentina, Brazil, Guatemala, Uruguay, and the Dominican Republic and held hostage for the release of political prisoners. Canada, Spain, and Turkey, containing dissident political factions, soon joined the ranks of South American countries in consular abductions.

There are several alternative explanations for the abrupt decline of contagious aggression. First, the targets of aggression develop effective countermeasures. As hijacking escalated, airlines added screening procedures as deterrents. College administrators similarly improved their methods of countercontrol through court injunctions and new judicial procedures on the basis of repeated experience in dealing with coercive group action. Just as aggressive tactics are widely modeled, so are the methods of countercontrol. Second, the discrepancy between anticipated and experienced consequences plays an important role in determining the future courses of aggression. Direct observation and media reports of mass aggression are largely confined to the dramatic episodes, not to the intervening long hours of boredom and fatigue. What is seen of the group's functioning generally conveys the sense of camaraderie and principled dedication rather than the stress of pressures for conformity, the feeling of isolation that accompanies estrangement from the larger community, and the discouragement arising from failure to achieve desired changes. Participants who are drawn into protest activities mainly by their apparent excitement may drop out after experiencing firsthand the full consequences of the endeavor. Third, a new style of behavior rapidly loses its positive value through overuse. When the same rhetoric and tactics are utilized repeatedly, protest activities take on the quality of staged productions rather than genuine expressions of principle. As leaders reduce their authenticity by trite rhetoric, their appeals tend to be viewed as manipulative and increasingly resisted. Some of the more idealistic followers may eventually become disillusioned by the contriving of power plays dictated more by strategic than by moral considerations.

Learning by Direct Experience

People rarely teach social behaviors that are never exemplified by anyone in their environment. Although modeling influences are universally present, patterns of behavior can also be shaped through a more rudimentary form of learning that relies on the rewarding and punishing consequences of trial-and-error performance. There have been few experimental attempts to fashion novel forms of aggression by differential reinforcement alone. It would be foolhardy to instruct novices how to handle firearms or hand grenades by selectively reinforcing their trial-and-error efforts. Where the consequences of errors can be dangerous or fatal, demonstration rather than unguided experience is the best teacher.

Learning through combat experience has been explored to a limited extent in experiments with lower species designed to train docile animals into ferocious fighers (Ginsburg & Allee, 1942; Scott & Marston, 1953). This outcome is achieved by arranging a series of bouts with progressively more experienced fighters under conditions in which the trainee can win fights without being hurt. As fighting skills are developed and reinforced through repeated victories, formerly noncombative animals become more and more vicious in their aggressive behavior. Whereas successful fighting produces brutal aggressors, severe defeats create enduring submissiveness (Kahn, 1951).

Patterson, Littman, and Bricker (1967) reported a field study illustrating how passive children could be shaped into aggressors through a process of victimization and successful counteraggression. Passive children who were repeatedly victimized, and whose counteraggression often proved effective in halting attacks, not only increased defensive fighting but eventually began to initiate attacks of their own. In contrast, passive children who were seldom maltreated because they avoided others, and those whose counteraggressive responses were unsuccessful, remained submissive in their behavior.

Modeling and reinforcement influences operate jointly in the social learning of aggression in everyday life. Styles of aggression are largely learned through observation and refined through reinforced practice. The powerful effects that these two determinants have on the form and incidence of aggression are graphically revealed in ethnographic reports of societies that pursue a warlike way of life and those that display a pacific style of behavior. In cultures lacking aggressive models and devaluing aggressive conduct people live peaceably (Alland, 1972; Levy, 1969; Mead, 1935; Turnbull, 1961). In societies that provide extensive training in aggression, attach prestige to it, and make its use rewarding, people spend a great deal of time threatening, fighting, maiming, and killing each other (Bateson, 1936; Chagnon, 1968; Gardner & Heider, 1968; Whiting, 1941).

INSTIGATORS OF AGGRESSION

A theory must explain not only how aggressive patterns are acquired but also how they are activated and channeled. Most of the events that provoke people to aggress, such as insults, verbal challenges, status threats, unjust treatment, and inciting actions, gain this activating capacity through learning experiences rather than from genetic endowment. People learn to dislike and to attack certain types of individuals either through direct unpleasant encounters with them or on the basis of symbolic and vicarious experiences that conjure up hatreds. In addition to paired experiences, stimuli gain aggression directing functions through association with differential response consequences. When aggression is treated differently depending on the times, places, or persons toward whom it is directed,

such informative cues come to signify probable consequences and people regulate their behavior accordingly. They tend to aggress toward persons and in
contexts where it is relatively safe and rewarding to do so, but they are
disinclined to act aggressively when to do so carries a high risk of punishment.
The different forms that aggression elicitors take are discussed separately in the
sections that follow.

Modeling Influences

Human behavior is extensively under modeling stimulus control. Therefore, an
effective way to prompt people to aggress is to have others do it. Results of
numerous laboratory studies generally show that both children and adults
behave more punitively after they have seen others act aggressively than if they
have not been exposed to aggressive models (Bandura, 1973; Goranson, 1970).
The eliciting power of modeling influences is enhanced under conditions where
observers are angered (Berkowitz, 1965; Hartmann, 1969; Wheeler, 1966), the
modeled aggression is socially justified (Berkowitz, 1965; Meyer, 1971), or the
victim invites attack through prior association with aggression (Berkowitz,
1970). The findings of laboratory studies are essentially corroborated by well-
designed field experiments. People who are repeatedly exposed to combative
models tend to be more physically assaultive in their social interactions than
those who observe nonviolent styles of conduct.

Social learning theory distinguishes four processes by which modeling influences can activate aggressive behavior. One mode of operation is in terms of the
discriminative function of modeled actions. In many instances, behaving as
others do is rewarding because the prevalent modes have proved most functional,
whereas divergent courses are less effective or may even bring disapproval. Thus,
through association with past reinforcement, modeled acts come to serve as
informative prompts for others to behave in a similar fashion.

Aggressive behavior, especially when cruel and lacking justification, is socially
censured if not self-condemned. Anticipated punishment exerts a restraining
influence on injurious conduct. Seeing people respond approvingly or even
indifferently toward aggressors conveys the impression that such behavior is not
only acceptable but even expected in the situation. The same modeled aggression
is much more effective in reducing restraints if it is socially legitimated than if it
is portrayed as unjustified. Moreover, it has been shown that exposure to models
engaging in threatening activities without adverse consequences has disinhibiting
effects on observers by extinguishing their fears vicariously (Bandura, 1971a). In
aggressive conduct that is regarded as emulative and therefore unemcumbered by
restraints, aggressive modeling is primarily instigational, whereas it serves a
disinhibitory function in the case of injurious behavior that is fear provoking.
Because aggression usually incurs severe punishment costs, both instigational and
disinhibitory processes are likely to be involved.

Seeing others aggressing generates *emotional arousal* in observers. Under conditions in which individuals are prone to behave aggressively, any source of emotional arousal can enhance aggressive responding (Tannenbaum, 1972; Zillman, 1971). Some of the instigative effects of modeling may very well reflect the emotional facilitation of aggressive behavior.

Aggressive modeling can additionally increase the likelihood of aggressive behavior through its *stimulus enhancing effects*. Modeled activities inevitably direct observers' attention to the particular implements being used. This directive attentional influence may prompt observers to use the same instruments to a greater extent, although not necessarily in an imitative way. In one experiment (Bandura, 1962), for example, children who had observed a model pummel a plastic figure with a mallet spent more time pounding other objects with a mallet than those who did not see it used for assaultive purposes. In sum, the combined evidence reveals that modeling influences, depending on their form and content, can function as teachers, as elicitors, as disinhibitors, as stimulus enhancers, and as emotion arousers.

Aversive Treatment

Frustration, which is widely invoked as a principal cause of aggression, subsumes such a diverse set of conditions that it no longer has a specific meaning. There exists a large body of evidence that painful treatment, deprivation or delay of rewards, personal insults, failure experiences, and obstructions, all of which are regarded as frustrations, do not have uniform behavioral effects (Bandura, 1969). Even the same treatment can elicit different responses at different intensities and under different learning histories. The heterogeneous events included under the omnibus term "frustration" do have one property in common—they are all aversive in varying degrees.

In social learning theory, instead of frustration generating an aggressive drive that is reducible only by injurious behavior, aversive treatment creates a general state of emotional arousal that can facilitate a variety of behaviors, depending on the types of responses the person has learned for coping with stress and their relative effectiveness (Bandura, 1973). When subjected to adversity some people seek help and support; others increase achievement efforts; others display withdrawal and resignation; some aggress; others experience heightened somatic reactivity; still others anesthetize themselves against a miserable existence with drugs or alcohol; and most intensify constructive efforts to overcome sources of distress. The major differences among the instinctual, aggressive drive, and social learning theories in how they conceptualize the motivational component of aggression are depicted schematically in Fig. 3. Several lines of evidence, reviewed in detail elsewhere (Bandura, 1973), lend greater validity to the *arousal-prepotent response* formulation than to the *frustration–aggression* view.

Different forms of aversive stimulation often have dissimilar behavioral effects.

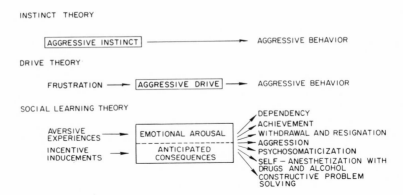

FIG. 3 Diagrammatic representation of motivational determinants of aggression in instinct, reactive drive, and social learning theories.

Therefore, in the social learning analysis injurious behavior is related to different classes of aversive antecedents.

Physical assaults. If one wished to provoke aggression, one way to do so is simply to hit another person, who is likely to oblige with a counterattack. To the extent that counteraggression discourages further assaults it is reinforced by pain reduction and thereby assumes high functional value in social interactions. Although naturally occurring contingencies favor the development of a strong pain–aggression relationship, there is some dispute over whether it is innate or acquired.

Azrin (1967) and Ulrich (1966) are major proponents of the nativistic view that pain-induced aggression is an unlearned reflexive behavior. As the determinants of pain–attack reactions are examined more closely, however, they begin to lose their reflexive status. Young animals rarely, if ever, fight when shocked unless they have had some fighting experience, and in some studies shocks produce little or no fighting in 20–30% of mature animals (Hutchinson, Ulrich, & Azrin, 1965; Powell & Creer, 1969). If aggression is an unlearned dominant response to pain, then initial shocks should produce attack, which is not generally the case (Azrin, Hutchinson, & Hake, 1963). Contrary to the reflexive elicitation hypothesis, when attack responses are shocked the painful stimulation reduces and eliminates rather than provokes aggression (Azrin, 1970; Baenninger & Grossman, 1969). The most striking evidence that pain–aggression reactions are determined more by situational factors than innate organization is the finding that in a small enclosure approximately 90% of the shocks provoke fighting, whereas in a larger chamber animals ignore each other and only 2% of the shocks elicit attack (Ulrich & Azrin, 1962). As environmental inducements to fight are removed, avoidance and flight responses to painful treatment take priority over attack (Knutson, 1970; Logan & Boice, 1969). Physically painful experiences are facilitative but clearly not sufficient to provoke aggression in animals.

Painful stimulation is an even less consistent elicitor of aggression in humans. Nonsocial sources of pain rarely lead them to attack bystanders. Whether or not they counteraggress in the face of physical assaults depends on their combat success and the power of their assailant. Those who have been successful in controlling people through force escalate their counterattacks to compel acquiescence (Edwards, 1967; Peterson, 1971). Given other options, low aggressors are easily dissuaded from making counterattacks under retaliative threats.

Verbal threats and insults. Social interchanges are typically escalated into physical aggression by verbal threats and insults. In analyzing the dyadic interchanges of assault-prone individuals, Toch (1969) found that humiliating affronts and threats to reputation and manly status emerged as major precipitants of violence. Their high sensitivity to devaluation was usually accompanied by deficient skills for resolving disputes and restoring self-esteem by verbal means without having to dispose of antagonists physically. The counterattacks evoked by physical assaults are probably instigated more by humiliation than by physical pain. Indeed, it is not uncommon for individuals, and even nations, to pay heavy injury costs in efforts to "save face" by combat victory.

Insult alone is less effective in provoking attack in those who eschew aggression, but it does heighten aggressive responding given hostile modeling and other disinhibitory influences (Hartmann, 1969; Wheeler & Caggiula, 1966). In subcultures in which social ranking is determined by fighting prowess, status threats, from either challengers within the group or rival outsiders, are quick to provoke defensive aggression (Short, 1968).

The most plausible explanation of how insults acquire aggression-eliciting potential is in terms of foreseen consequences. Affronts that are not successfully counteracted can have far-reaching effects for victims. Not only do they become easy targets for further victimization but they are apt to forfeit the rewards and privileges that go with social standing. To the extent that punishment of insults by counteraggression reduces the likelihood of future maltreatment, the insult—aggression reaction becomes well established.

Adverse reductions in level of reinforcement. Aversive conditions of life can also provoke people to aggressive action. Explanations of collective aggression characteristically invoke impoverishment and discontent arising from privations as principal causal factors. Considering that most discontented people do not aggress, the view that discontent breeds violence requires qualification, however. This issue is well illustrated in interpretations of urban riots in ghetto areas. Despite condemnation of their degrading and exploited conditions of life, comparatively few of the sufferers take active measures to force warranted changes. A vast majority of the disadvantaged do not engage in disruptive public protest, and even in cities experiencing civil disturbances, only about 15–20% of ghetto residents actively participated in the aggressive activities (Lieberson & Silverman, 1965; McCord & Howard, 1968; Sears & McConahay, 1969).

The critical question for social scientists to answer is not why some people who are subjected to aversive conditions aggress, but why a sizable majority of them acquiesce to dismal living conditions in the midst of affluent styles of life. To facilely invoke the frustration—aggression hypothesis, as is commonly done, is to disregard the more striking evidence that severe privation generally produces feelings of hopelessness and widespread resignation. Pervasive discontent may be a necessary but not a sufficient cause of collective aggression.

Comparative studies indicate that discontent produces aggression not in those who have lost hope but in the more successful members, whose assertive efforts at social and economic betterments have been periodically reinforced. Consequently, they have some reason to expect that coercive action can force additional social change (Caplan, 1970; Crawford & Naditch, 1970).

Current explanations of violent protest emphasize relative deprivation rather than the actual level of aversive conditions as the instigator of collective aggression. In an analysis of conditions preceding major revolutions, Davies (1969) reports that revolutions are most likely to occur when a period of social and economic advances that instills rising expectations is followed by a sharp reversal. People do not only judge their present gains in relation to those they secured in the past; they also compare their lot in life with the benefits accruing to others (Bandura, 1971b). Unfavorable discrepancies between observed and experienced outcomes tend to create discontent, whereas individuals may be satisfied with limited rewards as long as they are as good as, or better than, what others are receiving.

Because most people who feel realtively deprived do not resort to violent action, aversive privations contribute to aggression in interaction with other inducements rather than as an independent determinant. Gurr (1970) examined three determinants of the magnitude of civil disorders. These included the level of social discontent, traditional acceptance of forcible tactics to achieve desired reforms, and the balance of coercive power between the regime and the challengers. The multifaceted analysis disclosed that when forcible tactics are considered acceptable and challengers possess coercive power they will use collective force to change social practices within a system regardless of the level of discontent. Revolutionary violence, however, requires widespread discontent and dissident coercive power, whereas tactical traditions are of less importance.

Response to inequitable deprivation is further influenced by, among other factors, the social justification and promise of social reforms. Considering the complex interplay of influences, it is hardly surprising that level of deprivation alone, whether defined in absolute or in relative terms, is a weak predictor of collective aggression (McPhail, 1971).

Thwarting of goal-directed behavior.   Proponents of the frustration-aggression theory define frustration in terms of interference or blocking of goal-seeking activities. In this view, people are provoked to aggression when obstructed, delayed, or otherwise thwarted from getting what they want. Research bearing on this issue shows that thwarting can lead people to intensify their efforts, which, if sufficiently vigorous, may be construed as aggressive. However, thwarting fails to provoke forceful action in people who have not experienced sufficient positive reinforcement to develop reward expectations and in those who are blocked far enough from the goal that it appears unattainable (Bandura & Walters, 1963; Longstreth, 1966).

In instances where thwarting provokes aggression it is probably attributable more to the implied personal insult than to blocking of ongoing behavior. Consistent with this interpretation, people report more aggression to thwartings that appear unwarranted than to those for which excusable reasons exist, even though both involve identical blocking of goal-directed behavior (Cohen, 1955; Pastore, 1952).

The overall evidence regarding the different forms of aversive instigators supports the conclusion that aversive antecedents, although they vary in their activating potential, are facilitative rather than necessary or sufficient conditions for aggression.

Incentive Inducements

The preceding discussion was concerned solely with aversively motivated aggression, which occupies a more prominent role in psychological theorizing than is warranted empirically. The cognitive capacity of humans to represent future consequences enables them to guide their behavior by outcomes extended forward in time. A great deal of human aggression in fact is prompted by anticipated positive consequences. Here, the instigator is the pull of expected reward, rather than the push of painful treatment. This positive source of motivation for aggression represents the second component in the motivational analysis depicted schematically in Figure 3.

The consequences that people anticipate for their actions are derived from, and therefore usually correspond to, prevailing conditions of reinforcement. The powerful anticipatory activation and reinforcement control of aggression receives detailed consideration later in this chapter. It should be noted, however, that expectation and actuality do not always coincide because anticipated outcomes are also partly inferred from observed consequences of others, from what one reads or is told, and from many other cues that in past experience have been reliable forecasters of likely outcomes. Judgments are fallible. Aggressive actions are therefore sometimes prompted and temporarily sustained by erroneous anticipated consequences. Habitual offenders, for example, often err by overestimating the chances of success for transgressive behavior (Claster, 1967). In collective protest, coercive actions are partly sustained, even in the face of punishing consequences, by expectations that continued pressure may eventually produce social reforms.

Instructional Control

During the process of socialization, people are trained to obey orders. By rewarding obedience to directives and punishing noncompliance, orders eventually acquire eliciting power. After this form of social control is established, legitimate authorities can successfully command aggression from others, especially if actions are presented as justified and necessary and the agents possess strong coercive power. As Snow (1961) has perceptively observed, "When you think of the long and gloomy history of man, you will find more hideous crimes have been committed in the name of obedience than in the name of rebellion" (p. 24).

In his studies of obedient aggression, Milgram (1974) has shown that well-meaning adults will administer increasingly severe shocks on command despite their victims' desperate pleas. Adults find it difficult to behave counter to peer pressures calling for increasingly hurtful actions just as they are averse to defying legitimized authority. Seeing others carrying out punitive orders calmly likewise increases obedient aggression (Powers & Geen, 1972).

It is relatively easy to hurt people on command when their suffering is not visible and when causal actions seem physically or temporally remote from their deleterious effects. Mechanized forms of warfare, where masses of people can be put to death by destructive forces released remotely, illustrate such depersonalized aggression. When the injurious consequences of one's actions are fully evident, vicariously aroused distress and loss of self-respect serve as restraining influences over aggressive conduct that is otherwise authoritatively sanctioned. Milgram (1974) obtained diminishing obedience as the harmful consequences of punitive actions became increasingly more salient and personalized. Results of these, and other studies to be cited later, show that it requires particular social conditions rather than monstrous people to produce heinous deeds.

Delusional Control

In addition to the various external instigators, aggressive behavior can come under bizarre symbolic control. Every so often tragic episodes occur in which individuals are led by delusional beliefs to commit acts of violence. Some follow divine inner voices commanding them to murder. Others are instigated to self-protective attacks by paranoid suspicions that others are conspiring to harm them (Reich & Hepps, 1972). Still others are prompted by grandiose convictions that it is their heroic responsibility to eliminate maleficent individuals in positions of power.

A study of presidential assassins (Weisz & Taylor, 1970) shows that, with one exception, the murderous assaults were partly under delusional control. The assassins acted either under divine mandate, through alarm that the President was in conspiracy with treacherous foreign agents to overthrow the government, or on the conviction that their own adversities resulted from presidential persecution. Being unusually seclusive in their behavior, the assassins effectively shielded their erroneous beliefs from corrective influences.

MAINTAINING CONDITIONS

The third major feature of the social learning formulation is concerned with the conditions that sustain aggressive responding. It has been amply documented in psychological research that behavior is extensively controlled by its consequences. This principle applies equally to aggression. Aggressive modes of response, like other forms of social behavior, can be induced, eliminated, and reinstated by altering the effects they produce (Bandura, 1973).

People aggress for many different reasons. Essentially the same aggressive actions may thus have markedly different functional value for different individuals, and for the same individual on different occasions. In traditional theories, reinforcement influences are largely confined to the effects of external outcomes impinging directly on the performer. Social learning theory, however, distinguishes three forms of reinforcement control: they include the influence of direct external reinforcement, vicarious or observed reinforcement, and self-reinforcement.

Direct External Reinforcement

Aggression is strongly influenced by its direct consequences, which take many forms. Extrinsic rewards assume special importance in interpersonal aggression because such behavior, by its very nature, generally creates some painful costs. A person who gets into fights may suffer injury even though he eventually triumphs over his opponents. Under noncoercive conditions, positive incentives are needed to overcome inhibitions arising from the aversive concomitants of aggression.

Tangible rewards. People often resort to aggressive actions because it is an effective means of securing desired tangible rewards. Ordinarily docile animals will fight when aggressive attacks produce food or drink (Azrin & Hutchinson, 1967; Ulrich, Johnston, Richardson, & Wolff, 1963). Observation of children's interactions shows that approximately 80% of the aggressors' assaultive actions produce rewarding consequences for them (Patterson *et al.*, 1967). Given this surprisingly high level of positive reinforcement of aggressive behavior, there is no need to invoke an aggressive drive to explain the prevalence of such actions. Aggressive behavior is especially persistent when it is reinforced only intermittently, which is usually the case under the variable conditions of everyday life (Walters & Brown, 1963).

There are other forms of aggression that are sustained by their material consequences although, for obvious reasons, they are not easily subject to systematic analysis. Delinquent and adult transgressors, for example, can support themselves on costly drug habits on income derived from aggressive pursuits; protesters can secure, through forceful collective response, social reforms that affect their lives materially; and nations are sometimes able to gain control over prized territories through warfare.

Social and status rewards.   Some aggressive behaviors are maintained because they win approval and status rewards. People commended for punitive actions toward others become progressively more aggressive, whereas they display a relatively low level of aggression when their actions are not treated as praiseworthy (Geen & Stonner, 1971; Staples & Walters, 1964). Aggressive responses, if socially reinforced, not only increase in frequency but the reinforcement tends to enhance other forms of aggression as well (Geen & Pigg, 1970; Loew, 1967).

Analyses of social reinforcement of aggressive behavior in natural settings are in general agreement with results of laboratory studies. Parents of assaultive children are generally nonpermissive for aggressive behavior in the home but condone, actively encourage, and reinforce provocative and aggressive actions toward others in the community (Bandura, 1960; Bandura & Walters, 1959). In aggressive gangs, members achieve status and recognition through their skills in fighting (Short, 1968). During wartime, otherwise compassionate societies offer medals, promotions, and social commendations on the basis of skill in killing. In the Nazi structure of reinforcement, where enslavement and execution of racial minorities were viewed as meritorious acts of patriotism, promotions in concentration camps were made partly on skill in performing mass murders. Camp commandants proudly compared execution rates as if they were industrial production figures (Andrus, 1969).

Lest the Nazi atrocities be dismissed as an anomalous product of a deranged social system, it should be noted that otherwise socialized people can be led to behave brutally and to take pride in such actions when reinforcement practices are instituted that favor inhuman forms of behavior (*San Francisco Chronicle*, 1970).

Alleviation of aversive treatment.   People are frequently subjected to distressing treatment from which they seek relief. Coercive action that is not unduly hazardous is the most direct and quickest means of alleviating adverse conditions, if only temporarily. Defensive forms of aggression are often reinforced by their capacity to terminate humiliating and painful treatment. Reinforcement through pain reduction is well documented in studies cited above showing that children who are often victimized but terminate the maltreatment by successful counteraggression eventually become highly aggressive in their behavior (Patterson *et al.*, 1967).

In the social learning analysis, defensive aggression is sustained to a greater extent by anticipated consequences than by its instantaneous effects. People will endure reprisals on expectations that their aggressive efforts will eventually remove deleterious conditions. Aggressive actions may also be partly maintained in the face of painful counterattack by anticipated costs of timidity. In aggression-oriented circles, failure to fight back can arouse fear of future victimization and humiliation. A physical pummeling may, therefore, be far less distressing than repeated social derision or self-contempt. In other words, humans do not behave as unthinking servomechanisms directed solely by immediate response feedback. Under aversive conditions of life, people will persist, at least for a time, in aggressive behavior that produces immediate pain but prospective relief from misery.

Expressions of injury. Proponents of drive theories contend that the purpose of aggression is injury. It is therefore widely assumed that aggressive behavior is reinforced by signs of suffering in the victim. According to Sears, Maccoby, and Levin (1957) pain cues become rewarding through their repeated association with tension relief and removal of frustrations. Feshbach (1970), on the other hand, interprets the rewarding value of pain expression in terms of self-esteem processes. Perception of pain in one's tormentors is experienced as satisfying because successful retaliation restores the aggressor's self-esteem.

A contrasting view is that signs of suffering ordinarily function as inhibitors rather than as positive reinforcers of aggressive behavior. Because of the potential dangers of violence all societies punish cruel and destructive acts, except under special circumstances. In the course of socialization most people adopt for self-evaluation societal standards in which ruthless aggression is morally reprehensible. Consequently, aggression that produces suffering in others elicits both fear of retaliation and self-condemnation, which tend to inhibit injurious attacks.

Studies on how pain expressions affect assaults on suffering victims support the inhibitory view. Aggressors behave less punitively when their victims express anguished cries than when they suffer in silence (Baron, 1971a,b; Geen, 1970). Contrary to drive theory, pain cues reduce aggression regardless of whether the assailant is angered or not. People are even less inclined to behave cruelly when they see their suffering victims than when they merely hear the distress they have caused them (Milgram, 1974).

The scope of the experimental treatments and the populations studied are too limited to warrant the strong conclusion that pain expressions never serve as positive reinforcers of aggressive behavior. A gratuitous insult from a stranger in a laboratory may not create sufficient animosity for the victim to derive satisfaction from injurious retaliation. It is a quite different matter when an antagonist repeatedly tyrannizes others or wields his power in ways that make life miserable for them. In such instances news of the misfortune, serious illness, or death of an oppressor is joyfully received by people who ordinarily respond more compassionately to the adversities befalling others. However, the alleviation of aversive treatment from an injured oppressor rather than his suffering may be the primary source of satisfaction. In experimental investigations pain expression occurs without the other extraneous rewards accompanying victory over antagonists.

From the standpoint of social learning theory, suffering of one's enemies is most apt to be rewarding when hurting them relieves discomfort or benefits aggressors in other ways. When aggressors suffer repirsals or self-contempt for harming others, signs of suffering function as negative reinforcers that deter injurious attacks.

There are certain conditions under which pain expressions may assume positive reinforcing properties. Examples can be cited of societal practices where cruel, monstrous acts are considered praiseworthy by those in positions of power. Such bizarre reinforcement contingencies can breed people who take pleasure in inflicting pain and humiliation. Some of the most horrid illustrations of this phenomenon are documented in the proceedings of the Nuremberg trials. Rudolph Hoess, a former commandant of Auschwitz, for example, had a window installed in a gas chamber so he could watch the gruesome massacres (Andrus, 1969). Additionally, clinical studies of sexual perversion have disclosed cases in which pain expressions acquire powerful rewarding value through repeated association with sexual gratification. As a result, erotic pleasure is derived from inflicting pain on others or on oneself.

There are no conceptual or empirical grounds for regarding aggression maintained by certain reinforcers as more genuine or important than others. A comprehensive theory must account for all aggressive actions whatever purposes they serve. To restrict analysis of aggression to behavior that is reinforced by expressions of injury is to exclude from consideration some of the most violent activities where injury is an unavoidable concomitant rather than the major function of the behavior.

Questions also arise about the distinction traditionally drawn between "instrumental" aggression, which is supposedly aimed at securing extraneous rewards, and "hostile" aggression, the sole purpose of which is presumably to inflict suffering (Feshbach, 1970). In all instances, the behavior is instrumental in producing certain desired outcomes, be they pain, status rewards, or material gain. It would be more accurate to designate aggressive behaviors in terms of their functional value rather than whether or not they are instrumental.

Vicarious Reinforcement

People repeatedly observe the actions of others and the occasions on which they are rewarded, ignored, or punished. Observed outcomes influence behavior in much the same way as directly experienced consequences (Bandura, 1971b; Kanfer, 1965). People can, therefore, profit from the successes and mistakes of others as well as from their own direct experiences. In general, seeing aggression rewarded in others increases, and seeing it punished decreases, the tendency to behave in similar aggressive ways (Bandura, 1965; Bandura, Ross, & Ross, 1963b). The more consistent the observed response consequences, the greater are the facilitatory and inhibitory effects on viewers (Rosekrans & Hartup, 1967).

Vicarious reinforcement produces its behavioral effects through several mechanisms (Bandura, 1971c). Response consequences accruing to others convey information to observers about the types of actions likely to be approved or disapproved and the specific conditions under which it is appropriate to perform them. Observed reinforcement is more than informative. Seeing others' successes can function as a motivator by arousing in observers expectations that they can gain similar rewards for analogous performances. Some of the changes in responsiveness may also reflect vicarious conditioning or extinction of fears through the affective consequences accruing to models. Indeed, the legal system of deterrence rests heavily on the restraining function of exemplary punishment (Packer, 1968). In addition to the aforementioned effects, valuation of certain people can be significantly altered by observing their rewarding and punishing interactions.

There are a number of social factors that may substantially alter the customary effects of observed consequences. Models and observers often differ in distinguishable ways so that behavior considered approvable for one may be punishable for the other, depending on differences in sex, age, and social status. When the same behavior produces unlike consequences for different members, observed reward may not enhance the level of imitative aggressiveness (Thelen & Soltz, 1969).

Under some circumstances, observed punitive treatment raises rather than lowers aggression. When societal agents misuse their power to reward and punish they undermine the legitimacy of their authority and generate strong resentment. Seeing inequitable punishment, instead of prompting compliance, may free incensed observers from self-censure of their own actions and thus increase aggressive behavior. Indeed, leaders of protest movements sometimes attempt to rally supporters to their cause by selecting aggressive tactics calculated to provoke authorities to punitive actions.

Ordinarily, observed punishment tends to devalue the models and their behavior, whereas the same models assume emulative qualities when their actions are rewarded. However, aggressors may gain rather than lose status in the eyes of their peers when they are punished for a style of behavior valued by the group or when they aggress against social practices that violate the professed values of society. It is for this reason that authoritative agencies are usually careful not to discipline challengers in ways that may martyr them.

The manner in which aggressors respond to the consequences of their behavior can also influence how observers later react when they themselves are rewarded for displaying similar responses. Ditrichs, Simon, and Greene (1967) report that children who observe models express progressively more hostility for social approval later increase their own output of hostile response under positive reinforcement. However, when models appear oppositional by reducing hostile responses that bring them praise, or react in random fashion as though they are uninfluenced, observers do not increase their expression of hostility even though they are praised whenever they do so. Susceptibility to direct reinforcement, therefore, can be increased by observed willing responsiveness but reduced by observed resistance.

Self-Reinforcement

A theory that viewed the performance of aggression solely in terms of external rewards and punishments would be incomplete because humans can, and do, regulate their own actions to some extent by self-produced consequences. They do things that give them self-satisfaction and a feeling of self-worth, and refrain from behaving in ways that result in self-criticism and other self-devaluative consequences. Because of self-reactive tendencies, aggressors must contend with themselves as well as with others when they behave in an injurious fashion.

Self-Reward for Aggression

One can distinguish several ways in which self-generated consequences enter into the self-regulation of aggressive behavior. At one extreme are individuals who have adopted self-reinforcement codes that make aggressive behavior a source of personal pride. Such individuals readily engage in aggressive activities and derive enhanced feelings of self-worth from physical conquests (Bandura & Walters, 1959; Toch, 1969). Lacking self-reprimands for hurtful conduct, they are deterred from cruel acts mainly by reprisal threats. Idiosyncratic self-systems of morality are not confined to individuals or fighting gangs. In aggressive cultures where prestige is closely tied to fighting prowess, members take considerable pride in aggressive exploits.

Self-Punishment for Aggression

In the course of socialization most individuals acquire, through example and precept, negative sanctions against cruel conduct. As a result, they are restrained from injurious aggression by anticipated self-censure. There is no more devastating punishment than self-contempt.

Results of the study by Bandura and Walters (1959) have revealed how anticipatory self-reproach for repudiated aggression serves as a motivating influence to keep behavior in line with adopted standards. Adolescents who are compassionate in their dealing with others responded with self-disapproval, remorse, and attempts at reparation even when their aggressive activities have been minor in nature. In contrast, assaultive boys experience relatively few negative self-reactions over serious aggressive activities.

Disengagement of Self-Deterring Consequences

Rarely is aggression uniformly self-rewarded or self-punished, irrespective of the victim, or the circumstances under which it is performed. Although self-reinforcing influences serve as regulators of conduct, they can be dissociated from censurable deeds. By engaging in self-absolving practices humane, moral people can behave cruelly without self-condemnation. The self-exoneration takes many different forms.

Reconstruing aggression by palliative comparison. A practice that is widely employed is to minimize one's aggressive conduct by pointing to more outrageous practices. The more harmful the comparision activities, the more likely are given aggressive acts to appear trifling. When aggression is portrayed as fighting gross inhumanities, injurious behavior becomes laudable. In contests of power, reciprocal aggression usually escalates with each side extolling its own violence as benevolent countermeasures but condemning the violence performed by its adversaries as evil.

Justification of aggression in terms of higher principles. A closely related form of self-vindication is to construe one's aggression in terms of higher values. Given sufficiently noble aims, almost any form of aggression can be justified as righteous. To take a historical example, many massacres have been devotedly perpetrated by crusading Christians in the service of high religious principles. Similarly, in contemporary times violence is frequently espoused in the name of freedom, righteous ideologies, and social order. In everyday transactions, euphemistic labeling is a handy linguistic device for masking reprehensible activities or according them a respectable status. Moral justifications and palliative comparisons serve as especially effective disinhibitors because they not only eliminate self-generated deterrents, but also engage self-reward in the service of inhumane conduct.

Displacement of responsibility. People can be led to behave in an injurious way provided that a legitimate authority is willing to assume responsibility for their actions. Participants in studies who have been deterred from intensifying obedient aggression by distress over the suffering they have inflicted, continue to escalate shocks to hazardous levels despite their victims' agonizing cries, after the experimenter has assured them he will be fully accountable for the consequences of their behavior (Milgram, 1974). Responsibility for cruel deeds is not always assumed so explicitly because no one wants to be answerable for such acts. To reduce risks to themselves, superiors usually invite and condone reprehensible conduct by their subordinates in insidious ways that allow them to claim ignorance for what was happening in the event that disclosures arouse public condemnation.

Diffusion of responsibility.   Exemption from self-criticism can be achieved to some extent by obscuring and diffusing responsibility for aggressive practices. Collective aggression includes many task functions that must be supported by an organizational apparatus. Departmentalization of destructive activities works in several ways to reduce participants' sense of personal responsibility for their behavior. Through division of labor, division of decision making, and collective action, people can be contributors to cruel practices and bloodshed without feeling personally responsible or self-contemptuous for their part in it.

Dehumanization of victims.   A further means of protection against self-devaluation is to dehumanize the victim (Bandura, Underwood, & Fromson, 1975). People selected as targets can often be divested of human qualities by being viewed not as individuals with sensitivities, but as stereotyped objects bearing demeaning labels, such as "gooks" or "niggers." If dispossessing victims of humanness does not fully eliminate self-reproof, it can be further reduced by attributing subhuman or degrading characteristics to them. Foes become "degenerates," "pigs," and other bestial creatures. After victims have been so devalued, they can be cruelly attacked without much risk of self-condemnation.

Attribution of blame to victims.   Attribution of blame to victims is still another expedient that can be used for self-assuaging purposes. In this process, aggressors see themselves as essentially persons of good will who are forced into punitive actions by villainous adversaries. Victims are condemned for bringing the suffering on themselves either by their character defects or by their witless and provocative behavior. Observers of victimization can be affected in much the same way as the aggressors. Seeing victims suffer punitive treatment for which they are held partially responsible leads observers to devalue them (Lerner, 1971; Piliavin, Hardyck, & Vadum, 1967). The indignation aroused by ascribed culpability, in turn, provides moral support for even more brutal acts by aggressors.

Misrepresentation of consequences.   After people have aggressed, additional self-placating measures are available that operate principally through misrepresentation of the consequences of their actions. When people are prompted to self-disapproved conduct under conditions in which they have some choice on whether or not to behave that way, they tend to minimize injurious consequences and to recall potential benefits but not the harms of punishing courses of action (Brock and Buss, 1962, 1964). As long as the damages that aggressors cause are disregarded or belittled, they have little reason to engage in self-censuring reactions.

Graduated desensitization. The aforementioned practices do not instantaneously transform a gentle person into a brutal aggressor. Rather, the change is usually achieved through a gradual desensitization process in which the participants may not fully recognize the marked changes they have undergone. Initially, individuals are prompted to perform aggressive acts they can tolerate without excessive self-censure. After their discomfort and self-reproof are extinguished through repeated performance, the level of aggression is progressively increased in this manner until eventually gruesome deeds, originally regarded as abhorrent, can be performed without much distress.

Examples taken either from military atrocities or political violence convey the impression that sanctioning of human cruelty occurs only under extraordinary circumstances. Quite the contrary. Many societal practices causing widespread harm are routinely performed for financial profit by decent people under self-exonerating disguises.

It is commonly assumed that violence is best prevented by instilling principled morality and a sense of fellowship in individuals. Friendly associations among people serve to inhibit aggression toward each other in the face of provocation from external sources (Davitz, 1952; Wright, 1942). However, just as high moral principles can be used to support ruthless activities, positive bonds can heighten aggressiveness, under certain conditions. The mutual support of close friendship reduces restraints against aggressing toward a common foe. As Wright (1942) has demonstrated, close friends are more abusive toward their antagonists than groups with weaker friendship ties.

Given the variety of self-disinhibiting devices, a society cannot rely solely on individuals, however noble their convictions, to protect against brutal deeds. Just as aggression is not rooted in the individual, neither does its control reside solely there. Humaneness requires, in addition to benevolent personal codes, safeguards built into social systems that uphold compassionate behavior and discourage cruelty.

Like so many other problems confronting man, there is no single grand design for lowering the level of destructiveness within a society. It requires both individual corrective effort and group action aimed at changing the practices of social systems. Because aggression is not an inevitable or unchangeable aspect of man, but a product of aggression promoting conditions operating within a society, social learning theory holds a more optimistic view of people's power to reduce their level of aggressiveness. But much greater effort is needed to ensure that this capability is used beneficially rather than detrimentally.

ACKNOWLEDGMENTS

Preparation of this chapter was facilitated by Research Grant M-5162 from the National Institutes of Health, United States Public Health Service. Some of the material contained in this chapter is drawn from Bandura (1973).

REFERENCES

Andrus, B. C. *The infamous of Nuremberg*. London: Fravin, 1969.

Azrin, N. Pain and aggression. *Psychology Today*, 1967, **1**, 27–33.

Azrin, N. Punishment of elicited aggression. *Journal of the Experimental Analysis of Behavior*, 1970, **14**, 7–10.

Arzin, N. H., & Hutchinson, R. R. Conditioning of the aggressive behavior of pigeons by a fixed-interval schedule of reinforcement. *Journal of the Experimental Analysis of Behavior*, 1967, **10**, 395–402.

Azrin, N. H., Hutchinson, R. R., & Hake, D. F. Pain-induced fighting in the squirrel monkey. *Journal of the Experimental Analysis of Behavior*, 1963, **6**, 620.

Baenninger, R., & Grossman, J. C. Some effects of punishment on pain-elicited aggression. *Journal of the Experimental Analysis of Behavior*, 1969, **12**, 1017–1022.

Bandura, A. Relationship of family patterns to child behavior disorders. Progress Report, Project No. M-1734. United States Public Health Service, Stanford University, Calif., 1960.

Bandura, A. Social learning through imitation. In M. R. Jones (Ed.), *Nebraska symposium on motivation, 1962*. Lincoln, Nebraska: University of Nebraska Press, 1962. Pp. 211–269.

Bandura, A. Influence of models' reinforcement contingencies on the acquisition of imitative responses. *Journal of Personality & Social Psychology*, 1965, **1**, 589–595.

Bandura, A. *Principles of behavior modification*. New York: Holt, Rinehart & Winston, 1969.

Bandura, A. Psychotherapy based upon modeling principles. In A. E. Bergin & S. L. Garfield (Eds.), *Handbook of psychotherapy and behavior change*. New York: Wiley, 1971. Pp. 653–708. (a)

Bandura, A. Vicarious and self-reinforcement processes. In R. Glaser (Ed.), *The nature of reinforcement*. New York: Academic Press, 1971. Pp. 228–278. (b)

Bandura, A. *Social learning theory*. New York: General Learning Press, 1971. (c)

Bandura, A. *Aggression: A social learning analysis*. Englewood Cliffs, New Jersey: Prentice-Hall, 1973.

Bandura, A., Grusec, J. E., & Menlove, F. L. Observational learning as a function of symbolization and incentive set. *Child Development*, 1966, **37**, 499–506.

Bandura, A., & Mischel, W. Modification of self-imposed delay of reward through exposure to live and symbolic models. *Journal of Personality & Social Psychology*, 1965, **2**, 698–705.

Bandura, A., Ross, D., & Ross, S. A. Imitation of film-mediated aggressive models. *Journal of Abnormal & Social Psychology*, 1963, **66**, 3–11. (a)

Bandura, A., Ross, D., & Ross, S. A. Vicarious reinforcement and imitative learning. *Journal of Abnormal & Social Psychology*, 1963, **67**, 601–607. (b)

Bandura, A., Underwood, B., Fromson, M. E. Disinhibition of aggression through diffusion of responsibility and dehumanization of victims. *Journal of Research in Personality*, 1975.

Bandura, A., & Walters, R. H. *Adolescent aggression*. New York: Ronald, 1959.

Bandura, A., & Walters, R. H. *Social learning and personality development*. New York: Holt, Rinehart & Winston, 1963.

Baron, R. A. Magnitude of victim's pain cues and level of prior anger arousal as determinants of adult aggressive behavior. *Journal of Personality & Social Psychology*, 1971, **17**, 236–243. (a)

Baron, R. A. Aggression as a function of magnitude of victim's pain cues, level of prior anger arousal, and aggressor–victim similarity. *Journal of Personality & Social Psychology*, 1971, **18**, 48–54. (b)

Bateson, G. *The Naven*. Stanford, Calif.: Stanford University Press, 1936.

Berkowitz, L. The concept of aggressive drive: Some additional considerations. In L. Berkowitz (Ed.), *Advances in experimental social psychology*. Vol. II. New York: Academic Press, 1965, 301–329.

Berkowitz, L. The contagion of violence: An S–R mediational analysis of some effects of observed aggression. In W. J. Arnold & M. M. Page (Eds.), *Nebraska symposium on motivation, 1970*. Lincoln, Neb.: University of Nebraska Press, 1970, 95–135.

Brock, T. C., & Buss, A. H. Dissonance, aggression, and evaluation of pain. *Journal of Abnormal & Social Psychology*, 1962, **65**, 197–202.

Brock, T. C., & Buss, A. H. Effects of justification for aggression and communication with the victim on postaggression dissonance. *Journal of Abnormal & Social Psychology*, 1964, **68**, 403–412.

Caplan, N. S. The new ghetto man: A review of recent empirical studies. *Journal of Social Issues*, 1970, **26**, 59–73.

Chagnon, N. *Yanomamö: The fierce people*. New York: Holt, Rinehart & Winston, 1968.

Claster, D. S. Comparison of risk perception between delinquents and nondelinquents. *Journal of Criminal Law, Criminology, & Police Science*, 1967, **58**, 80–86.

Cohen, A. R. Social norms, arbitrariness of frustration, and status of the agent of frustration in the frustration-aggression hypothesis. *Journal of Abnormal & Social Psychology*, 1955, **51**, 222–226.

Crawford, T., & Naditch, M. Relative deprivation, powerlessness, and militancy: The psychology of social protest. *Psychiatry*, 1970, **33**, 208–223.

Davies, J. C. The J-curve of rising and declining satisfactions as a cause of some great revolutions and a contained rebellion. In H. D. Graham & T. R. Gurr (Eds.), *Violence in America: Historical and comparative perspectives*. Vol. II. Washington, D.C.: U.S. Government Printing Office, 1969, 547–576.

Davitz, J. R. The effects of previous training on postfrustration behavior. *Journal of Abnormal & Social Psychology*, 1952, **47**, 309–315.

Ditrichs, R., Simon, S., & Greene, B. Effect of vicarious scheduling on the verbal conditioning of hostility in children. *Journal of Personality & Social Psychology*, 1967, **6**, 71–78.

Edwards, N. L. Aggressive expression under threat of retaliation. Unpublished doctoral dissertation, University of Iowa, Iowa City, 1967.

Feshbach, S. Aggression. In P. H. Mussen (Ed.), *Carmichael's manual of child psychology*. Vol. II. New York: Wiley, 1970. Pp. 159–259.

Friedrich, L. K., & Stein, A. H. Aggressive and prosocial television programs and the natural behavior of preschool children. *Monographs of the Society for Research in Child Development*. 1973, 38(4) (Serial No. 151).

Gardner, R., & Heider, K. G. *Gardens of war*. New York: Random House, 1968.

Geen, R. G. Perceived suffering of the victim as an inhibitor of attack-induced aggression. *Journal of Social Psychology*, 1970, **81**, 209–216.

Geen, R. G., & Pigg, R. Acquisition of an aggressive response and its generalization to verbal behavior. *Journal of Personality & Social Psychology*, 1970, **15**, 165–170.

Geen, R. G., & Stonner, D. Effects of aggressiveness habit strength on behavior in the presence of aggression-related stimuli. *Journal of Personality & Social Psychology*, 1971, **17**, 149–153.

Ginsburg, B., & Allee, W. C. Some effects of conditioning on social dominance and subordination in inbred strains of mice. *Physiological Zoology*, 1942, **15**, 485–506.

Glueck, S., & Glueck, E. *Unraveling juvenile delinquency*. Cambridge, Mass.: Harvard University Press, 1950.

Goranson, R. E. Media violence and aggressive behavior: A review of experimental research. In L. Berkowitz (Ed.), *Advances in experimental social psychology*, Vol. 5. New York: Academic Press, 1970, 1–31.

Gurr, T. R. Sources of rebellion in Western societies: Some quantitative evidence. *Annals of the American Academy of Political & Social Science,* 1970, **391**, 128–144.

Hartmann, D. P. Influence of symbolically modeled instrumental aggression and pain cues on aggressive behavior. *Journal of Personality & Social Psychology*, 1969, **11**, 280–288.

Hoffman, M. L. Power assertion by the parent and its impact on the child. *Child Development*, 1960, **31**, 129–143.

Hutchinson, R. R., Ulrich, R. E., & Azrin, N. H. Effects of age and related factors on the pain-aggression reaction. *Journal of Comparative & Physiological Psychology*, 1965, **59**, 365–369.

Johnson, A. M., & Szurek, S. A. The genesis of antisocial acting out in children and adults. *The Psychoanalytic Quarterly*, 1952, **21**, 323–343.

Kahn, M. W. The effect of severe defeat at various age levels on the aggressive behavior of mice. *Journal of Genetic Psychology*, 1951, **79**, 117–130.

Kanfer, F. H. Vicarious human reinforcement: A glimpse into the black box. In L. Krasner & L. P. Ullmann (Eds.), *Research in behavior modification*. New York: Holt, Rinehart & Winston, 1965. Pp. 244–267.

Knutson, J. F. Aggression during the fixed-ratio and extinction components of a multiple schedule of reinforcement. *Journal of the Experimental Analysis of Behavior*, 1970, **13**, 221–231.

Knutson, J. F. The effects of shocking one member of a pair of rats. *Psychonomic Science*, 1971. **22**, 265–266.

Lerner, M. J. Observer evaluation of a victim: Justice, guilt, and veridical perception. *Journal of Personality & Social Psychology*, 1971, **20**, 127–135.

Leyens, J., Camino L., Parke, R. D., & Berkowitz, L. Effects of movie violence on aggression in a field setting as a function of group dominance and cohesion. *Journal of Personality & Social Psychology,* 1975, **32**, 346–360.

Lieberson, S., & Silverman, A. R. The precipitants and underlying conditions of race riots. *American Sociological Review*, 1965, **30**, 887–898.

Loew, C. A. Acquisition of a hostile attitude and its relationship to aggressive behavior. *Journal of Personality & Social Psychology*, 1967, **5**, 335–341.

Logan, F. A., & Boice, R. Aggressive behaviors of paired rodents in an avoidance context. *Behavior*, 1969, **34**, 161–183.

Longstreth, L. E. Distance to goal and reinforcement schedule as determinants of human instrumental behavior. *Proceedings of the 74th Annual Convention of the American Psychological Association*, 1966, 39–40.

McCord, W., & Howard, J. Negro opinions in three riot cities. *American Behavioral Scientist*, 1968, **11**, 24–27.

McCord, W., McCord, J., & Zola, I. K. *Origins of crime: A new evaluation of the Cambridge-Somerville Youth Study*. New York: Columbia University Press, 1959.

McPhail, C. Civil disorder participation: A critical examination of recent research. *American Sociological Review*, 1971, **36**, 1058–1072.

Madsen, C., Jr. Nurturance and modeling in preschoolers. *Child Development*, 1968, **39**, 221–236.

Mead, M. *Sex and temperament in three savage tribes.* New York: Morrow, 1935.

Meyer, T. P. Some effects of real newsfilm violence on the behavior of viewers. *Journal of Broadcasting*, 1971, **15**, 275–285.

Milgram, S. *Obedience to authority: An experimental view.* New York: Harper & Row, 1974.

New York Times, November 13, 1966. Youth, 18, slays 4 women and child in beauty school. Page 1.

Packer, H. L. *The limits of the criminal sanction.* Stanford, California: Stanford University Press, 1968.

Parke, R. D., Berkowitz, L., Leyens, J., West, S., & Sebastian, R. The effects of repeated exposure to movie violence on aggressive behavior in juvenile delinquent boys: A field experimental approach. In L. Berkowitz (Ed.), *Advances in experimental social psychology*. Vol. 8. New York: Academic Press, 1975.

Pastore, N. The role of arbitrariness in the frustration-aggression hypothesis. *Journal of Abnormal & Social Psychology*, 1952, **47**, 728–731.

Patterson, G. R., Littman, R. A., & Bricker, W. Assertive behavior in children: A step toward a theory of aggression. *Monographs of the Society for Research in Child Development*, 1967, **32**(5) (Serial No. 113).

Peterson, R. A. Aggression level as a function of expected retaliation and aggression level of target and aggressor. *Developmental Psychology*, 1971, **5**, 161–166.

Piliavin, I., Hardyck, J. & Vadum, A. Reactions to the victim in a just or non-just world. Paper presented as the meeting of the Society of Experimental Social Psychology, Bethesda, Maryland, August, 1967.

Powell, D. A., & Creer, T. L. Interaction of developmental and environmental variables in shock-elicited aggression. *Journal of Comparative & Physiological Psychology*, 1969, **69**, 219–225.

Powers, P. C., & Geen, R. G. Effects of the behavior and the perceived arousal of a model on instrumental aggression. *Journal of Personality & Social Psychology*, 1972, **23**, 175–183.

Reich, P., & Hepps, R. B. Homicide during a psychosis induced by LSD. *Journal of the American Medical Association*, 1972, **219**, 869–871.

Rosekrans, M. A., & Hartup, W. W. Imitative influences of consistent and inconsistent response consequences to a model and aggressive behavior in children. *Journal of Personality & Social Psychology*, 1967, 7, 429–434.

San Francisco Chronicle. June 11, 1970. A badge for killing Reds. Page 23.

San Francisco Chronicle. November 26, 1971. Hijacker's slick parachute escape. Page 1.

Scott, J. P., & Marston, M. V. Nonadaptive behavior resulting from a series of defeats in fighting mice. *Journal of Abnormal & Social Psychology*, 1953, **48**, 417–428.

Sears, D. O., & McConahay, J. B. Participation in the Los Angeles riot. *Social Problems*, 1969, **17**, 3–20.

Sears, R. R., Maccoby, E. E., & Levin, H. *Patterns of child rearing.* Evanston Ill.: Row, Peterson, 1957.

Short, J. F., Jr. (Ed.). *Gang delinquency and delinquent subcultures.* New York: Harper & Row, 1968.

Silver, L. B., Dublin, C. C., & Lourie, R. S. Does violence breed violence? Contributions from a study of the child abuse syndrome. *American Journal of Psychiatry*, 1969, **126**, 404–407.

Snow, C. P. Either–or. *Progressive*, 1961, **25**(2), 24–25.

Staples, F. R., & Walters, R. H. Influence of positive reinforcement of aggression on subjects differing in initial aggression level. *Journal of Consulting Psychology*, 1964, **28**, 547–552.

Steuer, F. B., Applefield, J. M., & Smith, R. Televised aggression and the interpersonal aggression of preschool children. *Journal of Experimental Child Psychology*, 1971, 11, 442–447.

Tannenbaum, P. H. Studies in film- and television-mediated arousal and aggression: A progress report. In G. A. Comstock, E. A. Rubinstein, & J. P. Murray (Eds.), *Television and social behavior*. Vol. 5. *Television effects: Further explorations*. Washington, D.C.: U.S. Government Printing Office, 1972, 309–350.

Thelen, M. H., & Soltz, W. The effect of vicarious reinforcement on imitation in two social racial groups. *Child Development*, 1969, 40, 879–887.

Toch, H. *Violent men*. Chicago: Aldine, 1969.

Turnbull, C. M. *The forest people*. New York: Simon and Schuster, 1961.

Ulrich, R. E. Pain as a cause of aggression. *American Zoologist*, 1966, 6, 643–662.

Ulrich, R. E., & Azrin, N. H. Reflexive fighting in response to aversive stimulation. *Journal of Experimental Analysis of Behavior*, 1962, 5, 511–520.

Ulrich, R. E., Johnston, M., Richardson, J., & Wolff, P. The operant conditioning of fighting behavior in rats. *Psychological Record*, 1963, 13, 465–470.

Walters, R. H., & Brown, M. Studies of reinforcement of aggression: III. Transfer of responses to an interpersonal situation. *Child Development*, 1963, 34, 563–571.

Weisz, A. E., & Taylor, R. L. American Presidential assassinations. In D. N. Daniels, M. F. Gilula, & F. M. Ochberg (Eds.), *Violence and the struggle for existence*. Boston: Little, Brown, 1970, 291–307.

Wheeler, L. Toward a theory of behavioral contagion. *Psychological Review*, 1966, 73, 179–192.

Wheeler, L., & Caggiula, A. R. The contagion of aggression. *Journal of Experimental Social Psychology*, 1966, 2, 1–10.

Whiting, J. W. M. *Becoming a Kwoma*. New Haven: Yale University Press, 1941.

Wolfgang, M. E., & Ferracuti, F. *The subculture of violence*. London: Tavistock Publications, 1967.

Wright, M. E. Constructiveness of play as affected by group organization and frustration. *Character & Personality*, 1942, 11, 40–49.

Zillman, D. Excitation transfer in communication-mediated aggressive behavior. *Journal of Experimental Social Psychology*, 1971, 7, 419–434.

Subject Index